Reflections on the
Cuban Missile Crisis

RAYMOND L. GARTHOFF

Reflections on the Cuban Missile Crisis

Revised Edition

THE BROOKINGS INSTITUTION
Washington, D.C.

Library of Congress Cataloging-in-Publication Data:

Garthoff, Raymond L.
  Reflections on the Cuban missile crisis / Raymond
L.Garthoff.—Rev. ed.
    p.   cm.
  Includes bibliographical references and index.
  ISBN 0-8157-3053-5 (alk. paper)
  1. Cuban Missile Crisis, Oct.1962.   I. Title.
E841.G37   1989
972.9106′4—dc20   89-7343
                                                      CIP

        9 8 7 6 5 4 3 2

THE BROOKINGS INSTITUTION is an independent organization devoted to nonpartisan research, education, and publication in economics, government, foreign policy, and the social sciences generally. Its principal purposes are to aid in the development of sound public policies and to promote public understanding of issues of national importance.

The Institution was founded on December 8, 1927, to merge the activities of the Institute for Government Research, founded in 1916, the Institute of Economics, founded in 1922, and the Robert Brookings Graduate School of Economics and Government, founded in 1924.

The Board of Trustees is responsible for the general administration of the Institution, while the immediate direction of the policies, program, and staff is vested in the President, assisted by an advisory committee of the officers and staff. The by-laws of the Institution state: "It is the function of the Trustees to make possible the conduct of scientific research, and publication, under the most favorable conditions, and to safeguard the independence of the research staff in the pursuit of their studies and in the publication of the results of such studies. It is not a part of their function to determine, control, or influence the conduct of particular investigations or the conclusions reached."

The President bears final responsibility for the decision to publish a manuscript as a Brookings book. In reaching his judgment on the competence, accuracy, and objectivity of each study, the President is advised by the director of the appropriate research program and weighs the views of a panel of expert outside readers who report to him in confidence on the quality of the work. Publication of a work signifies that it is deemed a competent treatment worthy of public consideration but does not imply endorsement of conclusions or recommendations.

The Institution maintains its position of neutrality on issues of public policy in order to safeguard the intellectual freedom of the staff. Hence interpretations or conclusions in Brookings publications should be understood to be solely those of the authors and should not be attributed to the Institution, to its trustees, officers, or other staff members, or to the organizations that support its research.

Foreword

OVER THE quarter-century since the Cuban missile crisis, much has been written about the crisis itself and the lessons that can be learned from it. Yet there remains much that has not been addressed, and even today new facts about the events and deliberations continue to emerge.

In this book Raymond L. Garthoff, a participant in the crisis deliberations of the U.S. government, reflects on the nature of the crisis, its consequences, and its lessons for the future. He provides a unique combination of memoir, historical analysis, and political interpretation. He gives particular attention to the aftermath and "afterlife" of the crisis and to its bearing on current and future policy.

In the first edition of this book in 1987 the author presented a number of facts for the first time. Since then, yet more information has become available, particularly from Soviet sources, in part from conferences in which the author participated but even more from individual interviews and research. This new information, much of it presented here for the first time, helps to fill in gaps in our knowledge about events and motivations on the Soviet side. More important, it enlarges our understanding of the crisis interaction.

The author supplies a dimension of analysis usually neglected: the crisis as experienced by the Soviets, and the lessons they appear to have drawn from it. He emphasizes the need to include this integral element of the picture not only to broaden historical perspective but also to recognize the importance of the interaction of American and Soviet policymaking in the events leading up to the crisis, in the confrontation itself, and in the subsequent development of U.S.-Soviet relations.

Raymond Garthoff, now a senior fellow in the Brookings Foreign Policy Studies program, wishes to acknowledge his appreciation to many colleagues involved in the missile crisis, and other students of the episode, with whom he has on various occasions discussed aspects of the subject. He wishes also to express appreciation to the National Security Archive for making available its file of declassified documents, unparalleled for breadth of coverage of the crisis. Finally, he wishes to thank Jeanette Morrison for editing the manuscript of both editions, Mark R. Thibault and Amy R. Waychoff for verifying the published sources, and Louise Skillings for secretarial support.

Brookings gratefully acknowledges the financial support for this book provided by the Andrew W. Mellon Foundation, the Carnegie Corporation of New York, and the John D. and Catherine T. MacArthur Foundation.

The views in this book are those of the author and should not be ascribed to the persons or foundations whose assistance is acknowledged, or to the trustees, officers, or other staff members of the Brookings Institution.

BRUCE K. MAC LAURY
President

May 1989
Washington, D.C.

Contents

Contents

Now, as to Cuba—there's a place that could really lead to some unexpected consequences.

Nikita Khrushchev to Secretary of the
Interior Stewart Udall, September 6, 1962

Purpose and Perspective

DO WE NEED more reflections on the Cuban missile crisis? The historical event itself was sufficiently important, and the twenty-fifth anniversary seemed a suitable occasion to redirect attention to the crisis and the lessons we could learn from it. I therefore decided in 1987 to write the first edition of this book. I raised the question nonetheless because so much had already been written on the subject, including a spate of anniversary articles. Moreover, the past decade has seen the declassification and release of numerous documents related to the crisis, and they complement—and in some cases modify—the picture of the Washington deliberations that has heretofore rested principally on the memoirs and reminiscences of a number of the key participants.

For perfectly natural reasons, commentary on the crisis in this country has focused almost entirely on *the American experience* of the event and the lessons we Americans have learned, or should learn, from it. In addition, the main reason so much attention has been given to the crisis is that it has rightly been regarded as the most intensive, dangerous, and climactic crisis of the cold war, and has thus become a unique historical source for the study of *crisis management*.

For various reasons, mainly the unsatisfactory outcome from the Soviet standpoint, the event has until recently received much less attention in the Soviet Union. In the Soviet Union it is known as the "Caribbean crisis" rather than the "Cuban missile crisis"— a difference stemming from more than mere Soviet preference not to highlight the role of their missiles, as shall be shown. The paucity of Soviet discussion has contributed to the relative American slighting of the Soviet role, but it has not been the main cause. The primary reason has been the intensity of the American decision-making experience, above all to the participants, who have dominated the discussion not only directly but also by providing the extensive record used by political scientists and historians—a biasing factor compounded by the release of extensive declassified documentary sources on the American handling of the crisis.

Many events bearing on the unfolding of the crisis have not been adequately taken into account in histories and analyses, and indeed in a number of cases have not even been known. In the first edition, and still more in this one, I provide new information on a number of events affecting the course and outcome of the crisis that have been neglected or unknown.

I was a participant in the missile crisis, as a staff-level adviser in the State Department with experience in Soviet affairs, intelligence analysis, and politico-military affairs. While playing only a supporting role in the crisis policymaking, I was privy to facts about several developments during the crisis that have not heretofore been published, including information not known to more senior participants who have written about the crisis.

In sum, the first aim of this study is to broaden the historical analysis. A second is to supply both new information and a somewhat different perspective, bringing in Soviet perceptions to a larger extent than has been done. A third is to contribute to the fund of memoir material, including a number of analytical and action memoranda I wrote during the crisis, now declassified, that are noted in the discussion and the texts of which are appended. Finally, I shall discuss the direct and indirect consequences of the Cuban missile crisis in the months and years following its resolution, also an important subject that has been given too little attention.

One principal objective of this volume is to address the *interaction* of American and Soviet perceptions and actions in entering the crisis, and in resolving it. The lack of appreciation of such interaction will become apparent in later discussions of the differing retrospective evaluations of the crisis and lessons drawn from it by the two sides. The very title of this study—and all other American accounts—draws attention to an important difference in Soviet and American perceptions and perspectives. Any reference to this subject in the United States is routinely to the "Cuban missile crisis" of October 1962. The crisis is often seen as having lasted thirteen days (October 16–28), from the time Washington discovered construction was under way in Cuba on launch facilities for Soviet medium-range missiles, to the day Chairman of the Council of Ministers Nikita S. Khrushchev formally agreed to withdraw missiles from Cuba and President John F. Kennedy pledged not to invade that country. Fuller accounts also include the period from October 28 to November 20, when intensive negotiations more completely spelled out and modified the settlement that had been reached, the U.S. naval quarantine was lifted, and the special alert status of the military forces of the two countries ended.

Soviet (and Cuban) accounts of the "Caribbean crisis" emphasize the persisting American hostility to Castro's rule in Cuba, the failure of the Bay of Pigs invasion by American-armed Cuban emigrés in April 1961, and an alleged continuing American threat to invade Cuba. The more immediate crisis itself is seen as beginning, not on October 16, but on October 22, with President Kennedy's announcement that the Soviet Union was installing medium-range missiles in Cuba and his demand that they be removed, accompanied by a naval quarantine to prevent any further shipment of offensive arms to Cuba. That marked the beginning of an intensive six days of deliberation in Moscow. The resolution of the crisis in principle on October 28 is stressed, with little attention to the subsequent three weeks of negotiation before it was in fact settled.

Several things should be said about the underlying differences in perspective. First, contrary to claims often made in both countries, neither holds a monopoly on the truth. Both have some legitimate basis for attributing different values to different facts, and even to the same facts. The facts themselves, of course, however well known, interpreted, or ignored, are the same for both.

Another point I would make about the difference in perspective is that even today the crisis is not sufficiently understood. Analysts on both sides have focused on how the experience of the crisis has made successive leaders more prudent and more sharply aware of the need to avoid actions that could bring us again to the brink of war. But there is inadequate understanding in the United States as to why that event is called the "Caribbean crisis" in the Soviet Union, and how it could be seriously regarded as stemming even in part from *American* actions. There is inadequate understanding in the Soviet Union as to why it is properly thought of in the United States as a crisis brought about by the secret introduction of *Soviet* missiles into Cuba. And in both countries there is insufficient attention to and understanding of the whole process of interaction, involving not only differing perspectives but differing frameworks of relevant reality—or different sets of facts. Very different base levels of openness on source material in the two countries compound the problem of trying to achieve some sort of integrated political and historical perspective.

In this revised edition I have also introduced to a greater extent, although still only in a limited way, the Cuban perspective. In Cuba it is called the "October crisis," one in a series of events defined by episodes in Cuban-American relations. Without attempting to deal fully with the Cuban point of view, I have drawn on the information now available about some important Cuban actions and the Cuban role in the introduction of Soviet missiles into the island, as well as Cuban-Soviet interaction during the crisis itself.

To broaden the context of the analysis, I categorize the crisis in terms of six stages: (1) the developments before October 16, 1962, including the Soviet decision in the late spring to deploy medium-range missiles in Cuba; (2) October 16–22, the period of intense secret internal deliberation and decision within the U.S. government; (3) October 22–28, the superpower confrontation and negotiation climaxing in an agreement basically resolving the crisis; (4) October 28–November 20, the clarification, implementation, and also modification of the basic agreement, including crucial Soviet-Cuban negotiation over some issues; (5) the aftermath of the crisis, in particular the impact on U.S.-Soviet relations for the year until the assassination of President Kennedy on November 22, 1963; and (6) the "afterlife" or resurrection of the issue of possible Soviet offensive arms in Cuba, other than missiles, that arose on several occasions in the 1970s. Finally, I turn to the long-term legacy of the crisis, its importance in its own right, its impact on Soviet thinking, and the light it sheds in retrospectively evaluating the crisis itself and drawing lessons from it.

In this revised edition it has been possible to clarify many aspects of the crisis, including but not limited to Soviet decisions and actions, with the benefit of important revelations by Soviet participants and historians. This information came to light in a series of interviews and meetings I have participated in over the past several years, including two extraordinary international conferences that brought together Soviet and American experts, and in one case knowledgeable Cubans also, in a collaborative revision of history. The John F. Kennedy School of Government at Harvard sponsored the first, at Cambridge, in October 1987, and supported American participation in a tripartite follow-through conference in Moscow in January 1989, sponsored by the Institute of the World Economy and International Relations of the USSR Academy of Sciences.[1] Most of the new material, however, comes directly from Soviet sources. In addition, some newly declassified American documents have proven useful. The reanalysis compelled by the new information from all these sources has, I believe, yielded a number of deeper insights concerning both Soviet and American actions and reactions, and above all their interactions, during the crisis.

1. A detailed account of the Cambridge conference (and an American-only predecessor conference at Hawk's Cay, Florida, in March 1987) has recently been published. See James G. Blight and David A. Welch, *On the Brink: Americans and Soviets Reexamine the Cuban Missile Crisis* (New York: Hill and Wang, 1989), in particular chapters 1 and 5. A full account of the Moscow conference also is expected to be published in due course.

The Soviet Decision

SOVIET ACCOUNTS of the "Caribbean crisis" stress many indications that after the failure of the Bay of Pigs invasion in April 1961 the leaders of the United States continued to seek ways to remove Fidel Castro and communism from Cuba. That is generally true. Most such accounts, however, while more or less correctly noting various U.S. political, covert, and military actions in 1961–62, incorrectly conclude from that evidence that there was a policy and firm plan for a new invasion of Cuba by the United States' armed forces. Military contingency plans were prepared in 1961–62 for possible air attack and invasion, and under some circumstances, never precisely determined, there might have been an attack. But there was *no* firm American political decision or intention to invade Cuba before the crisis erupted in October 1962.

The United States did conduct a series of large-scale military exercises in the Caribbean in the spring, summer, and fall of 1962. Between April 9 and 24 a major Marine air-ground task force carried out an amphibious exercise, *Lantphibex 1-62,* with an assault on the island of Vieques. Exercise *Quick Kick* from April 19 to May 11 along the U.S. southeastern coast involved 79 ships, 300 aircraft, and more than 40,000 troops. While publicly announced, the fact that it was designed to test an actual CINCLANT (Commander-in-Chief, Atlantic) contingency plan against Cuba was not of course disclosed.[2] The Soviets and Cubans, however, correctly assumed that it was testing a war plan. These U.S. exercises in April and May were highly significant because that was the period when the

2. "Command History–CINCLANTFLT, 1962," OPNAV Report 5750-5, submitted May 21, 1963, p. 14 (now declassified).

6

Soviet leaders were considering and making important decisions about expanded military support for Cuba, including the decision to deploy Soviet missiles. Later Soviet accounts charged that these exercises were part of the preparation for further direct U.S. military action against Cuba under an October 1961 directive from President Kennedy to the Joint Chiefs of Staff to draw up plans for an invasion of Cuba.[3] This was a distorted perception, because the plans were contingency plans, *not* plans adopted in pursuance of a decision to invade. Nonetheless, they seemed to Cuban and Soviet intelligence analysts and leaders to reflect a firm intention, or at the least an active hostility with probable intent.[4]

Apart from overt military activities, the Kennedy administration was also responsible after November 30, 1961, for sending sabotage and diversionary units of Cuban emigrés on raids into Cuba under a covert action plan called "Operation Mongoose," and even for plotting to kill Castro.[5] Between late 1961 and August 1962 the main focus of actual operations was on intelligence infiltration, but other actions were also undertaken. A recently declassified Mongoose planning document of February 20, 1962, projected a program and timetable culminating in a wide popular revolt in Cuba, a development that in turn was expected both to require and to justify American military intervention, in October 1962.[6] Submitted by

3. See, for example, I. D. Statsenko, "On Some Military-Political Aspects of the Caribbean Crisis," *Latinskaya Amerika* (Latin America), no. 6 (November–December 1977), pp. 109–10. The late Major General Igor D. Statsenko was one of the commanders of Soviet forces in Cuba in 1962.

4. Not all U.S. military moves in the Caribbean were related to Cuba, although the Cubans may have thought so. In January 1962 a U.S. cruiser and Marine force afloat were sent to be near the Dominican Republic because of unrest there, and in March 1962 a carrier and Marine force afloat were deployed in the Caribbean after disorder in Guatemala.

5. The most important aspects of this program were disclosed in the report of the Church Committee hearings in 1975. See *Alleged Assassination Plots Involving Foreign Leaders,* An Interim Report of the Senate Select Committee to Study Governmental Operations with Respect to Intelligence Activities, S. Rept. 94-465, 94 Cong. 1 sess. (Government Printing Office, 1975), pp. 139–43. Many of the key Mongoose and Special Group (Augmented) documents were declassified and released in January 1989.

6. See Brig. Gen. [Edward] Lansdale, "The Cuba Project," February 20, 1962, 3 pp. plus 23 pp. annex (Eyes Only, Top Secret Sensitive; now declassified);

Brigadier General Edward Lansdale, the Mongoose chief of operations, the projected program was, however, not accepted by the administration, which at that time approved only the intelligence infiltration stage of the plan. Moreover, the approved guidelines, issued on March 14, while recognizing that "final success [in overthrowing the Castro regime] will require decisive U.S. military intervention," authorized only covert operations "short of those reasonably calculated to inspire a revolt within the target area, or other development which would require U.S. armed intervention."[7] Cuban and Soviet intelligence were, however, aware that the U.S. government was undertaking a concerted covert action program aimed at overthrowing the Castro regime.[8]

The United States also aggressively pursued a wide range of overt political and economic maneuvers against the Castro regime. In January 1962 at Punta del Este, Uruguay, the United States succeeded in gaining enough Latin American votes to suspend Cuba from membership in the Organization of American States (OAS). By the spring of that year some fifteen Latin American countries (although not the several largest) had followed the earlier American lead and broken diplomatic relations with Cuba. Soviet officials and commentators have described the exclusion of Cuba from the OAS as the "diplomatic preparation" for invasion.[9]

---

and *Alleged Assassination Plots,* pp. 143–47. The October date was described in the document itself as "the maximum target timing" deemed feasible by the operational planners, and "not a rigid time-table," pp. 1–2. Moreover, it notes that "a vital decision, *still to be made,* is on the use of open U.S. force to aid the Cuban people in winning their liberty," p. 2; emphasis added.

7. "Guidelines for Operation Mongoose," March 14, 1962, p. 1 (now declassified). See also *Alleged Assassination Plots,* p. 147.

8. See Statsenko, *Latinskaya Amerika* (November–December 1977), p. 110. Cuban intelligence infiltration of the Cuban emigrés recruited by the Central Intelligence Agency was attested by senior Cuban officials attending the Moscow conference on the crisis in January 1989.

Senior Cuban officials have also referred to the enlistment of Cuban emigrés into the U.S. Army after July 1961 as an ominous sign. Some were, in fact, assigned to Special Forces units that were alerted for possible commitment in October 1962 along with the regular troops of the U.S. Army and Marine Corps.

9. One is Sergo A. Mikoyan; see Blight and Welch, *On the Brink,* p. 238. This impression is widespread.

The United States also pressed economic warfare against Cuba. The restrictions on U.S. trade with Cuba established in 1960 and 1961 were expanded to a complete embargo on February 3, 1962. The ban on trade carried in American ships was later expanded to deny entry to U.S. ports to ships of other countries en route to or from Cuba. And behind the scenes the United States used diplomatic means in the first half of 1962 to frustrate Cuban trade negotiations with Israel, Jordan, Iran, Greece, and Japan.[10]

In short, by the spring of 1962 the United States had embarked on a concerted campaign of overt and covert political, economic, psychological, and clandestine operations to weaken the Castro regime. A covert destabilization operations program was under way, including attempts to assassinate Castro. Military contingency plans for air attack and invasion of Cuba had been drawn up, and a series of military exercises training for possible execution of those plans was taking place.

It was thus not unreasonable for Cuban and Soviet leaders to be concerned in 1962 over intensified U.S. hostile action against Cuba, including the possibility of an invasion.[11] There had not, however, been any decision by President Kennedy to invade Cuba or to overthrow the Castro regime if nonmilitary means failed to topple it. That was the situation in April–May 1962 when the Soviet and Cuban leadership began to consider more far-reaching measures of Soviet military assistance to Cuba.

Until recently, few experts, East or West, had much information

10. See Memorandum, Brig. Gen. Lansdale, for the Special Group (Augmented), "Review of Operation Mongoose," July 25, 1962, p. 5 (Top Secret; now declassified).

11. In a conversation in mid-September 1962 with an official in the Soviet Embassy serving as a special channel of communication with President Kennedy, Georgi N. Bol'shakov, Khrushchev displayed his own personal view that Kennedy wanted to avenge his defeat at the Bay of Pigs. Bol'shakov, when asked if he believed the United States was planning to attack Cuba, noted the political pressures on the president, especially since the Bay of Pigs, and said he believed the United States would attack. Khrushchev interjected that "he [Kennedy] himself wouldn't mind getting revenge." See Georgi Bol'shakov, "A Hot Line—How the Secret Channel of Communication between John Kennedy and Nikita Khrushchev Worked," *Novoye vremya* (New Times), no. 5 (January 27, 1989), p. 41. Bol'shakov's role is further discussed in note 76.

on the Soviet—and Cuban—decision to deploy Soviet medium-
and intermediate-range nuclear-armed missiles in Cuba. According
to Nikita Khrushchev's unofficial but authenticated memoirs (published in two volumes, in 1970 and 1974, in the United States under
the title *Khrushchev Remembers*),[12] he first thought of stationing
Soviet long-range missiles in Cuba in May 1962: "We were sure
that the Americans would never reconcile themselves to the
existence of Castro's Cuba. They feared, as much as we hoped,
that a Socialist Cuba might become a magnet that would attract
other Latin American countries to Socialism. . . . It was clear to
me that we might very well lose Cuba if we didn't take some
decisive steps in her defense. . . . It was during my visit to Bulgaria
[May 14–20, 1962] that I had the idea of installing missiles with
nuclear warheads in Cuba without letting the United States find
out they were there until it was too late to do anything about them."
Khrushchev stated, as he had officially in December 1962 to the
Supreme Soviet after the crisis, that the rationale for the missiles
was to deter an American invasion of Cuba. "The main thing was
that the installation of our missiles in Cuba would, I thought,
restrain the United States from precipitous military action against
Castro's Government." But in his memoirs he added an important
point not made in the official Soviet statements in 1962 or in later
Soviet commentaries: "In addition to protecting Cuba, our missiles
would have equalized what the West likes to call 'the balance of
power'." And he went on to spotlight a psychological-political
consideration: "The Americans had surrounded our country with
military bases and threatened us with nuclear weapons, and now
they would learn just what it feels like to have enemy missiles
pointing at you; we'd be doing nothing more than giving them a
little of their own medicine."[13]

12. Strobe Talbott, ed. and trans., *Khrushchev Remembers*, 2 vols. (Boston:
Little, Brown, 1970, 1974). The authenticity of the taped Khrushchev memoirs
was initially subject to skepticism in scholarly circles, but expert analysis
comparing the voice prints with recorded Khrushchev statements established
beyond doubt the authenticity of the memoirs. He may not, of course, have told
the whole truth, and did not always remember everything accurately, but his
memoirs remain a very useful source.

13. Talbott, ed. and trans., *Khrushchev Remembers* (1970), pp. 492–94.

We now know, as will be detailed in the pages following, that Khrushchev first thought of the idea in April, and that it was spurred by the American deployment of similar missiles in Turkey. One can see from contemporary reporting in *Pravda* that while in Bulgaria Khrushchev strongly criticized the installation of American intermediate-range missiles in Turkey.[14] A few days later he also criticized a statement by President Kennedy that the United States might under certain circumstances be the first to resort to nuclear weapons, an assertion the Soviets interpreted as representing American rhetoric supporting coercive use of its strategic nuclear superiority.[15]

Castro, on different occasions, made contradictory statements as to whether the initiative was Soviet or Cuban. The most plausible account was given in an interview with *Le Monde* several months after the crisis, in which he stated that the Soviets proposed stationing the missiles in Cuba "to strengthen the socialist camp on the world scale." He then added: "Since we were already receiving a large amount of assistance from the socialist camp, we decided that we could not refuse. That is why we accepted them. It was not in order to ensure our own defense, but primarily to strengthen socialism on the international scale."[16] He made the same points publicly in 1965, after Khrushchev's ouster, declaring that the Soviets had proposed the missile deployment, and despite the "risk," he had accepted the missiles "for the sake of strengthening the socialist camp"; this speech was published in *Pravda*.[17] Castro has attributed the idea to the Soviets on several other occasions as well.[18]

14. "Celebration of Fraternal Friendship on Bulgarian Soil, Speech by Comrade N.S. Khrushchev," *Pravda,* May 17, 1962.

15. "Rally of 250,000 Working People in Sofia in Honor of Soviet Party–Government Delegation, Speech by Comrade N.S. Khrushchev," *Pravda,* May 20, 1962.

16. Claude Julien, interview with Castro, "Kennedy-Castro," *Le Monde,* March 22, 1963.

17. "The Struggle against Imperialism Demands Unity and Solidarity of Revolutionary Forces, Speech by Fidel Castro at a Meeting at the University of Havana," *Pravda,* March 18, 1965.

18. For example, see Tad Szulc, "Castro on John Kennedy and the Missile

Over the past few years, Soviet sources have gradually disclosed much of the record of decisionmaking on the missile deployment. Some of this information has been presented in Soviet publications and in the conferences on the missile crisis in Cambridge in 1987 and Moscow in 1989. Other essential parts of this account have become known in interviews with participants knowledgeable about particular parts of the process. The overall picture has now emerged fairly clearly.

The first key step was a conversation in April in the Crimea between Khrushchev and Marshal Rodion Ya. Malinovsky, the defense minister. Malinovsky drew Khrushchev's attention to the installation of American missiles just over the horizon of the Black Sea in Turkey. He told Khrushchev that the American missiles in Turkey could strike the Soviet Union in ten minutes, whereas Soviet missiles needed twenty-five minutes to hit the United States. Khrushchev then mused on whether the Soviet Union shouldn't do the same thing in Cuba, just over the horizon from the United States. The Americans, after all, had not asked Soviet permission. It appears that Malinovsky had not been thinking of a possible Soviet missile deployment in Cuba, but the idea struck Khrushchev as he thought about the U.S. missiles in Turkey.[19]

Upon his return to Moscow, in late April, Khrushchev discussed the idea with his close colleague First Deputy Prime Minister Anastas I. Mikoyan, and then in late April or early May with a

Crisis," *Los Angeles Times,* April 15, 1984, an article based on an interview with Castro.

19. The source for this account of the Khrushchev-Malinovsky conversation in the Crimea is Fedor M. Burlatsky, then affiliated with the Party Central Committee, who edited a message from Khrushchev to Castro sent in January 1963 explaining more fully the background to the decision to deploy the missiles in Cuba. Khrushchev sent a letter because he had to cancel a previously planned visit to Cuba at that time. The message was written and sent from East Berlin, where Khrushchev was attending the Seventh Congress of the Socialist Unity (Communist) Party.

It is not known whether Malinovsky was prompted to draw Khrushchev's attention to the U.S. missiles in Turkey by knowledge that they had just become operational. The Jupiter missiles in Turkey became operational in April 1962; see James M. Grimwood and Frances Strowd, "History of the Jupiter Missile System," U.S. Army Ordnance Missile Command, July 27, 1962, p. 104 (now declassified).

small ad hoc group tailored to examine the issue and comprising, in addition to himself and Mikoyan, the next ranking Party leader, Frol R. Kozlov, Foreign Minister Andrei A. Gromyko, Marshal Malinovsky, and Marshal Sergei S. Biryuzov, the commander-in-chief of the Strategic Missile (Rocket) Forces. The account of these first discussions comes from Sergo A. Mikoyan, son of Anastas, who was given a detailed account by his father (not published until 1988). His statement is plausible, and is corroborated in part by other accounts of the next stages of the decision process. Khrushchev's idea was to deploy a small number of medium-range missiles in Cuba secretly and then suddenly disclose their presence to the United States and to the world as a fait accompli.

In the first private discussion Mikoyan argued against the idea on several grounds, including that it would be provocative to the United States. In the ad hoc group meeting, he posed two objections: he believed Castro would refuse to agree to the deployment, and he did not believe the missiles could be deployed without detection by the United States. Khrushchev decided, and the group as a whole accepted, that these objections could be dealt with by raising the matter with Castro, and dropping it if he did resist, and by sending an undercover military mission to scout out the terrain and conditions of shipment and emplacement to determine whether the deployment could be made in secrecy.[20] Sergo Mikoyan has reported that Marshals Malinovsky and Biryuzov approved of the missile deployment "as a deterrent measure."[21]

Gromyko, as foreign minister but not then a member of the Presidium or Party leadership, did not express his opinion in the meetings. We now know, from Aleksandr I. Alekseyev, that Gromyko did express to Khrushchev privately, when asked, his "concern and doubts as to the success of the operation" and negative opinion. And Gromyko himself, breaking his long silence

20. Sergo Mikoyan has described these meetings at the Cambridge and Moscow conferences, in several conversations with this author, and in an article, "The Caribbean Crisis Seen from a Distance," *Latinskaya Amerika,* no. 1 (January 1988), pp. 70–71. For his comments at the Cambridge conference, see Blight and Welch, *On the Brink,* pp. 238–42.

21. Mikoyan, *Latinskaya Amerika* (January 1988), p. 70.

on this matter, has lately acknowledged that Khrushchev did raise the idea with him before raising it in the Presidium and that he had warned: "It will cause a political explosion in the USA. That has to be taken into account." But Khrushchev evidently gave little heed to those well-taken doubts.[22]

Another meeting was held soon after, in early May, in which the same group was joined by Alekseyev and candidate Presidium member Sharaf R. Rashidov.[23] Alekseyev had been suddenly brought back from Havana, where he was press counselor in the embassy, because he was the Soviet official having the best rapport with Fidel and Raúl Castro. Summoned by Khrushchev, he was unexpectedly informed that he would be the new Soviet ambassador to Havana. At this meeting Alekseyev first learned of the idea of stationing Soviet missiles in Cuba. Khrushchev asked him how Castro would react to such a proposal. He expressed doubt, to which Marshal Malinovsky objected, the latter recalling (somewhat

22. Gromyko disclosed his doubts and advice against the venture privately in May 1962 to Ambassador Alekseyev, telling him that he had earlier so advised Khrushchev when asked. See "Lessons of the Caribbean Crisis," an interview with A. I. Alekseyev by Yu. Sigov, in *Argumenty i fakty* (Arguments and Facts), no. 10 (March 11–17, 1989), p. 5. His recent public acknowledgment was made in an interview with a British editor; see Donald Trelford, "A Walk in the Woods with Gromyko," *Observer* (London), April 2, 1989.

Gromyko's silence as to his own views at the time, and all aspects of internal deliberations within the leadership before or during the crisis, both in his memoirs published in 1988 and in early 1989 at the Moscow conference, had prompted a very critical reaction by a prominent Soviet journalist who had participated in the conference. Citing Gromyko's "unique experience of fifty years of participation in world politics," and specifically during the Cuban missile crisis, Stanislav Kondrashov complained, "How are we to explain such traditional taciturnity of our statesmen when history itself demands that they frankly share their experience. . . ." Stanislav Kondrashov, "More on the Caribbean Crisis, in the Critical Light of Glasnost," *Izvestiya*, February 28, 1989.

23. The principal source for the account that follows is an article by Alekseyev, "The Caribbean Crisis: How It Was," *Ekho planety* (Echo of the Planet), no. 33 (November 1988), pp. 27–28. Alekseyev's comment on Malinovsky's active support for the proposed deployment is in his interview in *Argumenty i fakty* (March 11–17, 1989), p. 5. Sergo Mikoyan has also referred to this meeting and its outcome, but in less detail. Alekseyev told me in January 1989 that he had kept this all "bottled up" in himself for over twenty-five years, until he recently had been encouraged to write up his account. He is preparing a full memoir. He has not, however, had access to the archives for his work to date.

irrelevantly) that republican Spain had accepted Soviet arms in the 1930s. Alekseyev reports that Malinovsky "rather actively supported" the proposed missile deployment. Khrushchev disposed of the matter by saying that if Castro did not want to accept the missiles, the Soviet Union would support Cuba "by all other means," although he doubted the efficacy of other means. According to Alekseyev's account, Khrushchev stressed the need to find "effective means of deterrence" because he was sure the Americans would invade, but also favored the missile deployment "to repay the Americans in kind" for surrounding the Soviet Union with military bases and missiles, "to learn what it's like to live under the sights of nuclear weapons." Faced with a fait accompli of secretly installed missiles, "the pragmatic Americans will not dare to take irrational risks" and would learn to live with them just as the Soviet Union had learned to live with American missiles in Turkey, Italy, and West Germany.[24]

Khrushchev then made known his decision to send Marshal Biryuzov (incognito) and Alekseyev along with a routine delegation of agricultural experts, headed by Rashidov, to provide cover for the mission to determine Castro's reaction and for Marshal Biryuzov's group of several missile construction and other military experts to determine whether the missiles could be deployed in secrecy. Before the delegation departed, in late May, Khrushchev convened a meeting of members of the Presidium present in Moscow to inform them of the plan and wish the delegation luck.[25]

In his memoirs Khrushchev claimed that the Soviet decision was, "from the outset, worked out in the collective leadership. It

24. The United States had not deployed intermediate-range ballistic missiles in Germany, but it did then have intermediate-range cruise missiles there (Matador, later Mace) until 1969.

25. Alekseyev, *Ekho planety* (November 1988), pp. 28–29. Alekseyev contends that the "complete unanimity [that] reigned in the meeting" of Presidium members disproves any allegations of opposition to the plan. Alekseyev mistakenly recalled the date of the mission as mid-May; they arrived in Havana on May 30.

I had earlier learned from another knowledgeable source about the Rashidov delegation cover. See Raymond L. Garthoff, "Cuban Missile Crisis: The Soviet Story," *Foreign Policy,* no. 72 (Fall 1988), p. 66. Alekseyev later recounted the same story to the Moscow conference.

wasn't until after two or three lengthy discussions of the matter that we decided it was worth the risk to install missiles on Cuba in the first place.'' In view of Mikoyan's and Alekseyev's accounts, and other indirect evidence, this statement is misleading. Khrushchev also said: ''I had wanted my comrades [in the Party Presidium] to accept and support the decision with a clear conscience and a full understanding of what the consequences of putting the missiles on Cuba might be—namely, war with the United States.''[26] I find that assertion unconvincing. Khrushchev in retrospect may have wished to recall that the risks of a serious crisis were foreseen, weighed, and accepted, but they were not. Khrushchev, in fact, met the objections of Mikoyan by proposing to drop the plan if Castro balked, and by leaving it to the military to determine if they could make the desired deployment clandestinely. It is clear that the military saw this as a task to be accomplished (for an objective they desired) rather than as an open technical question. And Khrushchev simply ignored Gromyko's concerns. The Presidium was brought in to display unanimity on the occasion of the delegation's departure, not to deliberate the pros and cons of a decision already made.

The message to Castro proposing the missile deployment was diplomatically phrased as an offer of military support "all the way up to . . . deploying . . . Soviet medium-range missiles" on Cuban territory, if the *Cubans* considered that would be a useful measure to deter "the potential aggressor" from attack. Castro promptly gave a preliminary positive response because, he said, such an action would defend not only the Cuban revolution but also the broader interests of world socialism in the struggle against American imperialism, but he did not give a definitive reply until the next day, after meeting with his Politburo colleagues.[27] Marshal Biryuzov and his team of experts decided that the deployment could be made expeditiously and secretly.[28] It was decided that more de-

26. Talbott, ed. and trans., *Khrushchev Remembers* (1970), pp. 498–99.

27. This account is based on Alekseyev's article in *Ekho planety* (November 1988), p. 29, and further discussions with Alekseyev and senior Cuban officials participating in the Moscow conference. Alekseyev interpreted for Rashidov in advancing the proposal to Castro.

28. Mikoyan was surprised at this judgment, as well as at Castro's acceptance.

tailed arrangements on the missile deployment and other Soviet military assistance would be made when Defense Minister Raúl Castro visited Moscow a few weeks later, in early July. Those talks included several meetings of Raúl with Khrushchev, as well as with Malinovsky, Biryuzov, and other military leaders.[29]

Ambassador Alekseyev has recently revealed, and knowledgeable Cubans have confirmed, that a formal five-year renewable agreement between Khrushchev and Castro was drawn up to cover the stationing of the Soviet missile forces, under exclusive Soviet control, but it was never signed. Originally drafted and initialed by Marshal Malinovsky and Raúl Castro in early July, with a few amendments it was taken to Havana in early August by Alekseyev as he formally assumed his duties as the new Soviet ambassador. Fidel Castro also made several changes, and the revised draft was taken back to Moscow by Ernesto Che Guevara at the end of August. But Khrushchev then pigeonholed the agreement, for reasons I shall discuss shortly, and it was never signed.[30]

Sergo Mikoyan reported at the Cambridge conference that his father was "amazed that Biryuzov thought there were places in the mountains where the Americans would not discover the missiles. I should say, Mikoyan's opinion of this marshal was not very good; he said he was a fool." Cited in Blight and Welch, *On the Brink*, p. 239.

Khrushchev's opinion was obviously different. Even after the Cuban missile fiasco in which both he and Biryuzov shared in a major miscalculation, five months later he promoted Biryuzov to chief of the General Staff.

Incidentally, the speculation of some Western Kremlinologists that Marshal Biryuzov's selection in early April 1962 to be head of the Strategic Missile Forces may have been occasioned by the decision to place missiles in Cuba, and reflected objection to the missile deployment by his predecessor, Marshal Kirill S. Moskalenko, is unfounded. Biryuzov was, however, inexperienced in his new command when the matter arose and he made his on-site assessment in Cuba.

29. Discussions with Alekseyev, Mikoyan, and others. Raúl Castro was in Moscow July 2–17, 1962.

30. Throughout the period from May to October, for reasons of security *no* communications about the proposed, planned, and actual Soviet deployments in Cuba were sent even by coded messages; everything was hand-carried by members of the small coterie of senior officials directly involved. Alekseyev and Raúl Castro even personally prepared the agreement in Russian and Spanish texts, and Alekseyev interpreted the discussions between Raúl and Malinovsky (and Khrushchev). See Alekseyev, *Ekho planety* (November 1988), p. 29, confirmed in part by Sergo Mikoyan and other participants. Alekseyev, however, glosses over the fact that Khrushchev did not find time to sign the agreement between August 30 and October 27.

The Havana discussions in May–June 1962 were not limited to the question of deploying Soviet missiles. Colonel General Dmitri A. Volkogonov, the chief of the Institute of Military History, who has been researching the Caribbean crisis in Ministry of Defense archives, recently informed me that the decisions of May–June also covered the deployment to Cuba of a substantial contingent of operational Soviet combat military forces. Besides the missiles, the Soviet contingent included four reinforced motorized rifle regiments, for security of the missile sites and other forces and as a "trip wire" in case of a large U.S. attack; an integrated Soviet air defense force comprising radars, twenty-four surface-to-air missile (SAM) antiaircraft batteries with 144 launchers, and a regiment of 42 MiG-21 interceptors; and a coastal defense force comprising a number of cruise missile batteries, twelve Komar missile-carrying PT boats, and a regiment of 42 IL-28 light bombers for attacking any invasion force.[31] From late August of 1962 on, well before discovery of the missiles in mid-October, most of this weaponry was sighted by American aerial reconnaissance, but U.S. analysts failed to realize that a major Soviet operational military deployment was under way, assuming instead that the arms were being provided for the Cuban armed forces. We can now see that the Soviet decision in May–June had *two* important elements: one was emplacing Soviet nuclear missiles, the other was deploying a substantial contingent of conventionally armed Soviet combat troops, in all numbering some 42,000 men by mid-October.

The Soviet military command structure was also far more extensive and senior than was realized in Washington at the time and for a quarter-century afterward. Only in 1988, after the first edition of this book, was I able to learn from a knowledgeable Soviet source, Sergo Mikoyan, that the overall Soviet commander was General of the Army Issa A. Pliyev.[32] Several other senior

31. Interview with Col. Gen. D. A. Volkogonov, Moscow, February 1, 1989. Some elements of the planned conventional force deployment were cut short by the quarantine blockade.

32. General Pliyev seems to have been a most incongruous choice for this command. Not only did he lack any experience with ballistic missiles, air defense,

Soviet generals were also dispatched to Cuba. Pliyev's deputy overseeing the Strategic Missile (Rocket) Forces component was Colonel General Pavel B. Dankevich, later for many years the deputy commander of the Strategic Missile Forces in charge of combat training. The air defense component was represented at Pliyev's headquarters by three very senior officers: Marshal of Aviation Yevgeny Ya. Savitsky, for many years before and after the Cuban assignment the deputy chief of the Soviet Air Defense Command in charge of fighter interceptor aviation; Colonel General of Aviation Viktor I. Davidkov; and Lieutenant General (soon Colonel General) Stepan N. Grechko, a few years later first deputy commander of the Moscow Air Defense District. Of greatest interest today was the fact that one of the four Army ground force regiment commanders was Lieutenant Colonel Dmitri T. Yazov— today the minister of defense.[33]

But in October–November 1962 no one in the Ex Comm knew

---

and concealment from aerial reconnaissance, but virtually his whole career had been as a cavalryman. His only experience as a military adviser abroad had been in Mongolia from 1936 to 1938. Apart from daring horse cavalry raids behind German lines during the Second World War, his chief distinction was leading the last major cavalry charge in history—the Soviet-Mongolian "Horse Cavalry-Mechanized Group" that crossed the Gobi Desert and the Greater Khingan Range to attack the rear of the Japanese Kwantung Army in Manchuria in August 1945. A few months after the Cuban crisis, he was quietly returned to the command from which he had been surreptitiously "borrowed," the North Caucasus Military District. Yet he was apparently Malinovsky's selection, with Khrushchev's approval, for the delicate Cuban mission.

One Soviet source, neither General Volkogonov nor Dr. Mikoyan but an active participant in 1962, has told me that Khrushchev deliberately chose Pliyev rather than entrust the command to a missile-man, but that may be speculation. Ambassador Alekseyev has given a possibly confused version of that report, stating that "Khrushchev thought that naming a cavalry general commander of the Soviet contingent in Cuba, rather than a missile specialist, would underline the fact that the Soviet Union did not intend to employ the nuclear weapons, but only to use them as a means of deterrence." Interview in *Argumenty i fakty* (March 11–17, 1989), p. 5. That Khrushchev would expect such an effect on American thinking is highly unlikely, even apart from the fact that Pliyev's designation was successfully kept secret.

33. These commanders were identified by General Volkogonov in interviews in January and February 1989. Yazov, identified as a lieutenant colonel in August 1962, had been promoted to colonel by the end of the year, perhaps in conjunction with the missile crisis.

who the Soviet commander was, nor the scale or rank of the command. It was incorrectly assumed that, except for the missile and protective army units, other Soviet military personnel were serving only temporarily or in an advisory capacity.[34]

General Volkogonov states that the official decision and orders to the Ministry of Defense to proceed with the deployments of the missiles and the other Soviet military forces were given on June 10, 1962.

Knowledgeable Soviet sources have indicated that Khrushchev's general idea had been to deploy a small number of "medium-range" missiles (a Soviet category that comprised both American-designated "medium-range" and "intermediate-range" missiles). He left it to the military to design the appropriate missile force, a point that has been underscored by Sergei N. Khrushchev, Nikita Khrushchev's son. The military decided on a composite division of the Strategic Missile Forces, comprising three R-12 (SS-4 medium-range) missile regiments, with eight launchers each, and two R-14 (SS-5 intermediate-range) missile regiments (also with eight launchers each). Each launcher would be provided with the standard two missiles. For the deployment in Cuba, one nuclear warhead for each launcher was planned, meaning that the eighty missiles would have forty warheads, and the second missile at each launcher was a spare to offset reliability problems, rather than a reload. The missile facilities were to be completed and made operational by a date (not specified) in November or December 1962.[35]

---

34. When Acting UN Secretary General U Thant visited Havana at the end of October 1962 to arrange for an inspection of the missile withdrawal, he and his military aide were introduced to Statsenko, who claimed that all Soviet forces in Cuba were under his command. This statement, as well as his claim that the overall Soviet military complement in Cuba was only 5,000 men, was not true.

U.S. intelligence had identified the presence in Cuba of several Soviet generals senior to him, but by means that kept the information from being disseminated beyond a few in the intelligence community.

35. General Volkogonov confirmed the organization of the Strategic Missile Forces division in Cuba, which corresponds precisely to American intelligence observations and estimates. He is the source of the information that the plan called for forty nuclear warheads. Not all of the force had reached Cuba when further transport was interdicted by the American blockade.

Among American analysts there has been a consensus that the principal reason for the Soviet decision to deploy medium-range nuclear missiles in Cuba was to redress the publicly revealed serious imbalance in the strategic nuclear balance.[36] No other explanation satisfactorily accounts for the action. No doubt the Soviet leaders hoped and even expected that such a dramatic increment to their strategic military power would have political and military dividends for an activist Soviet foreign policy. In particular, there is considerable evidence that Khrushchev planned to renew pressure on Berlin. But the strongest motive that would have led to a consensus among the Soviet leaders on taking a risk in the Cuban missile venture was almost certainly a perceived need to prevent the United States from using its growing strategic superiority to compel Soviet concessions on various issues under contention. Forty Soviet medium- and intermediate-range missile launchers in Cuba, while in no way conferring a decisive strategic advantage that would free Soviet hands, could be expected to help restrain American actions until the Soviet Union fielded enough intercontinental ballistic missiles to provide a more reliable deterrent.

Khrushchev personally had earlier been largely responsible for an exaggeration of the image of Soviet strategic power. This fact no doubt increased his personal stake in recovering Soviet standing. But it was the shared judgment of the leadership that world political perceptions of the strategic balance mattered, and that the Soviet Union's position in 1962 needed shoring up, that led to the decision.

The explanation for the deployment subsequently given by the Soviets—to deter an American attack on Cuba—was not only convenient but virtually necessary once the crisis had been resolved by withdrawing the missiles in exchange for an American pledge not to attack Cuba. It was a factor, but a supplementary and

36. There is no need here to recapitulate the many writings dealing with this subject. One of the first and best is Arnold L. Horelick, "The Cuban Missile Crisis: An Analysis of Soviet Calculations and Behavior," *World Politics,* vol. 16 (April 1964), pp. 363–89. There is also extensive discussion of Soviet motivations and actions in the most comprehensive overall analysis of the crisis, Graham T. Allison, *Essence of Decision: Explaining the Cuban Missile Crisis* (Boston: Little, Brown, 1971), esp. pp. 40–56, 102–17.

secondary reason for desiring the missile deployment. Deterrence of an American attack on Cuba, and reassurance of the Cubans, were, however, clearly the only reasons for deploying the Soviet air defense and coastal defense forces.

The idea that Khrushchev saw the missile deployment as a test of Kennedy's will, or as feasible because of a misjudgment of Kennedy's will (after the Bay of Pigs and their summit encounter at Vienna in 1961), is questionable.[37] There are indications that Khrushchev may have misjudged Kennedy's mettle after their Vienna meeting (and perhaps the earlier Bay of Pigs action). In particular, Fedor Burlatsky reports that Yuri V. Andropov so stated to a group on the Central Committee staff soon after Vienna. But by the spring of 1962, any such judgments would have been superseded by the tough and effective Western stand over Berlin, marked above all by the wide range of military initiatives taken by President Kennedy in 1961–62. Moreover, while Soviet miscalculation of the U.S. reaction clearly occurred, judgments on the American reaction may have encouraged the decision but would not have been its purpose.

Similarly, the idea that the Soviet leaders intended from the outset to trade the missiles in Cuba for U.S. missiles in Turkey is not credible or supported by any evidence. For one thing, it is rejected by Soviet officials who were involved in the 1962 deliberations. For another, it is belied by the fact that the secret Soviet-Cuban agreement was made for a renewable five-year term. This was strictly an ad hoc objective born of the crisis confrontation, and even then not made the central element of a compromise.

No official published Soviet commentaries since the crisis have acknowledged that the principal motivation for the decision to install the missiles in Cuba was to bolster Soviet strategic military power. Such a statement would require admitting not only that Soviet strategic power needed bolstering in 1962, but also that the Soviet Union had failed in the attempt and been compelled to settle

37. In particular, see the cogent arguments of Richard Ned Lebow, in "The Cuban Missile Crisis: Reading the Lessons Correctly," *Political Science Quarterly*, vol. 98 (Fall 1983), pp. 447–78, and in "Deterrence Failure Revisited," *International Security*, vol. 12 (Summer 1987), pp. 197–213.

for a lesser concession in the compromise settlement. The argument that the missiles were to deter invasion of Cuba logically accounts for the decision to remove them when the United States pledged not to attack; an admission that they were needed to support broader Soviet political-military standing or military deterrence would not justify their removal even if Cuban security was assured.

Though avowing the official argument, Khrushchev came close to such an admission in his earlier-cited unofficial and unauthorized memoirs. Castro has admitted it in his statements that the step was justified as one needed to strengthen the socialist camp in the global correlation of forces. There is a third witness: First Deputy Prime Minister and veteran Politburo member Anastas Mikoyan.

On November 30, 1962, on his way back to Moscow from important negotiations with Castro in Havana, Mikoyan spoke to the Warsaw Pact ambassadors in Washington. Mindful that the Soviet Union had not consulted with its Pact allies either on the decision to place the missiles in Cuba or on the decision to remove them, he explained that the missiles had been intended both to defend socialist Cuba, the official explanation, *and* to achieve a shift in the balance of power between the socialist and capitalist worlds. Mikoyan also told the ambassadors frankly that (in the recollection of one present) "after evaluating the strong American reaction during the crisis, however, the Presidium had decided against risking the security of the Soviet Union and its allies for the sake of Cuba." This account is by the then Hungarian chargé d'affaires, János Radványi, who later defected.[38]

Some Soviet officials involved in Soviet-Cuban relations in 1962 and since, including Sergo Mikoyan and Ambassador Alekseyev, insist that the deterrence of American attack on Cuba was the sole or at least primary purpose of the missile deployment. Others, including Burlatsky and Georgi Kh. Shakhnazarov at the recent Cambridge and Moscow conferences, and several privately, have

38. See János Radványi, *Hungary and the Superpowers: The 1956 Revolution and Realpolitik* (Stanford: Hoover Institution Press, 1972), p. 137. Radványi's account rings true, and he has been a reliable source on other developments he experienced firsthand. The East Europeans would have appreciated that *their* security had not been made subordinate to Cuban security.

said that a primary purpose was to bolster the sagging Soviet end of the strategic balance and move toward strategic parity. General Volkogonov states that was the main purpose. Sergo Mikoyan, despite his own view, acknowledges that "Malinovsky and others talked of the strategic balance."[39] While we may never have definitive evidence, I believe that the principal purpose was to redress the strategic imbalance, and that deterrence of an American attack on Cuba and a demonstrative gesture of movement toward political parity, toward removing the double standard permitting American but not Soviet forward-based military deployments, were both contributing considerations.

The decision to undertake the action in secrecy, rather than publicly announcing it in advance, had a more significant effect on the American reaction and the whole course of events than was appreciated in Moscow at the time, or even in retrospect.

In deciding to install the missiles secretly, Khrushchev failed to understand that while they had a good case for contending that the Soviet action was legal and comparable to the U.S. actions in establishing bases near the Soviet Union, their use of secrecy and deception would undercut the rationale of normalcy and legitimacy. If it was all aboveboard, why do it surreptitiously? That was *not* comparable to what the United States had done. Of course, one can appreciate their belief that a sudden fait accompli would maximize the impact, but they did not adequately recognize the risks of premature American discovery and the adverse impact on their position of a sudden *American* announcement of the secret Soviet activity. I have recently asked a number of the 1962 U.S. policymakers what they think the American position would have been if the Soviet Union and Cuba had announced plans for a limited deployment of Soviet missiles in Cuba (the forty launchers planned, for example, were not discrepant from the forty-five launchers the United States had deployed in Italy and Turkey). All believed it was much less likely that the U.S. government would have sought, or been able, to compel retraction of the Soviet decision and preclude deployment.

39. See Blight and Welch, *On the Brink*, p. 239.

At the Moscow conference in early 1989, Soviet missile crisis veterans also were queried on the point. They indicated that Khrushchev's initial idea of arranging the missile deployment secretly was never really challenged or debated. Some now believe it may have been a mistake, but others argue that the United States would have made it an issue in any case and the Soviet Union would probably not have been able to get a pledge against invasion merely for forgoing a proposed deployment.

It also became known at the Moscow conference that the Cubans had strongly urged making the missile deployment and other Soviet military assistance and support measures public from the outset, but Khrushchev had refused. Rebuffed on the occasion of Raúl Castro's visit, Fidel himself on July 26 in a public speech stretched the matter as far as he could (and more than the Soviets appreciated) when he stated enigmatically that "when our Revolution can say that it is in a position to repulse a direct attack, the last danger hanging over it will have disappeared."[40] This new element in Castro's speech was entirely absent from the account of it published two days later in *Pravda*.[41] In late August another high-level Cuban delegation, headed by Che Guevara, visited Moscow, and in a meeting with Khrushchev on August 30, Che attempted unsuccessfully again to persuade Khrushchev to make the missile deployment and other Soviet military support measures public. The most the Cubans could get was an unusual secret "communiqué" on the discussion, which did not become known for twenty years and has never before been noted in any American account of the crisis.[42] Indeed, I believe that the reason that Khrushchev never signed the Soviet-Cuban draft agreement on the deployment was that he feared Castro would leak it.

There were, in fact, leaks and hints of the secret Soviet-Cuban arrangement. The United States was, of course, aware of the visits by Raúl Castro and Che Guevara and the attendant flow of conven-

40. "Fidel en el noveno aniversario del 26–27," *Hoy* (Today), July 27, 1962.

41. V. Borovsky, "Cuba Will Not Retreat," *Pravda,* July 28, 1962.

42. I was informed of these discussions by Emilio Aragonés Navarro, a Cuban leader who was a member of the delegation, on the occasion of the Moscow conference in January 1989.

tional weaponry to Cuba, and correctly appreciated that these visits dealt with the military relationship. Intelligence was, however, equivocal, and in some cases misleading conclusions were reached. For example, an intelligence report stated that Raúl Castro had requested Cuban admission to the Warsaw Pact, but the request was rejected. Another report in early September stated that the Cubans had informed Panamanian Communist Party leaders that "Cuba had secretly concluded a bilateral defense pact with the USSR which was tantamount to bringing Cuba into the Warsaw Pact." But a Soviet broadcast commentary on Cuban events on September 3 that specifically denied Cuban membership in the Pact was noted as well, and the reported statement to the Panamanians was discounted as probably an exaggerated Cuban interpretation of the more equivocal Soviet public statement of September 11 specifically denying any "need" for a Soviet military base in Cuba.[43]

As early as June, Cuban officers had been reported to be fearful of an American attack and its outcome if it came before September; thereafter "the danger will be over."[44] And in late September the CIA distributed, without evaluation, a report that Castro's pilot had been overheard in a bar boasting that Cuba was acquiring nuclear missiles from the Soviet Union and would no longer have to fear American attack.[45] But these reports were not regarded in Washington as sufficient indicators to be taken seriously.

The Soviet leaders also no doubt persuaded themselves much more effectively than they did the Americans that defensive intent meant the missiles were not really "offensive." Each side, of course, tends to see its own weapons of all kinds as not being offensive, while regarding even tactically or strategically defensive

43. All of these reports and interpretations are in Central Intelligence Agency, Office of Current Intelligence, "Evidence of a Soviet Military Commitment to Defend Cuba," October 19, 1962, pp. 1–4, esp. p. 3 (Secret, No Foreign Dissemination; now declassified).

44. Quoted in ibid., p. 2.

45. Cited in Roger Hilsman, *To Move a Nation: The Politics of Foreign Policy in the Administration of John F. Kennedy* (Garden City, N.Y.: Doubleday, 1967), p. 175.

weaponry of the adversary as contributing to a threat. But by carrying this argument to the point of giving misleading and even false assurances to the American leadership, to be described shortly, the Soviets only ensured American attribution of a more hostile intent to themselves. The Soviet leadership was also undoubtedly moved by familiar psychological factors such as self-assurance of success and banishment from their thinking of the prospect or consequences of failure.

On September 17, at a time when Khrushchev and his colleagues must have been considering the possible American reactions to their missile deployment in the light of cautionary statements made by President Kennedy on September 4 and 13 (discussed below), Khrushchev took the occasion of a visit by Austrian Vice Chancellor Bruno Pittermann to try preemptively to deter an American blockade. There were, at the time, a number of calls by American political figures outside the administration for a blockade to put pressure on Cuba, and the subject was a natural one for Khrushchev to comment on without reference to the secret missile deployment under way. Khrushchev undoubtedly expected the Austrians to pass along to the Americans his statement on the issue, so he saw it as an opportunity to influence the thinking of the American leadership. He told Pittermann that the United States intended to blockade Cuba, and that a blockade was an act of war. The Soviet government, he said, had instructed Soviet ships to proceed despite any interference by American warships, and if necessary such attempts at interference would be met by Soviet military means. This was, as events were later to demonstrate, a bluff. Moreover, it became clear in October that while long aware of the possibility of an American blockade, the Soviet leaders had not seriously considered how to meet one.

On October 15, on the very eve of the crisis, when the Soviet attempt to install the missiles surreptitiously seemed likely to succeed, Khrushchev told another visitor, Finnish President Urho Kekkonen, that he "now" believed that the United States would not attack Cuba.

The next day, October 16, Khrushchev had a long conversation with the new American ambassador, Foy D. Kohler. Three items in the discussion were, in retrospect, indirectly relevant to the crisis soon to unfold. First, Khrushchev assured Kohler that a planned fishing port at Mariel, which Cuba had just announced (without clearing the announcement with Moscow) the Soviet Union would help it build, would be entirely nonmilitary. This response to an American expression of concern, in itself true, was clearly also intended to lull broader American concerns about Soviet military activities in Cuba. Second, Kohler expressed United States regret over the accidental intrusion of a U-2 high-flying reconnaissance aircraft into Soviet airspace over Sakhalin Island on August 30, an action the Soviets had protested. And finally, Khrushchev sharply objected to the American placement of Jupiter intermediate-range ballistic missiles in Turkey and Italy.[46]

By early September 1962 rumors and reports in the American press of Soviet missiles in Cuba were increasing. In addition, in March the U.S. government had established a combined CIA-military center at Opa-Locka base near Miami, Florida, to interview the steady stream of Cubans emigrating to the United States. This intelligence collection center received hundreds of reports of sightings of missiles. Many of these were sightings of surface-to-air missiles, which the Soviets began to deploy at the end of August; many were not of missiles at all. (Similar reports had begun to be received as early as 1959, before Cuba and the Soviet Union had even established diplomatic relations.) In retrospect, at least one report of a missile sighting on September 12 was almost certainly of a Soviet SS-4 medium-range missile—but at the time it could not be confirmed, and hundreds of other reports were in error or unsubstantiated.[47] The same was true of numerous reports from

46. Kohler's detailed report of his long discussion with Khrushchev was dispatched to Washington in a series of cables. One cable, reporting the Cuban fishing port and U-2 exchanges, has been declassified; other cables in a series reporting on the discussions, including the one dealing with the Jupiters in Turkey and Italy, have apparently not yet been declassified.

The reason that Khrushchev would have had the Jupiters in Turkey on his mind will be discussed later; briefly, they were just reaching full operational status.

47. The CIA chief of the collection center in 1962 has written an interesting

other sources. Nonetheless the administration came under increasing pressure. On August 31 Senator Kenneth Keating, a Republican from New York, began a steady campaign claiming that there were Soviet offensive missiles in Cuba and that the Kennedy administration was covering up this fact.[48]

By early September the Soviets opened a deliberate campaign to counter any American suspicions. On September 4, Ambassador Anatoly Dobrynin told Attorney General Robert Kennedy that Khrushchev had sent his assurance that the Soviet government would not make any trouble—for example, over Berlin—for the president before the impending American congressional elections. Two days later Dobrynin met with White House aide Theodore Sorensen and passed on another message to the president, that Khrushchev might visit the United Nations in the second half of November (that is, after the U.S. elections), thus hinting at the possible opportunity for a meeting, as well as again implying that there would be no challenges in the meantime. And the day after that, he met with U.S. Ambassador to the UN Adlai Stevenson in New York and reassured him that only defensive weapons were being supplied to Cuba. Dobrynin had been instructed to give these assurances. He had *not,* moreover, been informed by Moscow that missiles were being deployed.[49]

---

account that stresses this report but seriously overstates its impact in Washington. See Justin F. Gleichauf, "Red Presence in Cuba: The Genesis of a Crisis," *Army,* vol. 29 (November 1979), pp. 34–38. Only a few other reports, out of hundreds, retroactively could be judged valid.

48. Senator Keating steadfastly refused to divulge the sources of his information, even when pointedly asked by a fellow conservative Republican, CIA Director John McCone. Some of his information, accurate and not, was evidently leaked by one or more disgruntled activists in U.S. intelligence organizations. Some came from Cuban emigré organizations that had long played up the "threat" from Cuba. Some, not even available in U.S. official hands, probably came from a certain Western ambassador in Havana whose capital had shown no interest in his alarmist reports.

49. Dobrynin had earlier confirmed to me that he was not told about the missiles until after the crisis broke, and he said this on the record at the Moscow conference. Indeed, he commented to me (in May 1988) that the Soviet Embassy in Washington had been cut out of Moscow's deliberations and decisions before, during, and after the crisis. Khrushchev, he said, often made foreign policy decisions without the advice of Soviet diplomats.

On September 4 President Kennedy issued a public statement that there was no evidence of "offensive ground-to-ground missiles," or of "other significant offensive capability" in Cuba, but he pointedly added: "Were it to be otherwise, the gravest issues would arise."[50] On September 11, TASS carried a statement authorized by the Soviet government that seemed to deny there were or would be offensive arms in Cuba; it said: "The arms and military equipment sent to Cuba are designated solely for defensive purposes," and also that "there is no need for the Soviet Union to shift its weapons for the repulse of aggression, for a retaliatory strike, to any other country, for instance Cuba. . . . There is no need to search for sites for them beyond the boundaries of the Soviet Union."[51] The clear, and intended, impression was that Soviet strategic missiles would not be sent to Cuba. On September 13 Kennedy again made a public statement denying the presence of offensive missiles in Cuba, stressing the distinction from defensive arms, and seeking to sharpen the warning. He said that if Cuba should ever "become an offensive military base of significant capacity for the Soviet Union, then this country will do whatever must be done to protect its own security and that of its allies."[52]

Most American analyses of the crisis have not considered relevant another range of contemporaneous developments, although these events were especially noted in Moscow and Havana.

50. "U.S. Reaffirms Policy on Prevention of Aggressive Actions by Cuba: Statement by President Kennedy," September 4, 1962, *Department of State Bulletin,* vol. 47 (September 24, 1962), p. 450. (Hereafter *State Bulletin.*) Kennedy's statement was prompted both by concern over the public debate in the United States and, significantly, by skepticism over Dobrynin's assurance to Robert Kennedy earlier that same day. See Robert F. Kennedy, *Thirteen Days: A Memoir of the Cuban Missile Crisis* (New York: W.W. Norton, 1969), pp. 25–27.

51. "TASS Statement," September 11, 1962, *Vneshnyaya politika Sovetskogo Soyuza i mezhdunarodnyye otnosheniya, sbornik dokumentov, 1962 god* (The Foreign Policy of the Soviet Union and International Relations, A Collection of Documents, 1962) (Moscow: Institute of International Relations [IMO], 1963), pp. 356–57. (Hereafter *Vneshnyaya politika, 1962.*)

52. "The President's News Conference of September 13, 1962," *Public Papers of the Presidents: John F. Kennedy, 1962* (GPO, 1963), p. 674. (Hereafter *Public Papers: Kennedy, 1962.*)

On August 24, the anti-Castro emigré organization Alpha 66 launched a daring speedboat strafing attack on a Cuban seaside hotel near Havana where Soviet military technicians were known to congregate, killing a score of Russians and Cubans. Although this particular raid was apparently not sanctioned by the United States, the Cuban exile organization responsible was permitted to base itself in Florida. On September 10 the same group attacked two cargo ships, one British and one Cuban, just north of Cuba. Again on October 7 Alpha 66 carried out another raid against the island, and on October 12 another group strafed a Cuban ship near the coast.

American military exercises in the region continued apace through the summer and fall. An airborne assault was tested in *Jupiter Springs*. In August the U.S. Strike Command carried out *Swift Strike II*, a major limited war exercise in the Carolinas with four Army divisions and eight tactical air squadrons, some 70,000 troops in all. A strategic mobility command post exercise called *Blue Water* was conducted in early October, and a large Marine amphibious assault was planned for mid-October under the code-name *Phibriglex*.

On September 5 Secretary of State Dean Rusk told nineteen Latin American ambassadors in Washington that the United States would work to prevent the spread of communism in the Western Hemisphere. On September 8 Cuban exile leaders in the United States publicly called on the Kennedy administration to support resumption of large-scale subversive activities to bring down the Castro regime. Between September 14 and 18 former Vice-President Richard Nixon and Senators Barry Goldwater, Strom Thurmond, John Tower, Hugh Scott, and Keating all called for a blockade of Cuba to end any Soviet military assistance (and even liberal Senator Jacob Javits asked the president to demand an end to Soviet military assistance and take whatever action was necessary). On September 26 Congress passed a resolution sanctioning the use of force, if necessary, to restrain Cuban aggression and subversion in the Western Hemisphere. On October 3 President Kennedy signed it. That same day twenty Latin American foreign ministers issued a statement in Washington condemning any attempt to make Cuba an armed base for communist penetration of the Americas. On October 8 the U.S. Congress acted to withhold aid from any country that traded with Cuba (a move that evoked protests from such allies and neutrals as Great Britain and Sweden).

One development in this period, not (presumably) known to the Soviet leaders, nor for that matter to any but a very few American leaders, was a series of continuing meetings of the secret Special Group (Augmented) that had been established in November 1961 to conduct covert operations against Cuba under the code-name "Mongoose." Attorney General Kennedy was a driving force in this covert action program. A Washington headquarters group had been set up under General Lansdale and a CIA "Task Force W" in Florida under William K. Harvey, both veteran covert action managers. The operation came to involve 400 Americans, about 2,000 Cubans, a private navy of fast boats, and an annual budget of about $50 million. Task Force W carried out a wide range of activities, initially mostly against Cuban ships and aircraft outside Cuba (and non-Cuban ships engaged in the Cuba trade), such as contaminating sugar shipments out of Cuba and tampering with industrial imports into the country. A new phase, calling for more raids into Cuba, opened in September.[53] On September 27 a CIA sabotage team in Cuba was arrested.

On October 4, a meeting of the Special Group (Augmented) saw an argument between CIA Director John A. McCone and Robert Kennedy over why the program was going so slowly, which led to a decision to step up operations including the dispatch of sabotage teams into Cuba. At least three meetings followed, including one on October 16 in between the two meetings in the White House

---

53. See *Alleged Assassination Plots*, pp. 139–43; John Prados, *Presidents' Secret Wars: CIA and Pentagon Secret Operations since World War II* (New York: William Morrow, 1986), pp. 210–13; and Arthur M. Schlesinger, Jr., *Robert Kennedy and His Times* (Boston: Houghton Mifflin, 1978), pp. 477–80.

A Miami CIA station was also established, in probable violation of the law banning CIA operations in the United States, to say nothing of organizing activities that contravened the Neutrality Act. It was headed by Theodore G. Shackley and Thomas C. Clines, both later to become better known for questionable unofficial covert activities before and after their retirement. The CIA code-name for its Miami-Cuban operation was JM/WAVE.

that day on the missiles in Cuba.[54] With the advent of the missile crisis the attention of all the U.S. government leaders shifted to that event, although covert operations were not forgotten.[55]

On October 12 a State Department spokesman said that although the United States did not "sanction" emigré raids on Cuba, it was not prepared to act against the Cuban emigrés who undertook them, and warned that foreign shippers who traded with Cuba took a risk.

President Kennedy believed that in his two September statements he had made a clear and strong warning to the Soviet leaders, although he was also attempting to reassure the American people and refute those who were claiming that a Soviet offensive missile threat already existed in Cuba.

Theodore Sorensen was very close to the president and drafted his September statements and most public statements on the Cuban situation and his personal messages to Khrushchev. Even more important, he was able to gauge President Kennedy's thinking unusually well. In the March 1987 Hawk's Cay conference of veterans of the missile crisis and scholars studying it, Sorensen made a revealing statement. Of Kennedy's September statements in effect saying the United States would accept the large Soviet military assistance to Cuba then under way but would not accept strategic offensive missiles, Sorensen stated his belief that the president had "drawn the line" at what he thought the Soviets would not do. Everyone except McCone had agreed that the Soviets would not put offensive missiles in Cuba. Kennedy meant to draw

54. John A. McCone, "Memorandum of Mongoose Meeting Held on Thursday, October 4, 1962" (now declassified); and *Alleged Assassination Plots,* p. 147.

55. Robert A. Hurwitch, State Department coordinator of Cuban affairs, proposed in the first days of crisis deliberations that one solution to the missile problem might be to send Cuban exiles in unmarked aircraft to bomb the missile sites, with a cover story that they were targeting oil refineries. Whatever appeal there might have been for removing in a surreptitious way missiles that had been surreptitiously brought in was overcome by doubts as to the proposal's effectiveness and the memory of the Bay of Pigs. Secretary Rusk turned the idea down flat, and it did not go beyond him. See Robert A. Hurwitch, "The Cuban Missile Crisis," *Foreign Service Journal,* vol. 48 (July 1971), pp. 17–20.

a line that would preclude a serious change in the strategic balance, but believed *no* missiles was a safe place to draw it. Sorensen believes "the President drew the line precisely where he thought the Soviets were not and would not be; that is to say, if we had known that the Soviets were putting forty missiles in Cuba, we might under this hypothesis have drawn the line at 100, and said with great fanfare that we would absolutely not tolerate the presence of more than 100 missiles in Cuba."[56]

On October 3 Under Secretary of State George W. Ball testified to Congress that "our intelligence is very good" that the military equipment supplied to Cuba "does not offer any offensive capabilities."[57] And on October 14, McGeorge Bundy, national security adviser to the president, stated on national television: "I *know* there is no present evidence, and I think there is no present likelihood that the Cubans and the Cuban government and the Soviet government would in combination attempt to install a major offensive capability."[58]

In fact, U.S. intelligence on major deliveries of arms to Cuba on the whole was quite good. The focus of American concern, however, was almost entirely on offensive weapons capable of posing a threat to the United States. Virtually no consideration was given to the possibility of deployment of other Soviet combat forces on the island. The one notable exception was in President Kennedy's statement of September 4, in which he not only linked his warning of gravest consequences to Soviet offensive missiles, but also to "any organized combat force in Cuba from any Soviet bloc country," and any "military bases provided to Russia."[59] But, he said, there was "no evidence" of any such organized combat force.

56. Cited in "Proceedings of the Hawk's Cay Conference on the Cuban Missile Crisis," Marathon, Florida, March 5–8, 1987, p. 51; and Blight and Welch, *On the Brink*, p. 43.

57. Quoted in Hilsman, *To Move a Nation*, p. 176. Ball supplied a detailed listing of Soviet military transfers to Cuba.

58. Quoted in ibid., p. 180. Note that Bundy referred to "major" offensive capability; he was aware of the IL-28 bombers, which, if that was all that was coming, the administration was then prepared to accept as not alone constituting a threat. This matter is discussed under "Stage 4: The Settlement" in this volume.

59. *State Bulletin* (September 24, 1962), p. 450.

Most striking was the total absence from a Special National Intelligence Estimate (SNIE) of September 19, 1962, that evaluated the military buildup in Cuba of any consideration of the deployment of Soviet combat forces in Cuba, other than nuclear missiles. The estimate, like all official reviews, noted the various weapon systems arriving, but assumed they were all transfers of arms to the Cuban armed forces.[60]

One consequence of the American failure to recognize the buildup of a Soviet military contingent was a serious underestimation of the number of Soviet military personnel in Cuba. In September and early October the number was estimated at 4,000 to 4,500. By October 22, when the president made his speech, after identification of the missile bases, the total was estimated at 8,000 to 10,000. With the discovery by low-level aerial reconnaissance of four mechanized infantry regimental combat teams (in Soviet parlance, reinforced motorized rifle regiments) between October 25 and November 6, the estimate rose again. At first, however, these were assessed at about 1,000 to 1,500 men each; later estimates were 1,500 to 2,500. The actual size was probably about 2,500 (each with about thirty-five tanks and another thirty armored vehicles). By November 19 the intelligence estimate was some 12,000 to 16,000 Soviet military personnel overall, including 8,000 in the four regiments. Retroactive estimates in early 1963, never later revised, raised the total to 22,000 Soviet military personnel.

As earlier noted, except for the four regiments of ground troops, discovered after the missiles and presumed to provide local security for them, all the other elements were in 1962 (and indeed have been until now) believed to be arms and equipment being supplied to the Cuban armed forces. The SAM sites were recognized to be initially operated by Soviet personnel, Soviet personnel were identified as flying some MiG fighters, and in general Soviet military training and advisory personnel were assumed to be present with all of these systems.[61] But it was not known that there were operational

60. SNIE 85-3-62, "The Military Buildup in Cuba," September 19, 1962 (Top Secret; now declassified), 9 pp.

61. During the crisis the CIA published a daily special intelligence memoran-

Soviet forces comprising a substantial expeditionary contingent, indeed nearly double the highest retroactive American estimate.

In 1979, Castro publicly stated that 40,000 Soviet military personnel had been in Cuba during the 1962 missile crisis, but little attention was paid to the revelation.[62] Several Soviet sources have now confirmed that in fact 42,000 Soviet military personnel were in Cuba at the time of the crisis, all of course having arrived before the quarantine. Without it, the total would have been even higher.

Meanwhile, the first Soviet medium-range missile equipment had arrived in Cuba in the large-hatch freighter *Omsk* on September 8, and a second shipment on the *Poltava* a week later. By mid-October, we later learned, some forty-two of the planned eighty missiles and associated launch equipment had arrived in Cuba.[63] Construction was under way on four missile complexes.

---

dum for the Ex Comm, "The Crisis: USSR/Cuba"; the issue for November 1, 1962, p. 7 (Top Secret–Sensitive; now declassified), carried an annex on "Evidence on Possibility Cubans May Be Manning SA-2 SAM Sites in Cuba," concluding they were not and citing many sources and reasons to buttress the conclusion that they were manned exclusively by Soviet personnel, estimated to total some 3,000 to 6,000 men. But this Soviet manning was assumed to be merely a transitory necessity, given time pressures. The memorandum for November 3 (pp. 4–5) carried a supplement titled "Cuban SAM Program Unprecedented," describing the analogous and unprecedented nature of the Soviet manning of the SAM system, and of the air defense radars and MiG interceptors, "at least temporarily." Such manning was still regarded as "a deviation from the normal Soviet pattern of first training foreign personnel and then providing MIGs, radar and other air defense equipment to a country which is scheduled eventually to receive SAMs." The special nature of the situation was assumed ("it is quite apparent") to be because of the missile deployment— *not* as a Soviet deterrent to possible American invasion.

One CIA intelligence analysis, not prepared for the Ex Comm, did on November 16 note that air defense, coastal defense, and bomber components were Soviet-manned and "all of these forces are probably in addition to Soviet military personnel assisting and training Cubans . . . for naval ships, aircraft, and land armaments being turned over to Cuba by the USSR." But it did not note that this would imply a sizable Soviet combat contingent. See CIA, "Soviet Military Forces in Cuba," in *Current Intelligence Weekly Review,* November 16, 1962 (Secret; now declassified), p. 5.

62. Castro's statement was made in a television interview with Dan Rather of CBS, in Havana on September 30, 1979. In the earlier edition of this book, written before the new Soviet information became available, I noted Castro's claim might be true.

63. I have been using the standard Soviet term "medium-range missiles." In

It has not been conclusively determined to this day whether any of the nuclear warheads had actually arrived in Cuba by mid-October 1962. Curiously, the status of nuclear warheads for the missiles has occasioned more speculation in recent years than it did during the crisis. The fact is that in October 1962 the United States did not know if there were Soviet nuclear warheads for the missiles in Cuba. It was known that the Soviets were building standard nuclear warhead storage facilities at the missile launch sites, like those in the Soviet Union. The intelligence community

---

1962 the United States divided this class of missile into two categories: medium-range (600–1,500 nautical miles; 1,000–2,500 kilometers) and intermediate-range 1,500–3,000 nautical miles; 2,500–5,000 kilometers). The Soviet Union had a medium-range ballistic missile (MRBM) called in the West the SS-4 (Soviet designation R-12), with a maximum range of 1,020 nautical miles, and an intermediate-range ballistic missile (IRBM) called the SS-5 (R-14), with a maximum range of 2,200 nautical miles. The Soviet deployment under way in October 1962 was for twenty-four SS-4 MRBM launchers and sixteen SS-5 IRBM launchers, with two missiles for each launcher (as was standard in the Soviet Union). The IRBMs could reach Washington and New York from Cuba. All forty-two missiles in Cuba in mid-October were SS-4 MRBMs; none of the SS-5 missiles had yet arrived. Most of the remaining missiles and equipment were en route on five large-hatch ships when the quarantine interdicted their arrival. The missiles and equipment for the last IRBM regiment were still on the docks in Leningrad awaiting shipment.

In later accounts, particularly by revisionist publicists and scholars, a school of analysis has questioned the honesty of the administration's public statements as to the range of these missiles. Some writers have contended that the real range of the missiles was only a few hundred miles. The chief initial source cited by most of these writers (who include Ronald Steel, David Detzer, Ronald R. Pope, and Barton J. Bernstein) was Robert Hotz, "What Was the Threat?" *Aviation Week and Space Technology,* vol. 77 (November 12, 1962), p. 21. In fact, however, the U.S. intelligence agencies had very good information on the range of these systems. By the evening of October 16 it was established that the MRBMs were SS-4 missiles of 1,020 nautical miles range and not SS-3 missiles of 700 nautical miles range, and on October 17 the first SS-5 equipment was identified. There was no uncertainty or debate within the administration, and no exaggeration or invention in the information publicly released.

Some scholars of the crisis have also been led by the confusion over "medium-range" missiles into fantasies about a political-military conflict in the Soviet Union. Noting that Khrushchev had, in all his references, spoken only about "medium-range" missiles, these commentators posited the possibility that the appearance in Cuba of "intermediate-range" missiles also may have reflected Soviet military insubordination in going beyond the intentions of the political leadership. Awareness that the Soviet term covers *both* American categories dissolves that speculation.

had no evidence of the presence in Cuba, or of earlier transport to Cuba, of nuclear weapons of any kind. Nonetheless, there was no assurance that warheads had not been brought in without detection, possibly by ship, or perhaps by submarine or by air. On balance, this was judged unlikely, but the policymakers could only be advised that the United States had to assume the warheads were there, and in due prudence that was the consensus assumption.[64]

There *was* concrete intelligence that nuclear warheads for the missiles had been loaded on the *Poltava,* one of the large-hatch freighters engaged in the missile transfers, in Odessa, and that the *Poltava* was en route to Cuba at the time the quarantine was imposed. As with all the missile-transporting ships, the *Poltava,* on this occasion as it transited the Bosporus, declared for a false destination (Algeria), as well as having a false manifest. It was only a few sailing days from Cuba when the quarantine was imposed. The *Poltava* turned back on October 24 and soon returned to the Soviet Union, along with the other four ships carrying missiles and

64. A special national intelligence estimate submitted on October 20 stated that "the construction of at least one probable nuclear storage facility [later others were identified] is a strong indication of the Soviet *intent* to provide nuclear warheads. In any case, it is prudent to assume that when the missiles are otherwise operational, nuclear warheads will be available." SNIE 11-19-62, "Major Consequences of Certain U.S. Courses of Action on Cuba," October 20, 1962, p. 2 (Top Secret–Sensitive; now declassified); emphasis added.

Well into the crisis, on October 25, Dean Rusk again raised the question, saying, "We need to know whether warheads have actually been delivered to Cuba"; but we did not know and the question was not further pursued. See "Summary Record of NSC Executive Committee Meeting No. 5, October 25, 1962, 5 P.M.," p. 1 (Top Secret–Sensitive; now declassified).

Some accounts of the crisis have erroneously referred to the presence of "tactical nuclear weapons" with the Soviet troops in Cuba, and assumed these were intended to counter any invading American forces. (Most notably, and surprisingly, Hilsman, *To Move a Nation,* pp. 159, 227.) There was no intelligence to this effect. These accounts have been based on a misunderstanding, in that the Soviet troops were equipped with FROG (Soviet designation Luna) short-range (30-mile) rockets, a system that is "nuclear-capable," as are many other rockets and artillery guns. The FROG system was also widely deployed, as in Cuba, for conventional nonnuclear operations.

General Volkogonov has confirmed that there were no nuclear warheads with, or intended for, these tactical rockets or any other weaponry in Cuba other than the R-12 and R-14 missiles.

associated equipment, and the eleven additional ships with other military equipment.[65]

The first Soviet to assert publicly that the nuclear missile warheads were in Cuba by October 22, 1962, was Ambassador Alekseyev in his memoir article in November 1988.[66] When I challenged him on this point, just before the 1989 Moscow conference, he was angrily positive. Alekseyev's assertion, however, claimed too much. He said "*all* 42 missiles and their warheads, and the military personnel, were already in place" in Cuba. Ships still en route to Cuba had only "auxiliary equipment and provisions for the troop contingent which we could if necessary get along without."[67] Yet even in 1962 we knew that the forty-two missiles there were far from "all" the missiles; none of the SS-5 (R-14) missiles had arrived. Moreover, while we were uncertain about possible gaps in our intelligence information, we were quite certain about the intelligence that at least some of the nuclear missile warheads were still en route on the *Poltava* and never reached Cuba. On balance, Alekseyev's account was clearly wrong in several important respects, and therefore unconvincing as evidence that any nuclear warheads had reached Cuba.

At the Moscow conference, and in supplementary discussions then and later, General Volkogonov also contended that nuclear warheads were in Cuba. He had consulted the Ministry of Defense archives and had spoken with two surviving Soviet generals who had been in Cuba. Moreover, his information was precise and fully consistent with 1962 American intelligence information: forty-two R-12 missiles of forty-eight planned were in Cuba; none of the thirty-two R-14 missiles had reached there; twenty nuclear warheads, of the forty it was planned to send, one for each launcher for a single launcher salvo, had reached Cuba (by ship arriving at the end of September or the beginning of October); the other twenty warheads were en route on the *Poltava* and their arrival in Cuba

65. See the further discussion in "Stage 3: The Confrontation," below.

66. At the Cambridge conference in 1987, Burlatsky believed no nuclear weapons had reached Cuba, while Mikoyan believed they were there, but neither had direct information.

67. Alekseyev, *Ekho planety* (November 1988), p. 29; emphasis added.

was thus interdicted by the blockade. When queried on when and how the twenty warheads had been removed from Cuba, he said they were taken out by ship November 2–5.[68] U.S. intelligence knew in 1962 that on November 5 the *Aleksandrovsk* departed Cuba, and on November 23, upon its arrival at Guba Okol'naya in the Northern Fleet area of the Soviet Union, workers were observed unloading six nosecone transport vans. These vans, which had been sighted while still in Cuba, were designed for transporting a missile nosecone, with the warhead, from the nuclear storage facility to the launch pad, where the nosecone would be mated to the missile before its erection for firing. Also, there had been "tenuous" signs that the *Aleksandrovsk* was carrying radioactive material. This intelligence would seem to corroborate Volkogonov's assertion.[69]

General Volkogonov, and Soviet political officials in the 1962 crisis, all firmly assert that Moscow had given clear orders that none of the missiles in Cuba would be placed on alert or in firing position, that is, the missiles and warhead nosecones would not be mated and the missiles would not be erected. And despite heavy reconnaissance none was ever so observed in Cuba. Indeed, while General Volkogonov did not provide details on the location of the warheads, U.S. intelligence information at the time strongly suggested that any warheads in Cuba were never even brought to the missile launch bases. By October 28, when the dismantling began, only two of the seven nuclear weapon storage facilities had been essentially completed—one at an R-14 (SS-5) site, for which there

68. Most of this information was provided by General Volkogonov in my conversations with him in January 1989, and at an interview in the Institute of Military History in February, rather than at the Moscow conference.

69. See "The Soviet Bloc Armed Forces and the Cuban Crisis, A Chronology: July–November 1962," National Indications Center, June 18, 1963 (Top Secret; now declassified), pp. 91, 97. The reference to possible detection of radioactive material was deleted from the entry on p. 91, but is given in a cross-reference on p. 97.

In addition, on November 9 a U.S. helicopter registered an uncertain "possible" detection of radioactivity from the freighter *Bratsk* leaving Cuba, one of the ships taking missiles out, but a more sensitive check two days later found no radioactive emanations from the ship.

were no missiles, and one at a missile system transshipping facility at Punta Gerardo some fifty miles west of Havana. None of the weapon storage facilities at the four R-12 (SS-4) missile launch complexes, where the missile systems were deemed operational, were considered to be in operation.[70]

One other pertinent fact came to the surface from conversations with Cuban participants, although not at the Moscow conference itself. They stated that Castro had been told at the time of the crisis not to worry about the blockade, that "the missiles and warheads" were already in Cuba. This reassurance appears also to be the basis for Alekseyev's belief that all the missiles and warheads were there. It seems clear that the Soviet military command in Cuba, on its own or in accordance with instructions from Moscow, had informed the Cubans (and Alekseyev) that the missiles and warheads were there in order to avoid exacerbation of Castro's anger by informing him that half of the missiles and half (or all?) of the warheads were not yet there but on ships that turned around rather than run the blockade.

If none of the warheads had reached Cuba, and if Castro knew it, his anger and disenchantment with the Soviets would have been that much greater. That could constitute sufficient reason not only to lie to him in 1962, but even perhaps to avoid admitting in 1989 that no warheads had ever been in Cuba. General Volkogonov's account could have been tailored to fit what had been known by American intelligence, as detailed in declassified papers and published accounts (among them the first edition of this book, which presented a full account, including the information on the *Poltava*

---

70. Information drawn from CIA Memorandum, "The Crisis: USSR/Cuba," October 28, 1962 (Top Secret–Sensitive; "Sanitized" and declassified), p. I-1, and unnumbered map at p. 3. The CIA estimate was that *none* of the "probable nuclear storage facilities," as they were cautiously identified, at the missile launch sites was yet "believed to be in operation," and apart from the "secured port facility" nuclear storage installation at Punta Gerardo, one at the SS-5 base at Guanajay was "essentially complete."

These estimates involved more than the mere assembly of the prefabricated quonset-type structures, the first of which at an MRBM site at San Cristobal had been put together much earlier, by October 22. See "The Crisis: USSR/Cuba," October 24, 1962, p. 6.

and the *Aleksandrovsk*). There remains, therefore, the possibility
that the American quarantine actually interdicted the transfer of
all the nuclear warheads to Cuba. If so, Soviet leaders must have
believed that the United States had deliberately timed the public
disclosure of the missiles and the naval blockade in order to prevent
the arrival of the warheads. Yet, ironically, the American leaders
believed they had to assume the missile warheads were already in
Cuba.

On balance, I am inclined to credit General Volkogonov's
account, and reversing the judgment advanced in the earlier edition
of this book, I now believe that probably twenty nuclear warheads
were in Cuba, although probably not at the missile launch complexes. Nonetheless, there remains a possibility that no nuclear
warheads ever reached Cuba.

Whether or not any of the warheads had arrived, by mid-October
the Soviet leaders probably were confident that their gamble on
secretly installing the missiles in Cuba was succeeding. Either the
Americans were not aware of what was occurring, or, perhaps, the
administration was adjusting to the fact and preparing to come to
terms with the deployment. They should have been alert to the
growing possibility of American detection of the missile deployment activities. On October 15, the very day after the crucial U-2
reconnaissance mission, *Pravda* reported from Havana protests
over U.S. overflights of Cuba. Yet Soviet and Cuban veterans of
1962 today confirm, as their behavior at that time indicated, that
neither leadership had any intimation before President Kennedy's
speech of October 22 that the United States had penetrated their
secrecy and knew of the missiles.

STAGE 2

The U.S. Decision

ON THE MORNING of October 16 President Kennedy was shown photographs of Soviet SS-4 launching installations under construction in Cuba, taken two days earlier by a U-2 reconnaissance airplane. He held two long meetings that day, beginning an intensive series of meetings by the group of senior government officials later (from October 23) officially termed the "Ex Comm" (Executive Committee of the National Security Council, or NSC).[71]

A great deal has been written about these seven days of meetings culminating in President Kennedy's public address of October 22. Several of the participants have written accounts or provided information to journalists who soon wrote books on the crisis.[72]

---

71. NSC meetings, the only two held during the crisis, were convened on October 21 and 22 to ratify the initial decisions. The Executive Committee of the National Security Council was formally established by National Security Action Memorandum 196 on October 22 and held its first meeting the next day. The core of the Ex Comm had, however, been meeting in secrecy since October 16. The final meetings of the ad hoc Ex Comm were held in early 1963 and dealt mostly with policy matters other than the aftermath of the missile crisis. In February 1963 the Ex Comm was dissolved, but it had proved so effective that it was continued with a somewhat narrowed composition as the "Standing Group" of the NSC.

72. There is no need here to list all of these books, as several extensive bibliographies exist; in particular, see Lester H. Brune, *The Missile Crisis of October 1962: A Review of Issues and References* (Claremont, Calif.: Regina Books, 1985). The key volumes by participants were Arthur M. Schlesinger, Jr., *A Thousand Days: John F. Kennedy in the White House* (Boston: Houghton Mifflin, 1965), pp. 794–841; Theodore C. Sorensen, *Kennedy* (New York: Harper and Row, 1965, and Bantam, 1966); quotations in this study from the latter edition, pp. 752–809; and the aforecited books—Robert Kennedy, *Thirteen Days*;

43

There was never any doubt or debate about the U.S. objective. From the first day, the president never wavered from one basic decision: the Soviet missiles must be removed. There were differing views on the *military* significance of the missiles (Secretary of Defense Robert McNamara downplayed their significance to the strategic balance, while Assistant Secretary of Defense Paul Nitze and the chairman of the Joint Chiefs of Staff, General Maxwell Taylor, stressed their military significance).[73] But more basic was the common judgment that the secret, surreptitious Soviet attempt to install the missiles despite the president's clear warnings could not be accepted. There was little consideration of the fact that the Soviet decision must have been made at least four or five months earlier and could not have been easily reversed in September. But that would not have changed the basic decision.

The key issue for decision, then, over that week was not what the U.S. objective should be, but how to attain it. There were three basic paths: (1) *destroy* the missiles by attacking them; (2) *compel* the Soviet leaders to remove the missiles by pressure; and (3) *induce* the Soviets to remove the missiles by negotiation, probably involving a trade for American concessions. The latter two were not entirely exclusive; there could be pressure *and* negotiation, but there was a clear difference. As General Taylor later characterized the three alternatives, we could "take them

---

Schlesinger, *Robert Kennedy*; and Hilsman, *To Move a Nation*. Two other books by seasoned journalists benefited so extensively from background access to official information as to deserve mention here as well; see Elie Abel, *The Missile Crisis* (Philadelphia: J.B. Lippincott, 1966); and Edward Weintal and Charles Bartlett, *Facing the Brink: An Intimate Study of Crisis Diplomacy* (New York: Scribner, 1967). See also Henry M. Pachter, *Collision Course: The Cuban Missile Crisis and Coexistence* (New York: Praeger, 1963); Robert A. Divine, ed., *The Cuban Missile Crisis* (Chicago: Quadrangle Books, 1971); and David L. Larson, ed., *The "Cuban Crisis" of 1962: Selected Documents, Chronology and Bibliography* (Boston: Houghton Mifflin, 1963; 2d. ed., Lanham, Md.: University Press of America, 1986). Finally, two well-informed and thoughtful recent accounts are in a memoir *cum* history by McGeorge Bundy, *Danger and Survival: Choices About the Bomb in the First Fifty Years* (New York: Random House, 1988), pp. 391–462; and in John Newhouse, *War and Peace in the Nuclear Age* (New York: Alfred A. Knopf, 1989), pp. 165–84.

73. See the Appendix, "Commentary on Document D: A Retrospective Evaluation of the Soviet Missiles in Cuba in 1962."

out" by our own military action; "squeeze them out" by pressure; or "buy them out" by counterconcessions. That the Soviet action was seen as a political challenge and as the result of duplicity strengthened inclinations not to choose the third alternative.

Underlying these deliberations was another significant fact virtually never addressed in American discussions. It had to do with the perceived Soviet motivation. *No one* in the U.S. government believed that the deployment of Soviet missiles was intended to deter a U.S. invasion of Cuba. This was true of all those of us whose task was to estimate Soviet intentions and advise the leadership: the intelligence community, led by the CIA; Ambassador-at-Large Llewellyn E. ("Tommy") Thompson, Jr., personally advising the president and the Ex Comm; and several senior specialists in the Department of State, including myself. Most important, it was also the belief of President Kennedy, Secretary of State Dean Rusk, Secretary of Defense McNamara, national security adviser McGeorge Bundy, and other government leaders. Political and expert judgments coincided on this point.

We saw the principal Soviet objective as redressing a strategic inferiority, publicly revealed and growing in disparity.[74] There was no possibility for an early change in this strategic imbalance through building up intercontinental forces—ICBMs, submarine-launched ballistic missiles (SLBMs), or strategic bombers. While Soviet strategic weapons deployment programs then under way (the SS-7 and SS-8 ICBMs) could help, it would be several years before really satisfactory systems then under development would be ready for deployment (the SS-9 and SS-11 ICBMs, and the SS-N-6, the

74. Deputy Secretary of Defense Roswell L. Gilpatric had disposed of the alleged "missile gap" of American ICBM inferiority in a major speech just a year before (October 21, 1961), in which he stated that the United States could retaliate with equal or greater force even after being subjected to a Soviet first strike. The Gilpatric speech was a carefully considered statement intended to make clear to all, including the Soviet leaders, that the Kennedy administration no longer believed in a missile gap to American disadvantage—that, in fact, there was a growing gap to Soviet disadvantage. On the shift in intelligence estimates and the state of American government assessment, see Raymond L. Garthoff, *Intelligence Assessment and Policymaking: A Decision Point in the Kennedy Administration* (Brookings, 1984).

Soviet equivalent of the Polaris SLBM system). Soviet SS-4 MRBM and SS-5 IRBM missiles in Cuba could, however, provide an interim substitute, ersatz ICBMs, so to speak.

Beyond that basic agreement as to the strategic rationale underlying the Soviet decision, there was some divergence of views on whether this was more a defensive political-military measure, or an offensive one. All agreed that the Soviet leaders wanted in general to strengthen their standing in the correlation of forces; most analysts—and political leaders—believed that Khrushchev and the Soviet leadership intended to renew pressures over the Berlin issue from a position of greater strength. Many also believed that the Soviet leaders would use their missiles in Cuba as leverage to place pressure on American military bases around the Soviet Union. As noted earlier, it remains the judgment of most American analysts and historians today that the main Soviet aim in deploying the missiles in Cuba was to bolster Soviet strategic military power and diplomatic-political strength, and that deterrence of an American attack on Cuba was at most a secondary objective.

Notwithstanding the assessment of Soviet strategic inferiority, and the incentive or temptation for Soviet leaders to deploy intermediate-range missiles in Cuba, it was also the unanimous consensus of Soviet affairs experts in the intelligence community and elsewhere in the government that the Soviets would *not* attempt to deploy missiles in Cuba. It was reasoned that while Soviet strategic inferiority gave them an incentive to place missiles in Cuba, it also made that action too risky. In addition, the Soviets had never deployed nuclear weapons outside their own territory (except on naval ships), and exercised very strict controls. Risks even apart from the American reaction were deemed to make such a deployment unlikely. A special national intelligence estimate prepared in mid-September reaffirmed that judgment.[75] There was one notable exception: Director of Central Intelligence McCone, a conservative Republican, believed the Soviets were planning to deploy offensive missiles in Cuba, and so advised the president.

75. SNIE 85-3-62, "The Military Buildup in Cuba," September 19, 1962 (Top Secret; now declassified); and see National Intelligence Estimate (NIE) 85-2-62, "The Situation and Prospects in Cuba," August 1, 1962 (Secret; now declassified).

During the critical last weeks of September and early October he repeatedly sent such warnings from his honeymoon trip to Europe. But his judgment on this matter was discounted.

Minister of Foreign Affairs Andrei Gromyko visited Washington and met with President Kennedy on October 18. This meeting was important in several respects. Kennedy repeated his warnings of September 4 and 13, but did not ask Gromyko outright whether there were Soviet missiles in Cuba. Gromyko said the Soviet Union would not introduce "offensive arms," but did not say what the Soviet government meant by that term. Kennedy and his advisers considered Gromyko's position to have been duplicitous. They also, after October 16, regarded as disinformation the many assurances that the Soviet Union would not put offensive missiles into Cuba that had earlier been conveyed, including further assurances by Ambassador Dobrynin, most recently on October 13 to former Under Secretary of State Chester Bowles. The most rankling, with the possible exception of Gromyko's evasion, was an assurance through an established and trusted informal channel from Khrushchev personally to the president received by Robert Kennedy on October 22, several days after American discovery of the missiles. At that time, Robert Kennedy had been told by Soviet Embassy counselor Georgi Bol'shakov, after the latter's return from Moscow, that he had been summoned to meet with Khrushchev and Mikoyan and instructed to convey an assurance to the president that "no missile capable of reaching the United States will be placed in Cuba."[76]

76. See Sorensen, *Kennedy*, p. 753. Bol'shakov was conveying a message from Khrushchev responding to an oral message from President Kennedy transmitted through Bol'shakov in a meeting on August 31; Bol'shakov met with Khrushchev at Pitsunda on about September 15. Robert Kennedy, after hearing the message and asking Bol'shakov to repeat the passage about only defensive arms, had him repeat it again to a trusted intermediary the next day. The American accounts of Bol'shakov's assurance were very clear, especially from an interjection from Mikoyan that only surface-to-air missiles were being provided, that there could be no confusion about defensive *purposes*; the message was no missiles *capable* of striking the United States.

Bol'shakov has recently written his own account of his role as a back channel intermediary in 1961–62, and it coincides closely with American accounts except for one important detail: he does not refer to missiles incapable of striking the

The second aspect of Gromyko's visit was a proposal to the president for a summit meeting of the two leaders, some time following the American congressional elections in November. Although Kennedy made a vaguely positive response, he instructed Ambassador Thompson to tell Ambassador Dobrynin that same night at dinner that a summit would not be appropriate under current conditions and would require proper preparations. U.S. advisers and political leaders saw the Soviet proposal for a summit, and the earlier assurances that the Soviet Union would not cause any problems for the Kennedy administration before the November 7 elections, as signs that by the time of a summit meeting in late November or December, Khrushchev planned to make publicly

---

United States (nor does he refer to Mikoyan's interjection); rather, he now reports the message as an assurance that "the Soviet Union is sending to Cuba only weapons of a defensive character, to defend the interests of the Cuban revolution." See Bol'shakov, *Novoye vremya* (January 27, 1989), p. 42. This is clearly a "sanitized" public version of the message he actually passed in October 1962.

Bol'shakov had served as an intermediary in a private channel of personal exchanges between Khrushchev and President Kennedy begun a year earlier, so he was regarded as a trusted source. Bol'shakov, incidentally, was himself unaware of the missiles when he passed his deceptive message.

For background on Bol'shakov's role, see Schlesinger, *Robert Kennedy,* pp. 499–502; and Pierre Salinger, *With Kennedy* (Garden City, N.Y.: Doubleday, 1966), pp. 184, 197–200, 282. Bol'shakov was believed to be a KGB operative; see Salinger, *With Kennedy,* p. 198.

According to informed American accounts (in particular, Schlesinger, *Robert Kennedy,* p. 527), the Soviets later withdrew Bol'shakov after his role had been revealed by disclosure of his pre-crisis unwitting deception on the missiles in a news column by Joseph Alsop. Robert Kennedy even wrote him a personal letter of appreciation. Ibid.

Bol'shakov's role remained, of course, a carefully kept secret in Moscow. At least some quarters in the Soviet establishment believe that his departure from Washington was engineered by the United States. As I noted in the first edition of this book, I had been told by a Kremlin insider of that time that among themselves Khrushchev had told the following anecdote: first, he had been asked by the Americans to withdraw the missiles, and did. Then he was asked to withdraw the IL-28 bombers, and did. Finally, he was asked to withdraw Bol'shakov, and did—but put his foot down at that point, saying, "All right, Bol'shakov too, but nothing more!" Bol'shakov later remonstrated to me that in fact this was *his* joke. Khrushchev may have appropriated the joke, or the attribution to him may have been apocryphal. Bol'shakov has now reported the joke as one he told at a private dinner at the time of his departure. See Georgi Bol'shakov, "A Hot Line," *Novoye vremya,* no. 6 (February 3, 1989), p. 41.

known that the Soviet missiles were already deployed and operational in Cuba, and buttressed by this new position of strength, to make new demands, probably on the status of Berlin.[77]

Later critics of the president's handling of the crisis have asked why he did not tell Gromyko about the missiles, or send a private message to Khrushchev, and give the Soviet leader an opportunity to save face by withdrawing the missiles quietly. Ambassador Charles E. ("Chip") Bohlen had suggested a letter to Khrushchev on October 18. Kennedy and several of his close advisors did try for two days, October 18 to 20, to draft such a letter.[78] But they were unable to find a formula that would be sufficiently persuasive without itself precipitating a crisis. Moreover, there was a consensus that it would be undesirable to let the Soviets take the initiative. I believe the decision not to do so was sound. In any case, the decision not to raise the matter privately with Khrushchev (and still less with Gromyko) was deliberate and considered.

Within several days the members of the Ex Comm and the president himself decided on what they regarded as the middle course: a blockade (termed a "quarantine" to avoid the status of belligerency entailed under international law by imposing a naval blockade) to interdict any further shipment of Soviet offensive arms to Cuba. Advocates of an American air attack on the missile facilities (and Cuban air force bases and other large airfields, also

77. A plenary meeting of the Central Committee of the Communist Party of the Soviet Union was already scheduled to meet in Moscow on November 19–23. Some have speculated that Khrushchev wanted to have an international triumph from his missile venture by then. Others have noted that the SS-5 IRBMs would not have been fully operational by that date and thus could not yet have been revealed. It is not known if Khrushchev was seeking to bring matters to a head as early as that Central Committee plenum. We do know that Khrushchev had tentatively planned a trip to Cuba in late November, and Ambassador Alekseyev states that it was planned to make public the presence of the missiles in Cuba at that time. See *Argumenty i fakty* (March 11–17, 1989), p. 5. Also, Khrushchev had considered attending the UN General Assembly in New York in late November or December, and through Gromyko had proposed a summit meeting in that general time period. While we do not know the precise timing, and perhaps Khrushchev himself had not yet decided, the general judgment that he planned at some point suddenly to make known the deployment of the missiles and to make political capital of the surprise move was almost certainly valid.

78. See Schlesinger, *Robert Kennedy*, p. 513.

considered militarily necessary) were not helped in their case by
the U.S. Air Force judgment that this would require 500 sorties—
and that even then there could be no guarantee that all the missiles
would be destroyed, or civilians spared.

Some revisionist historical analyses of the crisis have stressed
American concern with urgency before the Soviet missiles would
become "operational," and the fact that the United States continued to press its position even after most of the missile facilities
were deemed operational as meaning that a sense of urgency was
maintained for ulterior purposes and that diplomacy could have
proceeded at less than crisis pressure. It is true that on the first day
or two some, in particular Secretary McNamara, stressed urgency
of decision before the missiles should become operational. In fact
on the first day he argued that an air strike should only be considered
"on the assumption that we can carry it off before these [missiles]
become operational."[79] But this did not drive a decision for early
attack, and by the end of the first week the concern was less over
the current status of the missile sites—by then estimated and
assumed, for reasons of prudence, to be operational—than over
the possibility that with time they would become accepted as a new
status quo.[80]

Contrary to Soviet and Cuban claims, no U.S. plan for an
invasion of Cuba was under way. Nonetheless, while those who
have most stressed the fact that the United States had not made a
decision to attack Cuba are correct, they have sometimes leaned
too far toward dismissing the relevance of this contingency planning
to the history of the times.[81] As earlier noted, contingency plans
existed, and indeed as a conventional arms buildup in Cuba
proceeded in the summer and fall, steps were taken to enhance
U.S. readiness to carry out those plans. A series of measures were

79. "White House Tapes and Minutes of the Cuban Missile Crisis," *International Security,* vol. 10 (Summer 1985), p. 176.

80. See the discussion in Bundy, *Danger and Survival,* pp. 424–26.

81. Robert S. McNamara, at the Cambridge and Moscow conferences, is one;
this author, in the first edition of this book, was guilty of the same error.
McNamara accepts that U.S. actions probably looked very threatening to the
Cubans and Soviets, but I am addressing also the point that under some
circumstances, never clearly established, the United States might have attacked
Cuba.

taken in September and the first half of October. In particular, on October 1, two weeks before discovery of the missiles, Secretary McNamara met with the Joint Chiefs of Staff and directed that readiness for possible implementation of the contingency plans be raised.[82] For example, U.S. Air Force tactical air units designated to meet the contingency war plan for an air strike (Oplan 312) were put under the operational control of CINCSTRIKE (Commander-in-Chief, Strike Command); U.S. Navy forces were earmarked for 6-hour, 12-hour, and 24-hour reaction times, and the war plan was revised to put the base at Mariel for Soviet Komar missile patrol boats on the air-strike priority target list. On October 6 increased readiness was also directed for forces earmarked for Oplan 314 and 316, the two war plan variants for invasion of Cuba.

Most important, on October 8 the Joint Chiefs referred to CINCLANT a memorandum from Secretary of Defense Mc-Namara listing the "contingencies under which military action against Cuba may be necessary and toward which our military planning should be oriented." One of these, to be sure, was "evidence that the Castro regime has permitted the positioning of [Soviet] bloc offensive weapons on Cuban soil or in Cuban harbors," but this was only one of six, and listed second. First remained "Soviet action against Western rights in Berlin calling for a Western response including among other actions a blockade of Communist or other shipping enroute to Cuba." Also included were "an attack against the Guantanamo Naval Base or against U.S. planes or vessels outside Cuban territorial air space or waters"; "a substantial popular uprising in Cuba, the leaders of which request assistance in recovering Cuban independence from the Castro Soviet puppet regime"; "Cuban armed assistance to subversion in other parts of the Western Hemisphere"; and, finally, a very open

82. See "Department of Defense Operations during the Cuban Crisis," Office of the Secretary of Defense, February 12, 1963 (Secret; now declassified), p. 1; and "CINCLANT Historical Account of Cuban Crisis—1963," Atlantic Command, Headquarters of the Commander-in-Chief, Norfolk, Va., April 29, 1963 (now declassified), pp. 39–48, 58. See also James G. Hershberg, "Before the Missiles of October," *Boston Phoenix*, April 8, 1988, and a forthcoming elaboration in *Diplomatic History*, for the most thorough research on this activity, although in my judgment he overdraws conclusions on the extent of the U.S. inclination to attack Cuba prior to discovery of the missiles.

"contingency" indeed: "a decision by the President that affairs in Cuba have reached a point inconsistent with continuing U.S. national security."[83] But no decision had been made to attack Cuba, and the intensified contingency planning from late August to mid-October was a preliminary response to the Cuban arms buildup.

During the crisis deliberations after October 16, however, there was some significant military and political sentiment that following an air strike it would probably be necessary to mount an invasion of the island to destroy Cuban military power, and that it would be desirable at the same time to end Castro's rule. An air strike remained a possible recourse if the quarantine was not successful in inducing the Soviet leaders to agree to remove the missiles, but it seemed better to begin with more limited actions and then, if necessary, escalate. Also, the third alternative, a diplomatic negotiating path, was in fact expected to develop. There was, however, reluctance to think in terms of American concessions in general, as well as any specific terms. The only top adviser who did so with any passion, Adlai Stevenson, was as a result considered too much a "dove." The leading "hawk," calling for an immediate air strike and defeat of Castro's rule, was former Secretary of State Dean Acheson, called upon for advice in the first days of the crisis. But others also held this view, especially in the first few days, when it was the majority view. Fortunately, there was a full week for deliberation.[84]

It should be stressed, as many have observed, that the ability to devote an entire week to deliberation and decision free of public pressure, and free of Soviet action or interaction, was crucial. It was also unique; no other past crisis has had, and none in the future can be expected to have, such a lengthy period for decision free from external and domestic political pressures.

The overriding issue in the first phase was to decide on the precise objective and course of action to deal with the surreptitious Soviet deployment of medium- and intermediate-range missiles in

83. See "CINCLANT Historical Account," pp. 41–42.

84. The current political connotations of the terms "hawks" and "doves" originated during the missile crisis.

Cuba. This stage was marked by secret meetings, most held in Under Secretary of State Ball's office in the State Department to avoid the attention that arrivals for meetings at the White House would entail.[85] "Scenarios" providing action-response sequences were developed for three major alternative courses of action: a "political path," for a diplomatic deal with the Soviet Union, probably through a summit meeting with Khrushchev; a "block-ade" (later termed a "quarantine"), a selective and possibly gradual tightening naval cordon to prevent the arrival of more missiles and to compel Soviet withdrawal of those already in Cuba; and an "air-strike option," to destroy the missiles and launch facilities, probably with land invasion to follow to ensure no reconstitution of a military threat to the United States—also, of course, disposing of Castro once and for all. Some members of the Ex Comm sought limited advice from their own staffs as the week progressed, and assistance was discreetly provided for some scenario writing. But by and large the order of the day was to limit participation to the select senior officials in frequent and often lengthy meetings. By the end of the week a great deal of staff support for certain key diplomatic actions was required: preparations for rallying the support of the Organization of American States for the quarantine; preparations for last-hour consultations with key allies; preparations to call a UN Security Council meeting; preparations for key congressional consultations; and the like.[86] Military contingency planning was under way, and preparations were made for implementing a blockade.

During the first stage, one key element was predicting the Soviet

85. Ball's office was referred to by some participants as the "think tank," coining a term later applied widely to intellectual centers cogitating and advising on policy matters.

86. For example, in the forty-eight hours from midnight October 20 to midnight October 22, the State Department, working around the clock, transmitted fifteen separate presidential letters or messages to 441 recipients, with appropriate instructions on delivery, gave oral briefings to ninety-five foreign ambassadors, and drafted or participated in drafting and dispatched most messages and the texts of the U.S. proposals for the OAS and UN forums and appropriate background messages to various embassies—including a warning to 134 U.S. embassies and consulates to take precautions against possible hostile demonstrations following the president's address.

response or, more accurately, estimating the range of possible Soviet responses, and the American actions that could help to channel such responses in desired directions and away from the most dangerous and undesired ones. The analyses and estimates of Soviet responses were all keyed to the alternative U.S. actions and related scenarios.[87]

Once the president had spoken, American attention shifted from our decision to the Soviet response. And the Soviet leadership suddenly realized it was in a first-class crisis.

87. Ambassadors Llewellyn E. Thompson, Jr., and (until his departure for Paris on October 19) Charles E. Bohlen gave their expert advice. Two special national intelligence estimates—SNIE 11-18-62, "Soviet Reactions to Certain US Courses of Action on Cuba," October 19, and SNIE 11-19-62, "Major Consequences of Certain U.S. Courses of Action on Cuba," October 20 (both originally Top Secret–Sensitive; now declassified)—represented the best judgment of the intelligence community on Soviet responses.

Interestingly, the intelligence estimates considered an air strike and gradually escalating military actions *more* likely to lead to local Soviet involvement in military counteractions than a prompt all-out invasion. See SNIE 11-19-62, p. 9.

In addition, the Board of National Estimates submitted to Director of Central Intelligence McCone two estimates not coordinated with other agencies as "national" intelligence estimates, one on the "Effect on Cuba of a Blockade Covering All Goods Except Food and Medicines," and the other on "Survivability of West Berlin," if access to that city were blockaded in reprisal. While references to them are no longer classified, to my knowledge these estimates have not been declassified.

The Confrontation

PRESIDENT KENNEDY's address on October 22 had firmly set the objective of the dismantling and withdrawal of Soviet offensive weapons from Cuba. He intentionally directed attention at Moscow, and ignored Castro and the Cuban role.[88]

The United States had prepared carefully for rapid action by the Organization of American States, including direct communication to the Mexican president and foreign minister while they were traveling in the Far East. The seriousness of the Soviet and communist challenge (as it was seen and depicted), and the strength of the U.S. government's resolve, contributed to a unanimous OAS vote on October 23 condemning the missiles as a threat to the peace and calling for their removal. This outcome was even better than Washington had anticipated. The State Department had been confident of obtaining the support of a majority, even the two-thirds majority needed for an OAS imprimatur on the quarantine, but not of rallying a unanimous vote. In the United Nations Security Council there was more hesitancy, but the Soviet failure until October 28 to acknowledge publicly the presence of its missiles in Cuba, counterposed to convincing American photographic evidence, weakened Soviet claims that it was a normal and justified action to station forces in the territory of a friendly state. Other key neutral states, as well as allies, also gave support.[89]

88. Consideration had been given to approaching Castro and seeking by threats—and possible incentives if he broke with Moscow—to work on getting the missiles out through a Cuban reversal. In retrospect as well as in judgment at the time, as an alternative to facing the Soviet leaders head-on that course would probably have been ineffective and unwise.

89. In a notable example, on October 23 the American ambassadors in leftist

The U.S. leaders were initially concerned above all about two things: Would the Soviet leaders attempt to send military shipments through the quarantine blockade and challenge the U.S. Navy? And would the Soviet leaders attempt to build counterpressure elsewhere, for example by imposing a "quarantine" blockade of West Berlin, or by threatening the American intermediate-range missiles in Turkey?

The first of the appended memoranda (Appendix document A) is a hasty analysis I prepared on October 23 in response to a request by Walt W. Rostow, then head of the policy-planning council in the State Department. While it represented my personal view, it provides something of a feel for the thinking at the time on both Soviet motivation in placing the missiles in Cuba and on the range of counteractions the Soviet leaders might consider. I sought to indicate the "cards" they might see themselves holding. (I did not, incidentally, believe they would respond by counterescalation in Berlin or Turkey, and so argued, although not in this memorandum.)

From all indications President Kennedy's speech on October 22 caught the Soviet leaders by surprise. Ambassador Dobrynin, called in by Secretary Rusk and given a copy of the speech just an hour before it was delivered, arrived in a relaxed mood but left "ashen-faced" and "visibly shaken." Robert Kennedy went to see him the next evening, and Dobrynin still "seemed very shaken, out of the picture," without instructions, and uninformed as to any instructions that might have been given to Soviet ships about stopping short of the quarantine line (the main point on which Kennedy was hoping to get some indication of Soviet intentions).[90]

There is more evidence the Soviets were unsuspecting. By coincidence, Foreign Minister Gromyko departed from the United States to return to Moscow on the afternoon of October 22, just a few hours before the president's announcement. When word

---

Guinea and in Senegal were instructed to request that no permission be given to the Soviet Union for air-landing rights at Conakry and Dakar. Both countries agreed to the American request, foreclosing to the Soviet Union the option of air supply of key military equipment to Cuba.

90. For Kennedy's visit, see Schlesinger, *A Thousand Days*, p. 817. Dobrynin's reaction to Rusk's message was noted by several news correspondents who observed him enter and leave; see also Kennedy, *Thirteen Days*, pp. 52–53.

reached officials in Washington that Gromyko would meet the press before boarding his flight, some speculated that he might make a dramatic preemptive statement about the missiles in Cuba, presumably having learned the subject of the president's address. But his departure remarks were routine, occasioning considerable relief.

It remains uncertain what the Soviets had observed during the American activities of October 16 through 22, and what meaning they ascribed to whatever activities they had become aware of. One would assume that they had noticed the greatly intensified aerial surveillance of Cuba, although that information might not have gone beyond their intelligence watch institutions. They should have been able to pick up some of the preliminary U.S. military movements at sea, by the U.S. Air Force, and in Florida despite our efforts to preserve an atmosphere of normalcy—although, again, taken alone these might not have attracted political attention in Moscow. Some of the military moves were explicable in terms of a previously announced amphibious exercise in the Caribbean. Finally, inasmuch as several alert American newsmen and one ally (Great Britain) became aware of the unique pattern of secret high-level government meetings, one might assume that Soviet intelligence in Washington would have gotten wind of something unusual too. But there is no indication from Soviet behavior that they had realized or even suspected what was under way. Moreover, Dobrynin and other Soviet officials then in Washington, New York, Havana, and Moscow all say that they had no information on the American discovery of the missiles before the president's speech.

The president's speech was of course the primary focus for Soviet attention. In it, he disclosed that U.S. intelligence had discovered the missiles in Cuba six days earlier. The president referred to the MRBMs, the IRBMs, and "jet bombers, capable of carrying nuclear weapons." Recalling his own September warnings, he cited public and private deceptive Soviet assurances, including Gromyko's, that seemed to deny that offensive missiles would be sent to Cuba and underlined the surreptitious nature of the deployment. He characterized "their sudden, clandestine decision to station strategic weapons for the first time outside of

Soviet soil" as "a deliberately provocative and unjustified change in the status quo which cannot be accepted by this country." He called upon Khrushchev "to halt and eliminate this clandestine, reckless, and provocative threat to world peace . . . and to join in an historic effort to end the perilous arms race and transform the history of man."[91]

The quarantine to interdict any further transfer of offensive weapons to Cuba was announced, although without specifying when it would take effect. It was identified as one of a series of "*initial* steps," along with an immediate call for convening of the OAS, and an emergency meeting of the UN Security Council to seek "the prompt dismantling and withdrawal of all offensive weapons in Cuba, under the supervision of United Nations observers" as a precondition for lifting the quarantine.[92]

The overt nuclear element of the confrontation was contained in Kennedy's declaration that "it shall be the policy of this nation to regard any nuclear missile launched from Cuba against any nation in the Western Hemisphere as an attack by the Soviet Union on the United States, requiring a full retaliatory response upon the Soviet Union."[93]

Finally, although virtually never noted in American commentaries on the crisis, the Soviet (and Cuban) leaders would have taken particular note of another passage of several paragraphs addressed to "the captive people of Cuba," declaring that "your leaders are no longer Cuban leaders inspired by Cuban ideals. They are puppets and agents of an international conspiracy which has turned Cuba against your friends and neighbors in the Americas— and turned it into the first Latin American country to become a target for nuclear war—the first Latin American country to have these weapons on its soil. . . . Your lives and land are being used as pawns by those who deny you freedom. . . . I have no doubt that most Cubans today look forward to the time when they will be

91. "Radio and Television Report to the American People on the Soviet Arms Buildup in Cuba, October 22, 1962," *Public Papers: Kennedy, 1962*, pp. 806–08.

92. Ibid., pp. 807–08; emphasis added.

93. Ibid., p. 808.

truly free. . . . And then shall Cuba be welcomed back to the society of free nations."[94]

The Soviet leaders certainly understood that President Kennedy was now publicly committed to the removal of their missiles from Cuba and was instituting "initial steps" to cut off any further buildup. They probably knew or were quickly briefed on the fact that an effective quarantine meant that all of the IRBM missiles, and at least some (possibly all) of the nuclear warheads for the missiles, had not yet reached Cuba. The fact that nuclear warheads were at that very time en route at sea still several days from Cuba may have led the Soviet leaders to believe that the United States had timed the action to prevent the arrival of those warheads. But this consideration affected at most their judgment as to whether a viable "freeze" short of the planned deployment, but not involving withdrawal, might be negotiable. The dramatic American threat of full retaliation for any missile fired from Cuba, which attracted so much attention in the West, and which was undoubtedly desirable as a sign of American determination, was irrelevant to Moscow's calculations. It seems clear that under *no* contingency did the Soviet leadership contemplate actually firing its Cuban missiles, even if the warheads had been there.[95]

Of much greater concern in Moscow was whether the United States would now use the Soviet missiles as an excuse to invade Cuba. It was from this standpoint that they probably weighed the president's words about a "captive" Cuba and the American call for its freedom. They had no way of knowing that Kennedy had rejected even stiffer language hinting at the removal of Castro— what they did hear seemed ominous enough.[96]

94. Ibid., p. 809.

95. All knowledgeable Soviet participants at the 1989 Moscow conference on the crisis, including General Volkogonov, state firmly that the Soviet military command in Cuba had strict and clear instructions under no circumstances to prepare the missiles for firing, much less to fire them—in contrast to the instructions to Soviet air defense, coastal defense, and ground forces in Cuba, who were authorized to fight if Cuba were attacked. In addition, as noted earlier, if any nuclear warheads were in Cuba, they were probably held at the secured port storage facility rather than at the missile-launching bases.

96. See Sorensen, *Kennedy*, p. 789.

In addition, the Soviet leaders no doubt reevaluated such facts as the planned American amphibious exercise (*Phibriglex-62*) aimed at liberating the Caribbean island of Vieques near Puerto Rico from a fictional dictator "Ortsac" (Castro spelled backwards).[97]

The American success the next day in gaining unanimous support of its OAS allies was undoubtedly a shock for the Soviets. Their hopes for an anti-Yanqui backlash in Latin America at the American action against Cuba evaporated.

Another event almost certainly noted in Moscow, but *not* in Washington, was the coincidence that on that very day, October 22, with ceremonial fanfare, the first Jupiter missile launch position in Turkey was turned over to Turkish command.[98] This fact, remarkably, has only recently been noted; it was not by the American leaders at the time. It explains why Khrushchev had felt it a timely thing to complain about to Ambassador Kohler on October 16. Similarly, that the Jupiter missiles in Turkey first became operational in April 1962, in American hands, was unnoted in Washington but may have prompted Marshal Malinovsky to draw it to Khrushchev's attention at that time, contributing greatly to the decision on missile deployment in Cuba and to the genesis of the crisis.

The very hour of the president's speech was chosen for instituting a Defense Condition (DEFCON) 3 alert of all major U.S. commands and for shifting from limited military preparations under wraps to open all-out buildup of the contingent air-strike and invasion forces of the U.S. Army, Navy, Air Force, and Marines.[99]

97. In what may have been a move in psychological warfare, the Ortsac/Castro designation was leaked to the press and appeared on October 22. See Jack Raymond, "Navy and Marine Force Heads for Exercise off Puerto Rico," *New York Times*, October 22, 1962.

98. See Martin E. James, *Historical Highlights: United States Air Forces in Europe, 1945–1979* (Office of History, Headquarters U.S. Air Forces in Europe, November 1980), p. 61.

99. There was one important exception to the U.S. worldwide alert. General Lauris Norstad, the Supreme Allied Commander, Europe, and simultaneously the Commander-in-Chief, U.S. Forces in Europe, sought and obtained approval for a much less complete alert by U.S. forces there. Since the United States had

This alert action was both incidental to the shift to open operations and intended to demonstrate the seriousness of U.S. preparations for possible further military steps beyond the quarantine. An alert of all major commands had not been activated since the Korean War and must have been regarded seriously in Moscow.

Among other highly visible actions in implementing this alert on October 22 was the dispersal of the B-47 medium bomber force to some thirty-three civilian airports. Unprecedented actions were taken by the U.S. Strategic Air Command (SAC). SAC was generated to still higher alert, DEFCON 2, for the first time ever, on October 24. This involved a further and unprecedented intensification of combat readiness measures, including a significant increase in the armed airborne alert portion of the B-52 heavy bomber force and a shift to military alert status of ICBM launchers undergoing checkout or for other reasons on off-line status.[100]

Most of this activity would have been observed in due course by various means of Soviet information collection. But in this case there was a unique difference: the SAC full-alert process was reported "in the clear" rather than in normal encoded messages. Soviet communications interception personnel must have been shocked suddenly to hear the SAC commander-in-chief address all his senior commanders in an unprecedented message in the clear, stressing the seriousness of the situation faced by the nation, and assuring them that SAC plans were well prepared and were being

---

not consulted its allies, Norstad feared a high-visibility, unilateral American military alerting action could raise questions and undercut Western European support for the American stand on Cuba. It was a wise move, and a good example of political-military "feedback" in decisionmaking.

Among measures undertaken, however, was a transfer of contingency nuclear strike targets from two U.S. Air Force, Europe, tactical fighter-bomber squadrons in Germany to two others in the United Kingdom, "freeing the European squadrons for conventional operations in the event of a Berlin contingency." USAF Historical Division Liaison Office, Headquarters USAF, *The Air Force Response to the Cuban Crisis* (December 1962), p. 26 (Top Secret; now declassified).

100. One out of every eight B-52s was always in the air, armed with nuclear weapons and ready to strike upon order; aerial tankers were ready to service the entire bomber fleet. Polaris ballistic missile-launching submarines in port went to sea.

executed smoothly.[101] Soviet political and military leaders must have been puzzled and alarmed at this flaunting of the American strategic superiority, so great that the United States could afford to ignore normal operational security in order to drive home the extent of its power.[102]

Equally extraordinary, and not known in Moscow, was that this remarkable display of American power was unauthorized by and unknown to the president, the secretary of defense, the chairman of the Joint Chiefs, and the Ex Comm as they so carefully calibrated and controlled action in the intensifying confrontation. The decision for this bold action was taken by General Thomas Power, commander-in-chief of SAC, on his own initiative. He had been ordered to go on full alert, and he did so. No one had told him *how* to do it, and he decided to "rub it in." Nor did he even inform higher authority after the fact (or, if he did inform General Curtis LeMay, chief of staff of the U.S. Air Force, LeMay in turn did not tell anyone in the government leadership). When I mentioned this incident at the Hawks Cay conference in early 1987, all the former Ex Comm members (including Bundy and McNamara) were startled to learn of it.

Caught unaware, the Soviet leaders' first inclination was to reassess the situation, probe at possible ways to recoup as much as they could, and in the meantime play for time, avoiding any

101. I was first told about this action soon after the crisis by Major General (then Colonel) George J. Keegan, Jr., USAF (ret'd), then an intelligence officer at SAC headquarters, who said he was present when General Power gave the order. According to Keegan, perhaps exaggerating, SAC alert messages were transmitted in the clear. It has not been possible to corroborate Keegan's version from available records or other senior Air Force officers. Official Air Force records do, however, confirm the unique message from General Power to all senior SAC commanders. The wording cited here has been paraphrased from the actual recorded message. Some SAC subordinate headquarters treated the message as "top secret" after receipt, even though transmission had been in the clear and without classification. H. R. Haldeman has reported a version of this incident according to which Power's instruction was: "Make a little mistake. Send a message in the clear." See H. R. Haldeman with Joseph DiMona, *The Ends of Power* (New York: Times Books, 1978), p. 93.

102. In 1989, General Volkogonov told me that the initial Soviet reaction on hearing General Power's message in the clear was to wonder if it was a bluff, but that question was swiftly dispelled by observation of the SAC actions.

provocative action that might trigger further American reactions. Not until fourteen hours after the president's speech did the Soviet government issue a public statement sharply critical of the American actions, but silent on Soviet moves.

One action, undertaken without delay, had extraordinary and unpredictable consequences. Colonel Oleg Penkovsky of Soviet Military Intelligence, an American (and British) spy in Moscow, was arrested on October 23 (Moscow time; October 22 in Washington). Penkovsky had been under suspicion by Soviet counterintelligence for some time, but they had permitted him to continue at liberty (under close surveillance) in order to see if there were other Soviet agents in a network and to monitor contacts with his Central Intelligence Agency (CIA) and Secret Intelligence Service (SIS) handlers in the U.S. and U.K. embassies in Moscow. Soviet counterintelligence did not know, however, until his arrest and interrogation precisely what he had turned over to the Western intelligence services. In particular, they did not know if he had acquired and passed on information on the Cuban missile deployment. In fact, while from April 1961 to September 1962 Penkovsky had provided a tremendous amount of important military information, he had not been aware of or able to pass on anything about the missiles in Cuba. But this was not yet known to the Soviet military, intelligence, and political leaders on October 22.[103]

103. Some intelligence provided by Penkovsky was useful background information during the crisis. In particular, he had provided information on the Soviet missile forces, including the SS-4 and SS-5 systems. U.S. intelligence identification of the sites in Cuba, however, was based on familiarity with such sites in the USSR from overhead reconnaissance. A British writer, in a popular history of the British Secret Intelligence Service (SIS), has written an account of the Cuban missile crisis strewn with errors and grossly exaggerating Penkovsky's role. See Anthony Verrier, *Through the Looking Glass: British Foreign Policy in an Age of Illusions* (New York: W.W. Norton, 1983), pp. 193, 221–43. Another British writer with a greatly exaggerated and distorted picture of Penkovsky's role is Gordon Brook-Shepherd, *The Storm Birds: Soviet Post-War Defectors* (London: Weidenfeld and Nicolson, 1988), pp. 135–37. At the opposite extreme, it has been alleged that Penkovsky was a KGB plant. See Chapman Pincher, *Their Trade Is Treachery* (London: Sidgwick and Jackson, 1981).

Two American intelligence-associated commentators have also credited Penkovsky with providing information valuable to the United States in the missile crisis. That is correct, although the implied degree of value is exaggerated. See

Penkovsky's arrest, promptly known to the U.S. and British intelligence services and thus to CIA Director John McCone, was regarded strictly as an operational intelligence matter and was not even brought to the attention of the Ex Comm. If the significance of one important operational detail had been evaluated differently by Penkovsky's CIA and SIS handlers, however, it could have had a profound effect in greatly heightening tension in the crisis. I disclosed this matter in the original edition of this book for the first time.[104]

Penkovsky maintained communication with his American and British contacts in Moscow principally through "dead drops," places where material was left to be picked up by the other party. Nonverbal telephone signals were used to indicate that such drops had been made. In addition, Penkovsky was given a few standard coded telephonic signals for use in emergencies, including one to be used if he was about to be arrested, and also one to be used in the ultimate contingency: imminent war. When he was being arrested, at his apartment, he had time to send a telephonic signal— but chose to use the signal for an imminent Soviet attack. This seemingly bizarre act rings true. Penkovsky had always been a man with unusual self-importance (for example, he had asked his SIS handlers, while in London on an official trip in 1961, to be introduced to Queen Elizabeth, and also to be whisked to Wash-

---

Frank Gibney, Introduction, in Oleg Penkovskiy, *The Penkovskiy Papers* (Garden City, N.Y.: Doubleday, 1965), pp. 4, 17. And without explicitly naming Penkovsky, CIA Director Richard Helms had him particularly in mind in a public reference; see Chalmers M. Roberts, " 'Well-Placed Russians' Aided U.S. in Cuban Missile Crisis," *Washington Post,* April 16, 1971. Despite the title of the article, what Helms is quoted as saying, correctly, is that the United States was aided by material in "intelligence files" provided *earlier* by "U-2 photography of the Soviet Union" and "a number of well-placed and courageous Russians who helped us," including "a wealth of information on Soviet missile systems."

104. I had been involved in intelligence analysis and specifically in the evaluation of Penkovsky's materials from the outset of his reporting in the spring of 1961. One of the key CIA clandestine service officers responsible for directly managing the Penkovsky case, whom I had come to know well as a reliable person, is my source for this information. He told me in strict confidence soon after the event. In the nature of such things, and given both continuing secrecy pledges and diminishing sources after a quarter of a century, I have not been able to confirm this report, but also not to disconfirm it. I believe it to be true.

ington to meet President Kennedy; and he liked to wear British and American colonels' uniforms at his clandestine debriefing sessions when he was traveling in the West). He had tried to egg the Western powers on to more aggressive actions against the Soviet Union during the Berlin crisis in 1961. So when he was about to go down, he evidently decided to play Samson and bring the temple down on everyone else as well. Normally, such an attempt would have been feckless. But October 22/23, 1962, was not a normal day. Fortunately, his Western intelligence handlers, at the operational level, after weighing a dilemma of great responsibility, decided not to credit Penkovsky's final signal and suppressed it. Not even the higher reaches of the CIA were informed of Penkovsky's provocative farewell.

The Soviet leaders sought to maintain a low-key atmosphere in Moscow. Desiring also to keep decisions in their own hands, Khrushchev and the inner core of leaders did not even assemble the whole of the Presidium (the 1962 Politburo)—those members resident elsewhere in the Soviet Union because they held regional leadership positions were not summoned to Moscow during the whole ensuing week of crisis. (Mikoyan, however, was promptly called back from vacation and arrived in Moscow on the 23d.) On October 23 five top leaders—Khrushchev, Leonid I. Brezhnev, Aleksei N. Kosygin, Kozlov, and Mikoyan—attended an opera performance, demonstrating their own solidarity and seeking to show normalcy. After the performance, Khrushchev made the gesture of visiting backstage the American basso Jerome Hines, displaying an absence of animus toward the American people. Life in Moscow, including government working patterns and rehearsals for the annual November 7 anniversary parade, was normal. Diplomatic travelers were called back to Moscow as a precautionary measure, and most trip requests denied, but diplomatic life was also normal. Similarly, while Soviet and Warsaw Pact alerts were prominently announced on October 23, they were in fact minimal in impact, mainly involving largely symbolic measures such as canceling leaves. There were no major redeployments or high-readiness measures of the strategic missile force, air force, army, or navy.

By contrast, the Cuban army, indeed virtually the whole Cuban nation, was rapidly mobilized on October 23. The army expanded by ten times, mobilizing 48 divisions (300 battalions) totaling 270,000 men. General Sergio del Valle Jiménez and Politburo member Jorge Risquet Valdes, in 1962 one of the three regional field commanders, both have stressed how determined Cuba was to put up a strong fight against the expected U.S. invasion force and, after losing the conventional combat phase, to fall back to wage an extended guerrilla campaign from the mountains.[105]

The first test of U.S.-Soviet confrontation after President Kennedy had thrown down the gauntlet was the Soviet reaction to the naval quarantine. Some Soviet sources have indicated that Khrushchev's angry initial reaction was to ignore the American quarantine and attempt to run the blockade.[106] In practice, however, the Soviets behaved very cautiously from the outset. President Kennedy, in his speech on the early evening of October 22, had declared that a strict quarantine "is being initiated." In fact the United States awaited approval by the OAS the next day, and only twenty-four hours later, at 7:06 p.m. on October 23, did he sign a proclamation on interdiction of offensive arms shipments to Cuba, to be effective at 10:00 a.m. (2:00 p.m. Greenwich time) on October 24. But Moscow did not take any chances and wait for the fine print. Several Soviet ships had changed course and started to return as early as noon on October 23, and all sixteen ships carrying military cargo, including five with missiles and in one case also

105. Conversations in Moscow, January 1989.

106. Roy Medvedev, with access to Kremlin corridor gossip, wrote in a book published in 1984 that Khrushchev had issued orders to the Soviet ship captains to go ahead. See Roy Medvedev, *All Stalin's Men,* trans. Harold Shukman (Garden City, N.Y.: Doubleday, 1984), p. 52. This might have been based on a Moscow rumor account of Khrushchev's bluffing statement to Knox (see p. 78). Sergo Mikoyan also has recently said that Khrushchev's initial decision was to ignore the blockade, but that his father dissuaded Khrushchev from that course. It is quite unlikely that Khrushchev ever issued such orders, but very plausible that his first impulse was to do so and Mikoyan (and perhaps others) may have persuaded him not to.

Blight and Welch, *On the Brink,* pp. 306, 366–67 notes 85, 89, and 90 go much too far in accepting Medvedev's account, replete with other errors, as accurate and indeed in going beyond it to suggest that Mikoyan somehow "preempted Khrushchev's order."

nuclear warheads, had stopped and begun to return by the time the quarantine went into effect. Only five tankers and two other ships with nonmilitary cargoes, most of them still far from the blockade line, stayed on course for Cuba.

This prudence on the Soviet part was well advised.[107] President Kennedy was very edgy about the quarantine and anxious to avoid any unnecessary clash. Secretary McNamara, checking with Admiral George Anderson, the chief of naval operations, with detailed questions about the quarantine procedures (such as asking in what language Soviet ships would be hailed, and whether Russian-speaking naval personnel were on the American ships), had a sharp exchange over the issue of delegated or continuing political direction for the naval operation.[108] President Kennedy himself assumed a personal role, establishing direct communications with the quarantine commander, Vice Admiral Alfred G. Ward. But while the president did not want any unnecessary confrontation, he did want the quarantine to be effective. If the Soviet leadership had not recalled the ships with military cargo, there can be little doubt that the first real "offending" Soviet ship would have been stopped and, if necessary, seized.

It is now possible, on the basis of declassified documents, to know that the U.S. Navy had prepared very carefully indeed to make the quarantine successful. Most revealing are notes from the secret personal diary of the quarantine commander, Admiral Ward.

107. Ambassador Alekseyev, in his recent memoir (and at the Moscow conference), has suggested that it was a paper blockade and that some Soviet ships went on through. See Alekseyev, *Ekho planety* (November 1988), p. 30. When I challenged Alekseyev on this, he cited the *Bucharest,* a Soviet tanker that was hailed and allowed to pass through, and the *Leninskii Komsomol,* a cargo ship in the arms trade. But the *Leninskii Komsomol,* while arriving in Cuba with a cargo of crated IL-28 bombers after the president's speech, had passed through and even arrived at port before the quarantine went into effect. Another ship, a passenger ship possibly with Soviet troops aboard, while followed by a U.S. naval ship on October 23 inside the quarantine line, also arrived before the quarantine went into effect. These arrivals were given heroes' welcomes by the Cubans. Alekseyev may be reflecting a bravado shared with Cuban comrades over these arrivals after the speech, but they were not signs of laxity.

108. See Allison, *Essence of Decision,* pp. 131–32; and Blight and Welch, *On the Brink,* pp. 63–64.

On October 21, even before the president's speech but after the executive decision to effect the quarantine, Ward wrote: "Verbal orders were received to establish a blockade, stating that the probable first target would be POLTAVA, expected to arrive in the Havana area on 29 October. Intelligence indicated that POL-TAVA had missiles in her hold and her cargo would be in the prohibited category." On October 23: "CINCLANTFLT designated the first two targets as POLTAVA and KIMOVSK." October 24: "[I] Directed [U.S. cruiser] NEWPORT NEWS with her two destroyers to intercept POLTAVA." October 24, afternoon: ". . . Block [sic] freighters were reversing course and returning toward Europe. Specifically, and of greatest interest, POLTAVA took an easterly heading. [U.S. destroyer] LAWRENCE, who had been directed to proceed ahead at maximum speed to effect intercept of POLTAVA, was recalled."[109] From other declassified intelligence reports, we know that the *Poltava*—with nuclear weapons aboard—was in fact not expected to reach the quarantine line until the late evening of October 26. *Kimovsk,* the other ship noted as a prime target, was expected to reach the quarantine line at 8:00 p.m. on the 24th—some forty-eight hours before the *Poltava.* Moreover, *Kimovsk* was also a large-hatch ship engaged in military deliveries to Cuba and probably had SS-5 missiles aboard. Informal NSC notes on the Ex Comm meeting on the morning of October 23 record that *Kimovsk* had been "carefully picked as the 'right one' " for a challenge. Yet *Poltava* was being designated by the Navy as the "first target" as early as October 21, and was being pursued by a U.S. destroyer "at maximum speed" on October 24, still outside the quarantine line, before it turned away.[110]

If the Soviet leadership had failed to order the ships with military cargo to return to the Soviet Union promptly, by October 25 the

109. "Personal History or Diary of Vice Admiral Alfred G. Ward, U.S. Navy, While Serving as Commander Second Fleet," n.d. [October–November 1962], pp. 6, 9, 10, 11 (Secret; now declassified).

110. The Navy had established the quarantine line 500 miles out from Cuba, notwithstanding a presidential order to draw it in closer. See "Department of Defense Operations during the Cuban Crisis," p. 3; "Personal History or Diary of Vice Admiral Alfred G. Ward," pp. 4–6, 10; and Allison, *Essence of Decision,* pp. 128–30.

Poltava, with its cargo of nuclear weapons and missiles, would probably have been in U.S. hands. It seems highly unlikely that President Kennedy would have objected if the Navy had informed him it was ready to board a Soviet ship, identified as inside the quarantine line, believed to be carrying missiles and warheads, and with a risk that failure to board would result in the Soviet captain scuttling the ship with its cargo and claiming that the U.S. Navy had sunk his ship. Boarding parties were on the U.S. ships, including helicopter-borne detachments on the carrier *Essex.*

But the Soviet Union did not challenge the quarantine, and prudently withdrew *Poltava, Kimovsk,* and all its ships with military cargoes.

One other aspect of the naval confrontation requires note. The president and Ex Comm did not initially attend to the matter of handling Soviet submarines, and when reports of a Soviet submarine in the area of the quarantine were received on October 23, the president gave general orders to the U.S. Navy to give "highest priority to tracking the submarines and to put into effect the greatest possible safety measures to protect our own aircraft carriers and other vessels."[111] He did not realize he was giving the Navy carte blanche to "sit" on Soviet submarines once located and use low-power depth charges to force them to surface—a procedure successfully pursued with such zest that one damaged Soviet submarine eventually had to limp back to the Soviet Union on the surface escorted by a sub tender.[112] The aggressive American naval measures to neutralize the Soviet submarine "threat" were undoubtedly read in Moscow as a serious sign of American resolve, but the risks entailed had not been recognized or weighed by the Ex Comm and the president.[113]

111. See Kennedy, *Thirteen Days,* pp. 61–62.

112. The fullest account of the gradual development over October 22–24 of U.S. policy on handling Soviet submarines, and of the incidents that occurred, is given in Scott D. Sagan, "Nuclear Alerts and Crisis Management," *International Security,* vol. 9 (Spring 1985), pp. 112–17.

113. An incident that fortunately did *not* happen deserves mention. Several days into the crisis, a member of the Ex Comm in his other duties by chance became aware of another routine ongoing operation that should have been

Thus within a few days it had become clear that the Soviet leaders would not either challenge the quarantine at sea or mount a countermove. There was no escalatory initiative elsewhere.

On the other hand, construction of the missile bases in Cuba continued, and there was no Soviet diplomatic or other move signaling any readiness to withdraw the missiles. Indeed the Soviets continued publicly to deny their very existence. The debate in the Ex Comm therefore turned to renewed consideration of additional steps to induce or compel removal of the missiles. The quarantine middle course had served a useful role, but advocates of a need for more diplomatic flexibility on the one hand, and for an air strike against the missiles on the other, the doves and hawks, again began to urge new decisions.

The most hotly debated issue, proposed by some as a diplomatic alternative to an air strike, was a trade of mutual concessions, in particular the idea that as a counterpart to Soviet withdrawal of its missiles from Cuba, the United States might agree to remove its comparable intermediate-range missiles from Turkey—adjoining the Soviet Union, just as Cuba virtually adjoined the United States, with only ninety miles of water between.[114] This idea had arisen very early in the secret deliberation of the first week, and publicly in the second week, of the crisis. On October 25 it was advocated by the distinguished commentator Walter Lippman. His public proposal of the idea led many, perhaps some in Moscow also, to wonder if it was a trial balloon by the administration. It was not.

---

reconsidered under crisis conditions. A U.S. intelligence-collection ship for intercepting communications was perilously close to Cuban waters. No one had remembered it until then; it was promptly ordered to move a safe distance away. No incident occurred. Robert Kennedy noted the incident, but presented a brief account that misleadingly implied it was an example of careful foresight. See Kennedy, *Thirteen Days,* p. 86.

There is a strong tendency to ignore lessons from near-misses; in 1967 a similar ship in a similar situation, the *Liberty,* was attacked by Israeli aircraft and ships, and in 1968 its sister-ship, the *Pueblo,* was captured by the North Koreans.

114. Another proposed concession, suggested by Stevenson but quickly dismissed by the president, was a U.S. return of Guantánamo Bay and its base to Cuba in exchange for Soviet withdrawal of its missiles and all other military presence, establishing a military neutralization of the island.

The chief objection to a mutual withdrawal was that the missiles in Turkey were there following a NATO decision and under bilateral U.S.–Turkish agreements, and the United States would seem to be backing away from a NATO commitment to relieve itself of a threat, and moreover one that NATO countries in Europe had all faced for several years.[115] More basically, there was strong sentiment against making a concession because it would show a lack of resolve to compel the Soviets to retract their unwarranted and surreptitious deployment. On the other side, it was argued that the missiles in Turkey were obsolete and were slated for removal as soon as it could be arranged diplomatically, and that it was absurd to risk war for the sake of some unneeded and unwanted hardware.

The second of the appended memoranda (Appendix document B) was written on October 25, again to Walt Rostow.[116] I believed that the Soviet leaders would back down and withdraw the missiles in the face of continued firmness and pressure. I was "hawkish" on the question of compelling this outcome, rather than seeking to

115. NATO had decided late in 1957, when Soviet primacy in missilery first seemed to portend a missile gap, to station American-made intermediate-range missiles in Europe. Great Britain and the United States had concluded an arrangement that had provided sixty Thor IRBM missiles to Britain. Italy agreed in 1959 to take thirty Jupiter IRBM missiles, and Turkey, fifteen. The whole process of negotiation, training, constructing facilities, and the like took several years. Meanwhile the missiles became increasingly obsolete, and other, more suitable weapons, ICBMs and SLBMs, became available in rapidly growing numbers. In August 1962 the British had announced that the Thors were being phased out, and they were all out by December. In Italy the Jupiters had become operational in 1961–62. As earlier noted, in Turkey the missiles became operational in April, but by remarkable coincidence the actual turnover of the first Jupiter missiles to the Turkish armed forces (the warheads, of course, remained under U.S. control in all cases) occurred on October 22, 1962—the very day of Kennedy's quarantine announcement. This fact was not, however, known to him and to the other top American leaders, who had instead been thinking of phasing out these missiles as obsolete. President Kennedy had urged that this be done on several earlier occasions in 1961 and 1962, most recently in August. Accounts suggesting that the president was shocked to find that the Jupiters were still in Turkey, or that earlier orders by him for their removal had not been carried out, are in error.

116. This memorandum was circulated to some Ex Comm members, and I was told that Robert Kennedy had read it and spoken approvingly of it. It was, incidentally, a unique and heady experience for staff officers to write memoranda, uncleared by anyone, that were circulated only hours later to top decisionmakers.

induce it through concessions. On the other hand, while prepared to contemplate use of military force if necessary to attain that objective, I was not among the hawks who *sought* to use military force or wished to set the extirpation of communism in Cuba as a new, more far-reaching objective.[117] But in opposing a "trade" of missile bases, I was a hawk. The third memorandum (Appendix document C), written on October 27 for Alexis Johnson, also makes that clear. It was written principally to support the "hang tough" school in the State Department, to which he too belonged, and which was prepared to resort to an air strike if necessary to get the missiles out of Cuba, while opposing a negotiated trade of missile bases.

One important aspect of the internal debate in midweek, around October 24–25, was the possibility of tightening the quarantine to cover not only all military supplies but above all petroleum, as a way to squeeze Cuba and prevent a stalemate. Even before the president's address of October 22, when the quarantine option was being thought through, consideration was given to the possibility of a Soviet counterblockade of Berlin and to whether Berlin or Cuba would be more vulnerable to a cutoff of outside food and energy supplies. By the end of the week, however, concern had focused on how to bring the crisis to a head before the Soviet missiles already in Cuba became accepted as an element in the status quo.[118] Accordingly, the emphasis had shifted to either a diplomatic deal involving a trade-off of missile bases, or unilateral American military action to destroy the missile complexes.

No one in the Ex Comm, in the period before October 26, even posed the possibility of a diplomatic resolution based on an American commitment not to invade Cuba—not because of opposition to the idea, but because none of the president's counselors con-

117. For example, I vividly recall one small "caucus" meeting of a few hardline State Department officers (and Dorothy Fosdick, then chief aide to Senator Henry Jackson) with Dean Acheson, in which I was the only non-hawk uncomfortably present.

118. On October 26 I was tasked after the Ex Comm meeting to draw up a memorandum on the military significance of the missiles in Cuba. See Appendix document D. A commentary on the memorandum and retrospective evaluation follows the document.

ceived of that as a trade the Soviet Union would seek or settle for. Nonetheless the president himself was thinking along those lines by midweek. On October 25 President Kennedy, in a conversation with British Prime Minister Harold Macmillan, wondered whether some acceptable political proposal could be made, such as a trade for withdrawal of the Soviet missiles of some international guarantee for Cuba against invasion.[119]

And on October 26, at the sixth meeting of the Ex Comm, the president noted a Brazilian proposal at the UN General Assembly for a guarantee of the territorial integrity of all Latin American states (and for their denuclearization), and asked if the United States should commit itself not to invade Cuba. Secretary Rusk replied that the United States had already committed itself not to invade Cuba under the UN Charter and the Rio Treaty of 1947.[120]

Preparations for an invasion, as well as an air strike, continued to be made as a possible recourse, if necessary, to resolve the problem. Besides military preparations (including mobilization of military civil government teams for occupation tasks), on October 25 President Kennedy authorized a program, christened "Bugle Call," to prepare leaflets to drop over Cuba, in anticipation of an invasion. By the 27th some five million leaflets had been printed in Spanish, and the U.S. Air Force was ready to drop them whenever ordered. The order was, of course, never given.

The American military buildup for a possible invasion of Cuba was impressive. At the height of preparations the invasion force included one Marine and five U.S. Army (two airborne) divisions (with another Marine brigade and one and one-third more Army divisions as a follow-on reserve if needed): more than 100,000 Army and 40,000 Marine combat troops. The Air Force and Navy tactical air forces had 579 combat aircraft ready; the Navy had 183 ships, including 8 aircraft carriers, on station. The air-strike plan called for 1,190 strike sorties on the first day. The airborne

119. Memorandum of conversation between President John F. Kennedy and Prime Minister Harold Macmillan, October 25, 1962; and see Harold Macmillan, *At the End of the Day: 1961–1963* (Harper and Row, 1973), pp. 210–11.

120. "Summary Record of NSC Executive Committee Meeting No. 6, October 26, 1962, 10:00 A.M.," p. 2 (Top Secret–Sensitive; now declassified).

paratroop force, 14,500 strong, to be dropped on the first day was comparable to the force dropped during the invasion of Normandy. Potential casualties were estimated at some 18,500 in ten days of combat. The buildup continued even after agreement on Soviet withdrawal of the missiles, peaking on November 15, and for most of the forces "standing down" began only late in November.[121]

Some covert CIA "assets" may have been introduced into Cuba during the crisis as part of the preparations for possible American invasion, although available declassified documents do not provide confirmation. Those assets were separate from the teams assigned sabotage and subversive missions under the Mongoose program. Rather, they were to serve as "pathfinders" for local reconnaissance, carrying out preparations to facilitate safe landings for later American Special Forces and regular airborne and perhaps also amphibious assault forces. Apart from the above-noted regular forces amassed for an invasion, U.S. Army Special Forces (Green Beret) troops were also ready for special operations (and, at a later stage, possibly counterinsurgency actions) against Cuban forces, and an interservice Joint Unconventional Warfare Task Force was established and set up two operating bases.[122]

One important area about which the American policymakers and their advisers had virtually no information during the crisis, and scarcely more even after twenty-five years, was the state of play within the Soviet leadership. Contemporary sources included official Soviet statements, the Soviet press, reports from the American Embassy in Moscow, and appearances of Soviet leaders.

121. The two principal sources are the official Defense Department postmortem on "Department of Defense Operations during the Cuban Crisis," esp. pp. 6, 12–14; and "CINCLANT Historical Account," esp. pp. 56, 58–85, 153–59, 165.

122. "Department of Defense Operations during the Cuban Crisis," p. 9, has a sparse two-sentence reference to the Special Forces and the creation of the joint task force. The "CINCLANT Historical Account" had a six-page section on the Joint Unconventional Warfare Task Force, deleted in its entirety in the declassified version. No declassified document has referred to operations inserting pathfinders into Cuba.

The joint task force and the U.S. Army Special Forces were under the command of Major General William P. Yarborough.

To my knowledge the copious literature on the Cuban missile crisis has heretofore included no reference to preparations for the employment of U.S. special or unconventional forces.

On October 23, as earlier noted, five of the top leaders attended the opera; on the 26th five attended a concert; on October 28, as the critical phase ended, ten top leaders demonstratively again together attended the theater (Khrushchev, Kozlov, Brezhnev, Mikhail A. Suslov, Kosygin, Mikoyan, Dmitri S. Polyansky, Petr N. Demichev, Leonid F. Ilychev, and Aleksandr N. Shelepin). But did that signal real unity, or a facade arranged precisely to cover up real differences?[123]

"Kremlinologists" in Washington picked up, three weeks later when it was first published, the intriguing fact that on October 25 the Ukrainian Supreme Soviet had renamed the town of Khrushchev, Kremges—an apparent slap at the Party first secretary. The newspaper *Izvestiya,* edited by Khrushchev's son-in-law, Aleksei Adzhubei, was notably more ready than *Pravda* to seek a compromise solution to the crisis; the military newspaper *Red Star,* on the other hand, was notably more militant and intransigent. For example, on October 27, when Khrushchev was trying to make a deal involving *no* reference to any American missile bases, and a Presidium consensus may have sought a trade for U.S. missiles in Turkey, *Red Star* published an article referring to the U.S. demands for removal of Soviet weaponry (not yet identified specifically as missiles) from Cuba and truculently asked, "Why then not remove American weaponry and troops from the *hundreds* of military bases surrounding the Soviet Union?"[124]

On November 3 the old defeated Stalinist Marshal Kliment Ye. Voroshilov was resurrected from political oblivion to be identified as author of an article in *Pravda* extolling Khrushchev's handling of the crisis.[125]

At the same time, there were many signs that the price for

123. Later, in his unofficial memoirs, Khrushchev remarked that on one of these occasions—probably October 26—he suggested to his colleagues that they attend the Bolshoi Theater to have a calming effect on the public. And he added, "We were trying to disguise our own anxiety, which was intense." He does not mention divisions in the leadership. See Talbott, ed. and trans., *Khrushchev Remembers* (1970), p. 497.

124. A. Leont'yev, "Ashes and a Cold Shower," *Krasnaya Zvezda* (Red Star), October 27, 1962; emphasis added.

125. K. Voroshilov, "The Cause of Great October Lives and Triumphs," *Pravda,* November 3, 1962.

support of conservative party leaders on the Cuban affair was an abatement of Khrushchev's internal political destalinization campaign. On November 1 *Pravda* had reprinted an editorial article from the Mongolian Communist party newspaper *Unen* criticizing the lately deposed Mongolian party secretary D. Tumur-Ochir for attempting to "use the struggle against the remnants of the cult of personality for his own far-reaching purposes"—precisely the concern of some Moscow party leaders over Khrushchev's designs and machinations.[126] Khrushchev also had to shift his position on October 25 from neutrality to support for China in the Indian-Chinese border war that had broken out during the missile crisis.

Several Western Kremlinological studies of Soviet politics have examined the Soviet press and internal policy turns of 1962 and 1963 in detail and focused on such indications as these.[127] Most of this analysis was, however, either not available during the missile crisis or not brought to the attention of the harassed Executive Committee.

Particular attention was given to signs of any divergence between the body of political leaders (and Khrushchev in particular) and the military leadership. Marshal Malinovsky, the defense minister, was not a member of the Presidium.

On November 7, at the parade on the anniversary of the revolution, Marshal Malinovsky praised Khrushchev personally for his role in saving the peace in the Caribbean crisis and endorsed peaceful coexistence as well as strength.[128] At diplomatic recep-

126. "For the Triumph of Marxism-Leninism, for Proletarian Internationalism," *Pravda*, November 1, 1962.

127. The most extensive later Kremlinological analysis was Michel Tatu, *Power in the Kremlin: From Khrushchev to Kosygin*, trans. Helen Keitel (New York: Viking Press, 1969; first published in France in 1967), pp. 229–97. See also William Hyland and Richard Wallace Shryock, *The Fall of Khrushchev* (New York: Funk and Wagnalls, 1968), pp. 45–65; and Carl A. Linden, *Khrushchev and the Soviet Leadership, 1957–1964* (Baltimore: Johns Hopkins Press, 1966), pp. 146–73.

The most detailed press analysis, and the exception in treating the whole subject in terms of the context of Soviet–Cuban policy, is Herbert S. Dinerstein, *The Making of a Missile Crisis: October 1962* (Baltimore: Johns Hopkins Press, 1976), pp. 150–229, 239–62.

128. "Speech by Marshal of the Soviet Union R. Ya. Malinovsky," *Pravda*,

tions at the Japanese Embassy in Moscow on November 1 and the Italian Embassy on November 5, several Soviet military officers showed cordiality to Americans and toasted the fact that peace had prevailed. On the other hand, an unidentified "reliable source" told a Western ambassador in Moscow on November 5 that Malinovsky, supported by some civilian leaders, had opposed the withdrawal of the missiles and been overridden. Khrushchev himself was reported to have said the same thing in an informal conversation at a reception. (Khrushchev also acknowledged in conversation at a reception on November 7 that Castro had opposed "his" decision to remove the missiles, and had been told that there was no choice, that *not* to have done so "would have meant war.") And Khrushchev told American editor Norman Cousins several months later that the Soviet military had opposed the missile withdrawal, and had looked at him "as though I was out of my mind or, what was worse, a traitor" for asking if they could guarantee that refusing would not result in a global nuclear war. "So I said to myself," Khrushchev continued, " 'To hell with those maniacs. If I can get the United States to assure me that it will not attempt to overthrow the Cuban government, I will remove the missiles.' "[129]

While there is very little direct information on the deliberations in Moscow in those critical days, there were some indirect indications in addition to Khrushchev's messages of October 23 and 24 to President Kennedy. In these letters, Khrushchev sought to

---

November 8, 1962. Other key comments by Malinovsky and in the confidential military press evaluating the crisis are discussed later.

129. [Norman Cousins], "The Cuban Missile Crisis: An Anniversary," editorial, *Saturday Review*, vol. 5 (October 15, 1977), p. 4.

An unconfirmed intelligence report stated that when the Supreme Soviet met on December 12, 1962, some thirty-five to forty high-ranking military officers who were members as a sign of displeasure absented themselves from the session at which Khrushchev justified his handling of the crisis. If true, that was a significant act of political indiscipline, but the absence of any other reports of this alleged demonstration or punitive reaction casts doubt on it.

On the other hand, there seems no reason to doubt Soviet and Cuban officials and officers who state that in Cuba after October 28 Soviet military men wept over the humiliating missile pullout and dismantling of the missile facilities they had been working so hard to construct.

persuade Kennedy of the legitimacy and peaceful, deterrent purpose of the deployments, with no hint of readiness to withdraw the missiles. His message of October 24 opened with a plaintive plea for the president to put himself in Khrushchev's shoes: "Just imagine, Mr. President, that we had presented you with the conditions of an ultimatum which you have presented us by your action. How would you have reacted to this?"[130]

In one instance Khrushchev resorted to an unorthodox channel of communication. A visiting American businessman, William E. Knox, on October 24 was suddenly ushered in for a three-hour meeting. Khrushchev admitted the presence of the Soviet missiles—something publicly still denied—and claimed their nuclear warheads were in Cuba, but that the Soviet Union had strict control and would never fire nuclear weapons first. Clearly, he wanted to reassure the American leadership on the latter point. He said that the United States might stop a few ships, but that at some point he would give orders to strike an American blockade ship, or perhaps stop American ships on the high seas somewhere else. Again, he wished to signal both that he would not immediately challenge the quarantine, but that Soviet acquiescence could not be assumed indefinitely. (As earlier noted, Soviet ships had by that time already begun to turn back.) Khrushchev then raised the matter of the U.S. missiles in Turkey. But rather than proposing a mutual withdrawal, he argued that the United States would have to learn to live with the Soviet missiles in Cuba, just as the Soviet Union had learned to live with American missiles in Turkey and elsewhere. Finally, he suggested that the best way to resolve the crisis would be a personal meeting with President Kennedy in Moscow, or Washington, or perhaps in a rendezvous at sea. Thus as of October 24 Khrushchev was at least still hoping that the U.S. leadership could be brought to accept the continued presence of Soviet missiles in Cuba.

130. This message, and all of the published Khrushchev messages of October 1962, and most subsequent Soviet commentaries to 1982, are conveniently compiled in Ronald R. Pope, ed., *Soviet Views on the Cuban Missile Crisis: Myth and Reality in Foreign Policy Analysis* (Lanham, Md.: University Press of America, 1982); for the quotation, see p. 32.

On October 25, several Soviet diplomats around the world began to break the silence that their initial lack of instructions had imposed.[131] Ambassador Nikita S. Ryzhov in Turkey saw Foreign Minister Feridun Erkin and raised the matter of the Jupiters in Turkey as parallel to Soviet missiles in Cuba, perhaps hinting at a trade, or an implied threat. But several other Soviet envoys began to stress the Soviet desire to end the confrontation peacefully and hinted at readiness to compromise.[132] The one who was most explicit, Ambassador Nikolai A. Mikhailov in Indonesia, told the Indian ambassador there that the Soviet Union would hold off its ships during negotiations and suggested that the removal of the missiles might be negotiable.[133] These conversations were noted with interest in Washington but were not—wisely—regarded as necessarily authoritative.[134]

131. Despite an absence of instructions, some Soviet ambassadors—including Dobrynin—in private conversations on October 22 through 24 predicted a stiff Soviet response, such as challenging the quarantine. Ambassador Valerian Zorin at the United Nations did have instructions—to *deny* the presence of Soviet missiles in Cuba.

132. Among the more unorthodox channels was a London osteopath on the raw edge of British political life. On October 24 Dr. Stephen Ward had lunch with Soviet Naval Attaché Captain Evgeny Ivanov at the latter's invitation and was asked to use his connections to pass along a suggestion that could give Britain a rare opportunity to serve world peace. Ivanov's bait was this: if the British government called a summit conference, Khrushchev would accept and would be ready to turn back Soviet ships and discuss removal of the missiles from Cuba. Ward did pass the message to Sir Harold Caccia, the permanent undersecretary of the Foreign Office, but the idea was not further pursued.

Dr. Ward and Captain Ivanov attained fleeting notoriety some eight months later when Ward's protégée Christine Keeler turned out to share the beds of both Secretary of State for War John Profumo and Captain Ivanov, to the detriment at least of the career of Profumo.

133. Telegram no. 742, Djakarta to State, October 25, 1962, p. 2 (Secret; now declassified). The identity of Mikhailov's interlocutor has been excised on the declassified cable, but had been earlier disclosed by other sources including the first edition of this book.

134. In the first edition of this book I assumed, as many of us did in 1962, that Mikhailov's remarks represented a "signal" authorized by Moscow. A senior Soviet official involved at the time now states this was not the case, which seems correct in view of other revelations noted below. Mikhailov had been a senior Communist Party official, indeed one of the Party Secretaries, before being banished to the diplomatic service in 1954 by Khrushchev.

At midday on Friday, October 26, a breakthrough was seen when Aleksandr Fomin, officially the Soviet Embassy public affairs counselor in Washington (but believed to be the KGB *resident*, or station chief), insisted on urgently arranging a meeting with ABC News correspondent John Scali. It seemed clear that the Soviets had sought to use a deniable and dispensable but trusted Soviet intelligence contact out of official channels to take a sounding and float a trial balloon. The Soviets—or, more precisely, whomever Fomin was representing, presumably Khrushchev—sounded out a potential deal: Soviet removal of the missiles from Cuba, under UN inspection, in exchange for a U.S. public commitment not to invade Cuba. Scali reported the conversation and was taken to Secretary Rusk. Rusk's reply, cleared with the president, was that the United States saw "real possibilities" along the lines suggested, but that "time is very urgent."[135]

New information requires modifying two important elements of this traditional account. First, contrary to the American assumptions in October 1962 and since, Fomin was apparently *not* instructed or authorized by Moscow to propose terms for a possible settlement; his probe was strictly his own.[136] The Ex Comm

135. See Hilsman, *To Move a Nation*, pp. 217–19; and Salinger, *With Kennedy*, pp. 271, 274–80. Scali's notes have also been declassified. Scali has written up his own account: John Scali, "I Was the Secret Go-Between in the Cuban Crisis," *Family Weekly* (October 25, 1964), pp. 4–5, 12–14.

136. Fomin himself informed a Soviet scholar in 1987 that he had been acting on his own authority, and he repeated this statement at the Moscow conference in early 1989. Independently of that, Georgi M. Kornyenko, political counselor in the Soviet Embassy in Washington at the time and later Dobrynin's deputy, told me during an interview in Moscow in May 1988 not only that Fomin had been operating on his own initiative, under a general guidance from Ambassador Dobrynin to try to sound out possible American positions, but also that Fomin had reported his discussion with Scali in a way that left unclear how much had been Scali's initiative and how much Fomin's, leaving Dobrynin and Kornyenko very dubious of the report. Fomin even claimed that Scali had initiated the contact. At the Moscow conference, Fomin himself presented an account that was even more bizarre, including an alleged contact with Scali on October 22 in which Scali had informed him of the missiles in Cuba even before the president's speech. Scali hotly denies such a meeting ever took place, and denies also Fomin's account of their meeting on October 26.

Fomin's, Kornyenko's, and Dobrynin's denials of authorization for Fomin's

assumption that Fomin's more precise offer represented a filling in of Khrushchev's proposal and that the two were "really a single package"[137] was not warranted. Moreover, his report on the American reaction was not received in Moscow in time to inspire or even influence Khrushchev's message.

On October 26 also UN Secretary General U Thant suggested to Ambassador Adlai Stevenson and John J. McCloy that an American assurance that it would not attack Cuba might be an appropriate quid pro quo for a Soviet withdrawal of its missiles. That suggestion was also thought to have been discreetly planted by the Soviets.

Hours later, between 6:00 and 9:00 p.m., a message from Chairman Khrushchev to the president was received piecemeal. It bore all the marks of Khrushchev's personal style and raised speculation in Washington that it might have been sent without clearance by the Presidium. Khrushchev proposed that, if the United States would undertake not to invade Cuba (with its own or proxy forces), the reason for the Soviet stationing of missiles there would be eliminated, and implied that the missiles could then be withdrawn. While the potential deal was not fully explicit, in the light of the Fomin message it seemed clear and to provide the basis for an agreement.

As the president and his Ex Comm advisers were preparing on the morning of the 27th to respond favorably, a second message was received at about 10 o'clock, this time adding a demand for the withdrawal of the American missiles in Turkey.[138] The new

---

exploratory sounding with Scali are not of course proof certain that Fomin was not making a probe authorized through KGB channels. In retrospect, however, it seems very unlikely that it was. Why would Khrushchev (or anyone in the KGB) have authorized a probe and then not waited for the results? Conditions may of course have compelled a more speedy action than initially anticipated. But why would Khrushchev (or the KGB) have promised more through Fomin than they wanted to offer or could deliver (UN inspection)?

137. Hilsman, *To Move a Nation,* p. 219.

138. This message was also sent later on October 26, but owing to the time difference between Moscow and Washington arrived only on the morning of the 27th. Contrary to the speculation of some American analysts, however, it was not written and sent earlier than the message received the previous evening.

message caused great concern. The mood became even more grim when, minutes later, word was received that a U-2 reconnaissance plane had been shot down over Cuba and the pilot killed. Moreover, in the next few hours, for the first time two low-level reconnaissance flights were also fired upon. Meanwhile, one of the Soviet ships, the tanker *Grozny,* had resumed movement toward the quarantine line. Some speculated that Khrushchev might no longer be in control or able to agree to a deal on the basis of the first message.

New light has recently been thrown on the question of the hardening of terms in the second Khrushchev message, the one received on October 27. A senior Soviet source explained that the first letter, with its vague but attractive offer, written in haste early on October 26, was sent after Soviet intelligence had reported an American attack on Cuba was possibly imminent. The Soviet leaders believed time had run out. When later intelligence modified that estimate and time seemed to be available for some diplomatic bargaining, the second letter with its stiffer demands was sent.[139]

The full story behind the shooting down of the U-2 by an SA-2 surface-to-air missile (SAM) has also lately emerged. None of our speculations at the time were correct: it was not an action taken by Khrushchev (under pressure or otherwise), nor by a more hard-line element in the leadership in Moscow, nor under standing instructions, nor by the Cubans.

That someone in the Soviet leadership, necessarily high in the military or able to give an order to the military, had created the incident in an unsuccessful attempt to forestall Khrushchev's efforts to arrange a compromise was seriously considered as a possible explanation.

Another possibility given some credence in the Washington intelligence community during the crisis was that the air defense system radars had simply been unable to engage the high-flying U-2s earlier. A deficiency in Cuban high-altitude radar capability had delayed activation of the SAM system; October 27 might just have been the first time it was able to intercept.

139. This information was provided by a senior and knowledgeable Soviet official in an interview in May 1988, first reported in Garthoff, *Foreign Policy* (Fall 1988), p. 74.

The possibility that the Cubans had shot down the U-2 was rejected by U.S. intelligence analysts at the time because they believed, correctly, that the SAM system was entirely under Soviet manning and control.[140] Nonetheless, years later a former aide to Castro, Carlos Franqui, held that Fidel Castro himself, while on an inspection visit to a Soviet SAM site, asked how the system operated and how to fire the missiles. When shown, he suddenly fired the missile. This story, for a number of reasons, including the improbability that the Castro inspection would have coincided with a U-2 flight within range, can be dismissed. Castro himself denied that he fired the missile and has stated that, although he had ordered the antiaircraft gunfire, the Soviets had shot down the U-2 with a SAM missile without clearing it (although, he added, he would not have objected).[141]

Most intriguing was the suggestion, advanced in 1987 in an article based on leaked National Security Agency (NSA) intercepts of Soviet military communications in Cuba, that Cuban forces had overrun a Soviet SAM site and shot down the U-2.[142] The NSA intercepts did not cover the actual shootdown but disclosed Soviet casualties and dispatch of a Soviet military security detachment on the night of October 26 from another post in the general area of the SAM site. Authoritative Soviet and Cuban sources have since revealed that an accidental explosion at a munitions dump caused the casualties and triggered dispatch of a security detachment as well as medical personnel before the possibility of an attack had been dispelled. The Cubans probably could not have fired a SAM

---

140. Khrushchev himself had confirmed Soviet control in his conversation with Knox on October 24. A later-reported statement by Soviet negotiator Vasily Kuznetsov in New York on October 31 that "all antiaircraft means" in Cuba were in Cuban hands was either misstated or misunderstood; only antiaircraft artillery useful against low-flying aircraft were in Cuban hands. See CIA Memorandum, "The Crisis: USSR/Cuba," November 1, 1962, p. 2.

141. For the original claim by Franqui, see *Time,* March 16, 1981, p. 51. For Castro's denial, see Jim Hoagland, "Cuba Reconsiders 1962 Understanding: Castro Sheds Light on Downing of U.S. Reconnaissance Plane during Missile Crisis," *Washington Post,* February 3, 1985.

142. See Seymour M. Hersh, "Was Castro Out of Control in 1962?" *Washington Post,* October 18, 1987.

missile even if they had seized the site; no Cubans had yet begun training with the SAM system.

An even more bizarre explanation had surfaced briefly soon after the crisis. The *New York Times* reported rumors circulating among Communist diplomats that *Chinese* military personnel had manned the site and shot down the American plane.[143] Actually, this public rumor was grounded in a secret report by a senior Polish general to a military audience in Warsaw on November 12, 1962, on what he had been told in Moscow. It was transparently a disinformation attempt by Soviet intelligence to fan anti-Chinese sentiment in response to the sharp Chinese attacks on the Soviet handling of the crisis.

In fact, the plane was shot down as the result of a decision taken by two local Soviet air defense commanders in Cuba, without authorization from Moscow and contravening at least the intent of their standing orders. In explanation of this action, some Soviet sources, in particular Ambassador Alekseyev, say they were influenced by Castro's orders to his forces on October 27 to shoot down the U.S. reconnaissance aircraft, and when a U-2 was in range decided out of solidarity to interpret their orders as allowing them to fire.[144] The local commander for the SAM units in the eastern part of the island, Major General Igor Statsenko, made the decision, cleared with Lieutenant General Stepan Grechko in Havana. Time did not permit clearance even with General Davidkov or General Pliyev, the air defense and overall commanders of Soviet forces in Cuba. Their standing air defense instructions had been to fire in the event of an American attack on Cuba; they interpreted this to allow firing at an American aircraft violating Cuban sovereign airspace, even though that had not been the interpretation earlier placed on the instructions. General Volkogonov has disclosed that Marshal Malinovsky promptly dispatched to the Soviet forces command in Cuba a mild reprimand and firm restatement of orders not to fire on U.S. reconnaissance aircraft,

143. See Arthur J. Olsen, "Chinese Gunners Reported in Cuba," *New York Times,* November 17, 1962.

144. See Alekseyev, *Ekho planety* (November 1988), p. 32.

explaining that they had fired "prematurely," and that efforts were under way to resolve the conflict through political means.[145]

General Statsenko, one of the two officers responsible, in an article written just before his death in October 1987, while not acknowledging his role in the incident, sought to defend his action, referring to it as a "justified rebuff" to the "American air pirates" and claiming that it "strengthened the faith of Cuban workers in a capability to defend their independence."[146]

It is disturbing that this kind of initiative by subordinate field officers was not treated more severely. General Volkogonov, and other responsible Soviet officials, state that the standing orders of the Soviet command in Cuba concerning the medium-range surface-to-surface missile forces were far more restrictive and clear than for the surface-to-air missiles: the medium-range missiles were not to be made capable of firing or placed in firing position, much less fired, without explicit instructions from Moscow.

In Washington, the conjunction of the second, tougher, Khrushchev message with the shootdown of the U-2 intensified differences within the Ex Comm over what course of action to take, as well as underlining the urgency of decision. The Joint Chiefs recommended an air strike and invasion. The State Department proposed a draft message flatly rejecting the Turkish missile trade demanded in the second letter. Others objected that it would be difficult for the administration to persuade world opinion, and perhaps opinion at home as well, that prolonging or intensifying the crisis was preferable to withdrawing obsolete missiles from Turkey. In the end, on

145. Interview with General Volkogonov, January 1989. Incidentally, Ambassador Alekseyev, the Soviet ambassador in Havana at the time, believed in 1962 and for many years thereafter that the U-2 had been shot down by the Cubans; he was not "cleared" for military operational information and not informed by the Soviet military command, or Castro.

146. See Maj. Gen. (res.) I. Statsenko, "The Invasion Did Not Take Place," *Kommunist vooruzhennykh sil* (Communist of the Armed Forces), no. 20 (October 1987), p. 84. Statsenko's role in the incident was first disclosed by Sergo Mikoyan shortly after the general's death. See Garthoff, *Foreign Policy* (Fall 1988), pp. 75–76; and Blight and Welch, *On the Brink*, pp. 310–11, 369 note 118. Fuller information has become available at the Moscow conference and in interviews since that time.

the basis of suggestions by Thompson, Sorensen, and Robert Kennedy, the president decided to respond positively to the first message and simply to ignore the second.[147]

On October 27 the president sent a message to Khrushchev in effect accepting his proposal of October 26. The president had his brother Robert, known to all as his close confidant, deliver the message through Ambassador Dobrynin also and orally give him several additional points. In conveying the message to Dobrynin, Robert Kennedy stressed both the president's readiness to give assurances against an invasion of Cuba and the urgency of a prompt Soviet acceptance. If the *Soviets* did not promptly agree to remove the missiles, "*we* [the United States] would remove them."[148] This was not a bluff. Plans had been set for a possible air strike on Monday or Tuesday morning (October 29 or 30), although the president had *not* made any final decision, even contingently.

Only six years later did it become known that Robert Kennedy had also informed Dobrynin that the president had long been thinking of phasing out the missiles from Turkey and Italy. With an improvement in relations after a resolution of the crisis, the president expected that "within a short time after this crisis was over, those missiles would be gone."[149] He noted, however, that the stationing of the missiles in Turkey had been a NATO decision, and that the United States could not unilaterally decide to remove them. Disposition of the missiles in Turkey could therefore not be part of a U.S.-Soviet agreement on the missiles in Cuba.

---

147. Ambassador Thompson's role, which has not been adequately appreciated, was particularly important. As McGeorge Bundy has recently noted, the president's reluctance was not owing to any unreadiness on his own part, but to doubt that Khrushchev would still accept the terms of the first letter. Thompson's counsel that he would was influential, and correct. See Bundy, *Danger and Survival,* p. 431.

Transcripts of the October 16 and 27 Ex Comm meetings, from taped recordings, have been declassified and published; see *International Security,* vol. 10 (Summer 1985), pp. 171–94, and vol. 12 (Winter 1987–88), pp. 30–92. (Most Ex Comm meetings were not taped, but those held in the Cabinet Room of the White House were.)

148. Kennedy, *Thirteen Days,* pp. 103, 108; emphasis added.

149. Ibid., p. 109.

The essential elements of the American proposal of October 27 were an *ultimatum* (although Kennedy's published account does not indicate so precisely, the Soviets understood they had only some forty-eight hours), *coupled with a way out,* the noninvasion undertaking in exchange for removal of the missiles, *and accompanied by the additional sweetener* of the private assurance of an American intention to remove the missiles from Turkey and Italy. The prospect of a reciprocal American action, even if not as an integral or public quid pro quo, certainly made it easier for Khrushchev to accept the basic over-the-table settlement.

A new page in the crisis history is emerging from several recent Soviet disclosures. It now appears that there was a previously unreported earlier meeting of Robert Kennedy with Ambassador Dobrynin at the Soviet Embassy on October 26. In this meeting, after Dobrynin had argued against a double standard in considering American missile and other bases around the Soviet Union legitimate while denying the legitimacy of Soviet missiles in Cuba, Robert Kennedy reportedly asked if the missiles in Turkey were really that important, and took the initiative in informing Dobrynin that his brother had been planning to phase out the missiles in Turkey. He then left the room to talk with the president, and upon his return confirmed the president's intention to remove the missiles from Turkey if the overall situation was normalized. Dobrynin then reported this possibility to Moscow. It thus now seems likely that this indication of American intention to remove the Jupiters from Turkey, in conjunction with the revised intelligence estimate on the imminence of American action against Cuba, prompted introduction of the proposal for removal of the missiles from Turkey in the second message received on October 27.[150]

150. There has been no reference to a meeting between Robert Kennedy and Ambassador Dobrynin on October 26 in the American literature, and indeed none to any meetings during the crisis other than the evenings of October 23 and 27, but Dobrynin says they met several times during that week, often late at night, alternating between the Soviet Embassy and the Attorney General's office.

Dobrynin gave a slightly imprecise but extended account of this chain of events on October 26 and 27 to the Moscow conference, and one hopes he will clarify the record further when the transcript of that meeting is prepared for public release. Other Soviet sources have hinted or revealed parts of this account

Another recent revelation throws additional light on the situation. McGeorge Bundy has disclosed that the decision to have Robert Kennedy add the "sweetener" on the Jupiter missiles was made by the president in a small group of Ex Comm members in the Oval Office after the Ex Comm meeting on the 27th, and that it was Dean Rusk who proposed it. As Bundy notes, the fact that Rusk, stalwart on interests of the NATO alliance, made the proposal encouraged rapid consensus and presidential decision. Whether Rusk was aware of the earlier Robert Kennedy–Dobrynin discussion of this matter is not clear, but he was aware of the president's own favorable inclination and saw it as appropriate to assist the president in using this diplomatic asset. This is the newly revealed background to Robert Kennedy's conversation with Dobrynin late on October 27 when he confirmed the president's intention to remove the Jupiter missiles from Turkey and Italy.[151]

The hours between the president's message of October 27 and the Soviet reply the next morning were extremely tense in Washington (and no doubt in Moscow too). This was the day called

---

earlier. Georgi Shakhnazarov, after having discussed the crisis with Dobrynin, reported to the Cambridge conference in October 1987 that "the Turkish idea was born here [in the United States] in the Soviet Embassy, in a conversation, maybe with Robert Kennedy. It was suggested to Moscow, and then it came back. . . . Dobrynin got the impression from this conversation that this could serve as a basis for agreement." Cited in Blight and Welch, *On the Brink*, pp. 256–57. Georgi Kornyenko, Dobrynin's political counselor in 1962, informed me in May 1988 that the first edition of this book had been wrong in saying the key Dobrynin–Kennedy conversation on the missiles in Turkey had been brought up by Dobrynin; moreover, it had taken place not in the Justice Department but in the Soviet Embassy. Regrettably, Kornyenko didn't then make clear he was referring to an earlier conversation. See Garthoff, *Foreign Policy* (Fall 1988), p. 75, not there attributing this account of Dobrynin's report to Kornyenko.

Apparently Robert Kennedy did not make written accounts of all his discussions with Dobrynin. The Robert Kennedy papers in the Kennedy Library include only notes (still classified) to the two meetings of October 23 and 27 during that week. In addition, his book *Thirteen Days* was edited after his death, and both omissions and deletions were made from the rough notes he had compiled.

This disclosure further underscores the determination of President Kennedy to resolve the crisis by negotiation.

151. See Bundy, *Danger and Survival*, pp. 432–35. Rusk, recently queried on this point, does not now recall whether he was aware of an earlier Robert Kennedy–Dobrynin discussion.

"Black Saturday" because of the disappointment and deep concern after the second Khrushchev message. There was an FBI report that the Soviet Mission in New York was preparing to destroy its records, a precautionary measure if diplomatic relations were going to be suddenly severed.[152] And in Moscow for the first time "popular" demonstrations were mounted in front of the U.S. Embassy. Was Khrushchev still in charge, and could he now accept the deal he himself had proposed? Also on October 27–28 communists in Venezuela, heeding a public call from Castro, bombed four U.S. oil company power stations in the Lake Maracaibo region. While not controlled by Moscow, and probably not by Havana either, this action added to the sense of tension in the Ex Comm.[153]

Another incident that contributed to the tension was an unintended American military action. On October 27 a U-2 reconnaissance plane, apparently on a routine air-sampling nuclear detection mission, strayed over the Chukhotsk peninsula in northeastern Siberia and caused a local Soviet air defense reaction. The pilot had made a navigational error and returned to Alaska under U.S. fighter escort without incident.[154] President Kennedy, when told of it, broke the tension with a harsh laugh and comment, "There is always some so-and-so [sonofabitch] who doesn't get the word."[155]

Moscow probably saw the U-2 intrusion as yet another crass American reminder of its strategic superiority. The location of the incident argued against its being taken as a serious military recon-

152. See Kennedy, *Thirteen Days,* p. 93. Ambassador Dobrynin, and a senior Soviet official in their UN Mission in October 1962, while denying that any files were destroyed, have said that preparations were made for various contingencies.

153. Under the circumstances, even quite innocent events were cause for concern. On October 27 a Soviet transport plane was permitted to fly through Dakar for Brazil. It was feared in Washington that the plane would go to Havana, despite its flight plan, and might have nuclear weapons aboard. In fact it did fly to Rio de Janeiro as declared, to take home the body of the Soviet ambassador to Brazil, who had perished in a drowning accident.

154. The U.S. Air Force fighter interceptors scrambled to escort and protect the U-2 on its return were, under new standing orders from October 22, armed with air-to-air nuclear missiles, so an incident could have been very serious.

155. See Hilsman, *To Move a Nation,* p. 221.

naissance mission of the type that might be made on the eve of hostilities, if it was soberly evaluated. But it undoubtedly contributed to the rising tension.

Khrushchev complained about the overflight in his next message, asking if it were a "provocation," happening "at a time as troubled as the one through which we are passing, when everything has been put into combat readiness." Kennedy expressed regret for the intrusion by the unarmed plane, attributed it to a serious navigational error by the pilot, and said he would "see to it that every precaution is taken to prevent recurrence." The next day a standdown of all U-2 flights around the Soviet Union was ordered.

Rusk arranged for Scali to contact Fomin again and give him hell for the "double cross" of the Soviet step back in the second message, which threatened to drive the crisis again to a dangerous point. Scali, without instructions to do so, even overstated by saying that "an invasion of Cuba is only a matter of hours away." Fomin's message to Moscow after this second conversation may well have reinforced Khrushchev's determination and strengthened arguments to accept the American proposal, as Fomin later told Scali.[156]

Soviet sources, including Gromyko at the Moscow conference, despite many disclosures concerning the crisis, have been unwilling or unable to provide information on the deliberations of Khrushchev and his "Ex Comm" in those critical days of the crisis.[157] Nonetheless, we now know a good deal about the considerations in the forefront of Khrushchev's thinking at that time, in particular on the crucial day, October 27.

156. Ibid., pp. 222–24; and Bundy, *Danger and Survival*, p. 439.

157. A small window into the atmosphere of the deliberations is provided by Melor Sturua, a correspondent of *Izvestiya*. He has recounted how on October 26 he was suddenly summoned to the Kremlin, along with Mikhail Kharlamov, then head of Moscow television and radio. They were the only civilians in a sea of military men outside Khrushchev's office, which, when the door was opened, showed Marshal Malinovsky with map and pointer briefing members of the Politburo (Presidium), presumably on U.S. preparations to invade Cuba. They had been called in to publicize promptly Khrushchev's latest message to Kennedy, the so-called second letter, received in Washington early on October 27, and the first message made public. Sturua told this story at the Moscow conference on the crisis, and then in "Dialectics of the Caribbean Crisis," *Izvestiya*, February 6, 1989.

Above all, President Kennedy had offered to accept a commitment not to invade Cuba. Whatever Khrushchev's own view of that possibility—and as we have seen there are signs he took it seriously—an American commitment not to attack Cuba met three basic needs: it would justify both the deployment of Soviet missiles in Cuba and their withdrawal; it would assuage Castro; and it would remove the imminent dangers of more serious Soviet defeats in losing Cuba or risking war with the United States.

But beyond these were other considerations. One was a real danger that the situation would slip out of control. This risk was not merely in some unanticipated or even uncontrolled American action, but also in some uncontrolled Soviet or Cuban action. Several knowledgeable Soviet officials have emphasized that the unauthorized Soviet shootdown of an American U-2 came as a surprise and shock to Khrushchev.[158] This uncontrolled local Soviet action, plus coincidental Cuban initiation of antiaircraft firing on low-flying reconnaissance aircraft, almost certainly contributed to Khrushchev's determination on October 28 to end the confrontation quickly, without bargaining for better terms, before it could slip out of control.[159]

Of particular importance was a message from Castro that Khrushchev received on the morning of October 27. Castro, while long convinced that the United States was determined to overthrow the Cuban Revolution, had been confident during the crisis that the United States would back down, assuming (as he did) that the Soviet Union stood firm. On October 26, he received convincing intelligence that American military preparations were keyed to launching an air attack and invasion on October 29 or 30, and for the first time became alarmed at this situation. In fact, he became so alarmed that he went to the Soviet Embassy in Havana and spent the night of October 26 in a bomb-shelter there, during which time he wrote a message to Khrushchev (with, according to Ambassador Alekseyev, that envoy's assistance), which was urgently cabled to Moscow. Authoritative Cuban and Soviet sources

158. Among these is Sergei Khrushchev, son of the late leader.

159. On this point see also Daniel Ellsberg, "The Day Castro Almost Started World War III," *New York Times,* October 31, 1987.

are agreed on the above facts. There is, however, some uncertainty over what action (if any) Castro asked Khrushchev to take. My own reconstruction from several conflicting accounts is that Castro heatedly asked Khrushchev what he was going to do about the situation, which was supposed to have been dealt with by putting the missiles in Cuba.[160]

Khrushchev himself, in his speech to the Supreme Soviet in December 1962 in which he detailed (and sought to justify) Soviet actions in the crisis, while not of course referring to Castro's letter or any recommendations in it, cited information from Cuba as well as from Soviet intelligence as indicating the imminence of an American attack.[161] Castro's warning, and his alarm (however expressed), undoubtedly had a different effect than he had intended or expected. On top of Castro's order to his antiaircraft guns to fire, the unauthorized Soviet shootdown, the American U-2 intrusion over the USSR, and the reports of U.S. preparations for an imminent attack, the warning could only have encouraged Khrushchev to accept the deal Kennedy was offering. And he promptly did.

According to a senior Soviet diplomat, Khrushchev personally told him that the United States was ready on October 27 to invade Cuba, and that he decided to pull the missiles out because a

160. The Cuban delegation to the January 1989 Moscow conference, including Politburo member Jorge Risquet Valdes and senior Party leader Emilio Aragonés Navarro, were familiar with the message. So, too, of course, was Ambassador Alekseyev (and former Foreign Minister Gromyko, but he made no comment on it). Sergei Khrushchev, who has not seen the message, was cited in a Western press leak as having said that his father reported that Castro had asked him to fire the missiles. See Bill Keller, " '62 Missile Crisis Yields New Puzzle," *New York Times,* January 30, 1989. All others have vehemently denied that Castro made such a request. I believe that Sergei Khrushchev was accurately reporting something that his father later said in a considerable exaggeration of what Castro actually wrote.

161. "The Present International Situation and the Foreign Policy of the Soviet Union, Report by Comrade N. S. Khrushchev at the Session of the U.S.S.R. Supreme Soviet, December 12, 1962," *Pravda,* December 13, 1962. The nature of Soviet and Cuban intelligence (and I was told there was close coordination and agreement between the two military intelligence organizations in Cuba at the time) has not been specifically disclosed, but the extensive U.S. military preparations, plus even one leak or penetration revealing a full readiness target for operations on October 29 or 30, would have been sufficient.

communist Cuba without missiles was better for Soviet interests than a U.S.-occupied Cuba. While not confirmed, this account is very plausible.[162] It also accords with other information as to the Soviet decision.

The United States later received information from a reliable Soviet source that the Soviet leadership had by then decided not to go to war over Cuba even if America invaded, and formalized that decision in a signed top secret Central Committee directive.[163]

The Soviet leaders promptly agreed to the president's proposal, which is to say his recasting of the first Khrushchev proposal, on October 28 and publicly broadcast the fact.[164] President Kennedy in turn issued a statement welcoming Khrushchev's "statesman-like" decision to withdraw the missiles (omitting to mention that part of the deal was an American pledge of noninvasion of Cuba). Thus the crisis was essentially resolved that day.[165]

162. The statement was made privately by a Soviet ambassador accredited to a Western European country on October 31, 1962, and was promptly learned of by the United States. It is difficult to see how it would have been in Soviet interest to invent this statement for disinformation.

163. This intelligence report, received about six months after the crisis, was both plausible and from a well-placed source. It has, however, never been either corroborated or disconfirmed. Ordinarily, leaderships avoid making such decisions before having to do so, but in this case it may have been decided to reach consensus on an outer limit to support for Cuba.

164. The reply was broadcast on Radio Moscow at 9:00 a.m. (Washington time), about two hours before the official copy was received. The Soviet leaders were taking no chances on a delay that might see an American military move. Khrushchev's letter of October 26 had experienced a long delay in transmission to Washington from the U.S. Embassy in Moscow.

Burlatsky has said that Khrushchev, then at his dacha twenty kilometers outside Moscow, on October 28 dispatched the final message accepting the deal offered by Kennedy by courier directly to the Moscow radio-television broadcast station. According to another report, probably exaggerated, part of the message was sent to the radio station even before the whole text was completed. There is no question that Khrushchev did rush his reply to beat the deadline Kennedy had set by a good margin.

165. The Soviets moved promptly to begin dismantling the missile facilities, without even waiting for a response from Kennedy confirming agreement. Orders were received in Havana that afternoon, and observable work on dismantling began within two hours. Inexplicably, at one site *construction* continued the next day, before work there also shifted to dismantling; someone just didn't get the

From the Soviet (and Cuban) standpoint, the United States had made a major concession. If one believed that the United States had been intending to invade Cuba, an American pledge under the circumstances was an important step. On the other hand, if the U.S. leadership was not planning an invasion, a pledge of restraint was no real sacrifice, while obtaining the removal of the Soviet missiles *was* important, for domestic political, international political, and military reasons. Within the U.S leadership, there was no real debate over acceptance of a noninvasion commitment. There had been those who favored an air strike and invasion in order to remove both the missiles and Castro, but once the alternative of removing the missiles without resort to force was a real choice, *no one* in the Ex Comm argued for invading or even keeping an invasion option.[166]

What would have happened if the Soviet government had not agreed on October 28? If it had narrowed the possibilities for negotiation and insisted that the missiles would stay, the United States might well eventually have attacked the missile bases, followed by an invasion. If it had agreed to remove its missiles from Cuba, but insisted on a formal U.S. pledge to remove American missiles from Turkey, a diplomatic solution could probably have been found. But the risks were high.

No one can be absolutely certain what President Kennedy would have done if Khrushchev had rejected his proposal of October 27

---

word (or couldn't believe it). The dismantling was thorough; everything that could not be taken away was broken up and bulldozed.

166. This consensus included of course Secretary of Defense McNamara, who had consistently opposed an air strike or invasion, and also General Maxwell Taylor, the chairman of the Joint Chiefs and the only military man on the Ex Comm, who had earlier argued for an air strike and invasion. A few senior military men, notably General Curtis LeMay of the U.S. Air Force, continued to argue for an air strike on October 27 (and even on October 28!), and Admiral George Anderson, the chief of naval operations, complained that "we had been had." But these were a minority even among the military leaders. The strongest civilian advocate of an attack on the missiles in the early days of the crisis, Dean Acheson, no longer served as an adviser after October 20, but even he congratulated the president after the outcome. CIA Director John McCone, an advocate of military action and earlier reluctant to give up the objective of removing Castro, nonetheless joined the consensus.

and defied his tacit ultimatum. At the time, I and many others on the Ex Comm or working closely with it believed he would have ordered an air strike. Others, however, including Robert Mc-Namara and McGeorge Bundy, believed he would have tightened the quarantine by including petroleum, and perhaps taken other steps short of direct military action, while continuing to negotiate. Some of his closest advisers, Theodore Sorensen and Arthur Schlesinger, believed he would have made further concessions, including if necessary an outright deal trading our missiles in Turkey for the Soviet missiles in Cuba. It should be recalled that in 1962, and indeed until 1969, most members of the Ex Comm and all others except a handful of close advisers of the president knew nothing of the unilateral "sweetener" in Robert Kennedy's statement to Dobrynin of American intentions to phase out the missiles in Turkey and Italy.[167]

Only in 1987 did Dean Rusk disclose information that makes it appear highly likely that President Kennedy would not have launched an air strike but instead continued negotiations. Rusk revealed that on October 27, after sending Robert Kennedy to deliver the key message to Dobrynin, President Kennedy privately asked Rusk to call the late Andrew Cordier, the former deputy UN secretary general then at Columbia University, and ask him to be prepared to suggest to Secretary General U Thant that he propose to both the Soviet Union and the United States that they remove

167. On October 29, two days after their key conversation and after Khrush-chev's agreement, Dobrynin took an unsigned draft letter to Robert Kennedy. This draft from Khrushchev to the president sought to tie down the U.S. withdrawal of its missiles from Turkey and Italy as part of the deal, seeking a presidential letter to that effect. Robert Kennedy called Dobrynin back the next day, returned the draft Khrushchev letter, and categorically rejected any such written exchange. He informed Dobrynin that if the Soviet Union published anything claiming that there *was* such a deal, the U.S. intentions with respect to the Jupiter missiles would change, and it would negatively reflect on the U.S.-Soviet relationship. The Soviets dropped the matter. See Schlesinger, *Robert Kennedy,* p. 523. This account has been confirmed by a knowledgeable Soviet senior official.

In response to a question from Dobrynin, Kennedy had estimated the missiles would probably be gone in four or five months. Immediately after the crisis, the United States moved within the alliance to take the missiles out of Italy and Turkey, and they were gone by April 25, 1963, less than six months later.

their missiles respectively from Cuba and Turkey. Cordier was given a precise message to this effect, but told not to actually make the suggestion until receiving a signal from Rusk. Thus President Kennedy wanted to have in ready reserve a neutral request to which he could respond favorably much more easily than he could to a Soviet demand. While the whole question was rendered moot by Khrushchev's acceptance of the president's October 27 proposal, it is clear that Kennedy was more inclined to pursue additional negotiations and even to accept a compromise involving an explicit commitment to withdrawing U.S. missiles rather than attack Cuba.[168]

Nonetheless, the situation was fraught with dangers of slipping out of control. I believe that both the U.S. and Soviet leaderships reached a sensible and statesmanlike compromise resolution of the problem.

168. See James G. Blight, Joseph S. Nye, Jr., and David A. Welch, "The Cuban Missile Crisis Revisited," *Foreign Affairs,* vol. 66 (Fall 1987), pp. 178–79.

The Settlement

THERE WAS widespread relief and near euphoria over the success-ful conclusion of the crisis among the U.S. leaders and people, and among the Soviet leaders and people as well. Nonetheless, while the October 28 agreement was crucial, it did *not* end the crisis. Several issues remained or arose in the next three weeks requiring resolution, and there remained the need to implement the agreed terms. Intense and difficult negotiations were required to convert the October 27–28 exchange of messages into practice. One issue was the question of weapons that the United States considered "offensive" other than the missiles—principally, the IL-28 light bombers. Another was the question of inspection arrangements to assure the withdrawal of the missiles and dismantling of the launch facilities. A third was the question of means to provide assurance against future reintroduction of offensive arms. A fourth was the form and content of U.S. assurances against invasion of Cuba. And finally, only with resolution at least of the issue of which "offen-sive" weapons would be removed, and verification of the removal of the missiles, was the United States prepared to end the quaran-tine. This phase of the crisis lasted from October 28 to November 20. Indeed, in one important respect—an American assurance against invasion of Cuba—the final phase continued inconclusively until mid-January 1963, and was left in uncertainty for much longer.

Meanwhile, the United States relied heavily on extensive aerial reconnaissance—a unilateral impingement on Cuban sovereignty not covered in the agreement resolving the crisis.[169] While the

169. Aerial reconnaissance of Cuba by the United States had been conducted ever since October 1960, on an average of about two flights a month before the

Soviets raised only pro forma objections, there was considerable concern over what the Cubans might do—concern even on the part of the Soviets.[170]

One of the early potential dangers, then, was possible Cuban attack on American reconnaissance aircraft. A memorandum of November 5, 1962, appended to this study (Appendix document J) called for tit-for-tat reprisal to any attack (in practice, probably only in response to any successful attack) on overflying American aircraft. This memorandum was written mainly to counter calls for restraint on the grounds that the U.S.-Soviet crisis could be reignited if Soviet personnel were killed in such American reprisal attacks. Concern over Soviet reaction to Russian casualties had been introduced into the crisis debates as early as October 16 by Ambassadors Bohlen and Thompson. It was a valid point. Nonetheless, many of us regarded it as a factor that should not be permitted to exclude consideration of options. It had remained a factor weighed variously, along with others, by different members of the Ex Comm throughout the debate on an air strike. Now the question arose again, in a more limited way, in connection with consideration of contingency responses to the shooting down of another American reconnaissance plane. President Kennedy had overruled such reprisal when Major Rudolf Anderson, Jr., was shot down at the height of the crisis on October 27.[171] If another

---

heavy military buildup of August to October 1962. It continued after the missile crisis until early 1977, when President Jimmy Carter ended it as a gesture toward normalizing relations with Cuba. He resumed flights in 1979.

170. In his letter of October 27, in addition to protesting the accidental U-2 overflight of the USSR that day (and recalling the earlier one of August 30), Khrushchev also urged Kennedy "to bear in mind that a violation of Cuban air space by American aircraft may also have dangerous consequences." N. Khrushchev, "A Message from the Chairman of the Council of Ministers of the USSR to the President of the United States and the General Secretary of the U.N.," *Vneshnyaya politika, 1962*, p. 424. In addition, on October 30, First Deputy Foreign Minister Vasily Kuznetsov (in a discussion with Stevenson) urged that the United States limit itself to peripheral flights and oblique reconnaissance photography. As further insurance, the Soviets did not turn over control of the SAM sites to the Cubans until many months later.

171. The president's decision became known at the operating level in the Pentagon barely in time to prevent a planned air strike on the probable offending

aircraft had been shot down after the crisis had been essentially resolved, I am sure he would also have held back in the first instance. If the threat of continued air defense interference had threatened our ability to verify the removal and continuing absence of the missiles, however, it would have been necessary to assure continuing air reconnaissance. A tentative decision was made by the president on November 8 calling for careful examination of the particular circumstances in any incident, and for a presidential message to Khrushchev explaining the rationale for our limited military response, but endorsing the concept of measured retaliation that some of us had advocated.[172]

The president sent John J. McCloy to New York to work with Ambassador Adlai Stevenson on the American side as leaders of a bipartisan team that also included Under Secretary of State Ball and Deputy Secretary of Defense Roswell Gilpatric.[173] The Soviet government sent First Deputy Foreign Minister Vasily Kuznetsov to work with Ambassador Valerian Zorin. And, most important, the Presidium sent First Deputy Chairman of the Council of Ministers Anastas Mikoyan on November 1 to Havana to negotiate with Fidel Castro about the Cuban role in the settlement, and more generally to discuss Soviet-Cuban relations under the new circumstances.

---

air defense missile site that was about to be made in accordance with contingency plans approved by the president at the Ex Comm meeting on October 23.

172. See Executive Office, White House, "Memorandum for the NSC Executive Committee: Revised Course of Action in the Contingency that a Surveillance Plane Is Shot at or Destroyed," November 8, 1962 (Top Secret; now declassified).

173. McCloy was called back from a European trip. President Kennedy may have sent McCloy because he himself had doubts about Stevenson's firmness in negotiating with the Soviets (as Robert Kennedy did), or perhaps because he believed others had that perception. (Robert Kennedy, in fact, had urged the president to replace Stevenson; see Schlesinger, *Robert Kennedy,* p. 516.) Moreover, if any concessions had to be made, it would be better to have the conservative Republican McCloy make them. McCloy told me, years later, that "Washington" had considered Stevenson too soft, but "actually, he was tougher than I was. He was indignant at Gromyko having lied about no missiles in Cuba." Raymond L. Garthoff, "Memorandum for the Record: Conversation with John J. McCloy on the Cuban Missile Crisis," January 9, 1984.

Mikoyan's task was formidable. Castro was furious at the Soviet leadership for getting him to accept the missiles and then agreeing—without consulting him—to remove them.[174] He had been told the missiles would be a valuable sign of the Soviet commitment, in one sense a substitute for the Warsaw Pact alliance membership he had sought and been denied. And now they were being removed at the demand of his enemy.

Cuban troops apparently took up positions around the four Soviet missile bases on October 28 and remained there for three days (at one site reportedly until November 3, after Mikoyan arrived).[175]

174. Ambassador Alekseyev, in his memoir article in November 1988 and at the Moscow conference in January 1989, recounted how Cuban President Osvaldo Dorticós Torrado had called him early on October 28 and told him of the radio broadcast announcing Khrushchev's decision to withdraw the missiles. Alekseyev warned Dorticós against believing everything on the American radio, but when Dorticós told him it was *Moscow* radio, Alekseyev said, "I felt like the most unhappy person on earth, imagining Fidel's reaction." Castro would not see him for three or four days. See Alekseyev, *Ekho planety* (November 1988), p. 33. Even at the Moscow conference some twenty-six years later, Cuban officials could not understand why the Soviet leadership did not at least inform them, if not consult them, before announcing the decision publicly. Khrushchev's pleas of urgency might explain the decision, but hardly its handling with the Cubans. Clearly, Khrushchev was afraid of what Castro might do.

175. I reported this unequivocally in the first edition of this book, based on very good intelligence in 1962. At the 1989 Moscow conference, although this matter was never brought up at the table, a member of the Cuban delegation, and separately former Soviet ambassador to Havana Alekseyev, both took the initiative in raising it with me privately. Both advised that the *interpretation* reached by the United States—that Cuban troops had been ordered to surround the Soviet bases—had been in error while confirming that soldiers in Cuban uniforms *had* appeared around the Soviet missile bases. Alekseyev said they were *Soviet* troops in Cuban uniforms to provide perimeter security; the Cuban said they were *Cuban* troops providing perimeter security and local antiaircraft protection for the bases. Neither explained why such troops appeared *after* the crisis had peaked. Nor was there any explanation for the discrepancy in the two accounts. Possibly corroborating either account is another CIA intelligence report of October 28 that "automatic anti-aircraft weapons and personnel trenches have been prepared during the last few days. Camouflage is being extended and . . . dispersion of personnel and equipment also is evident." CIA Memorandum, "The Crisis: USSR/Cuba," October 28, 1962, p. I-1 (now declassified). Also, it is known that in Cuba (and other countries) Soviet military advisory personnel have often worn the uniforms of the host country to be less conspicuous.

On the other hand, Roy Medvedev, whose sources could only have been

Mikoyan was the only Soviet Presidium member to have visited Cuba (in February 1960), even before the Soviet Union and Cuba had established diplomatic relations on May 8, 1960. Mikoyan had negotiated economic and trade agreements then that helped Castro to wean Cuba away from economic dependence on the United States. The Soviet leadership hoped the same means would again help to mollify Castro. Mikoyan was accompanied by Artemy A. Alikhanov, deputy chairman of the State Committee for Foreign Economic Relations, in charge of aid and trade. But while new economic assistance presumably did help, it certainly did not solve Mikoyan's problems.

Mikoyan was in Havana for twenty-two days.[176] It took him sixteen days to obtain Castro's reluctant agreement to give up the IL-28 bombers. He was unable to secure Castro's acquiescence to any external inspection and verification measures in Cuba, and in turn the Soviet Union was unable to get from the United States formal assurances against invasion of Cuba to still Castro's abiding mistrust of American promises on that score.

Castro also sought to establish his own terms for any resolution of relations with the United States. Immediately after the public exchange of Khrushchev's and Kennedy's messages on October 28, Castro set forth in a letter to UN Secretary General U Thant, made public, his own five conditions. Castro demanded a cessation of the economic blockade imposed earlier by the United States, a cessation of all covert sabotage, subversion, and infiltration operations carried out by the United States and accomplices, an end to "piratical raids being carried out from bases in the United States

---

Moscow Party corridor gossip, and not American intelligence from 1962, referred to *Cuban* troops surrounding the Soviet missile bases. See Medvedev, *All Stalin's Men*, p. 51. While not in itself authoritative, the independent Moscow origin for his account strongly tends to corroborate the original American report.

176. Ambassador Alekseyev and Sergo Mikoyan have both attested to Castro's stubborn opposition to various proposals for withdrawing the IL-28s (and, initially, some other arms) as well as the missiles, and for inspection in Cuba, and the like. (Sergo Mikoyan had accompanied his father to Cuba.) At one point Castro refused for several days even to see Mikoyan, until the latter threatened to leave.

Anastas Mikoyan's devotion and skill in handling this difficult assignment was reflected in his decision to remain in Havana even when his wife died. Khrushchev left with him the decision whether to return to Moscow for the funeral, but Mikoyan considered it important that he stay.

and Puerto Rico," cessation of U.S. air intrusions, and U.S. withdrawal from and return to Cuba of the naval base at Guantánamo Bay.[177] Mikoyan and the Soviet leaders had no choice but to endorse publicly the justice of Castro's demands, while seeking in practice to steer toward a realistic settlement.[178]

The anger of Castro and the Cubans at the Soviet leaders went well beyond their chagrin and disappointment at Khrushchev's decision, without consulting or even informing Havana, to agree to take the missiles out. They correctly perceived then, and still believe to this day, that the Soviet leaders by settling the crisis through a superpower deal failed to let Cuba or its interests become part of the diplomacy of settlement. One result is that more than a quarter of a century later relations have still not been reestablished between Cuba and the United States. A realistic assessment of the gap between the interests of the two countries as perceived in Havana and Washington, and the constraints of prevailing sentiments and domestic political realities in the two countries, make it highly unlikely that any real accommodation could then have been attained. But the Cubans have rightly seen themselves as being dealt out of the picture altogether, and a degree of resentment toward Moscow on this issue is felt to this day.[179]

One intriguing question about Cuban objectives and diplomacy in October 1962 remains. On October 8, before the missile crisis, President Osvaldo Dorticós Torrado, in a speech to the UN General Assembly in New York that went virtually unnoticed at the time, had said: "Were the United States able to give us proof, by word and deed, that it would not carry out aggression against our country, then, we declare solemnly before you here and now, our weapons would be unnecessary and our army redundant," and "then Cuba

177. Letter, Fidel Castro to U Thant, UN General Assembly Document A/5271, October 28, 1962, pp. 1–2; reprinted in Larson, ed., *"Cuban Crisis" of 1962*, 2d ed., pp. 197–98.

178. Mikoyan publicly endorsed Castro's position on his own authority because there was no time to consult Moscow. See Mikoyan, *Latinskaya Amerika* (January 1988), p. 77; and cited in Blight and Welch, *On the Brink*, p. 269.

179. From conversations with senior Cuban and Soviet officials, Moscow, January 1989.

would not have to strengthen its defenses. Cuba would not even
need any army. . . ."[180] He said this in the context of a defense
against charges of a military buildup in Cuba, and accompanied it
by basically valid charges of American-sponsored acts of sabotage,
aggression, and mercenary invasion (at the Bay of Pigs). And Cuba
would no doubt have sought ironclad guarantees before disbanding
its army in whole or in part. But it seemed to offer a possible basis
for negotiation of reciprocal restraints.

On October 23, the day after President Kennedy's address,
when the UN Security Council began to debate the missile crisis,
the Cuban delegate, Ambassador Mario García-Inchaustegui, *repeated* these passages from Dorticós's speech, probably on his
own initiative rather than on instructions or even clearance from
Havana.[181] Again, it went unnoticed in Washington. Unnoticed,
that is, until Fomin's conversation with Scali on October 26. Fomin
said that the Cuban delegate in the UN Security Council debate
had asked for noninvasion assurances in return for dismantling the
missiles and had received no response.[182] This stretched the statement by Dorticós cited by García-Inchaustegui, but not beyond
recognition. It is clear in retrospect that the Cuban authorities had
not been pushing for such a deal on withdrawal of the missiles
during the crisis, but presumably Dorticós did have in mind some
broader diplomatic dialogue in which reciprocal restraints could
have been explored.

Following the Khrushchev-Kennedy deal of October 28, Castro

180. This passage was omitted in the abridged version of his speech printed
in the *New York Times,* October 9, 1962. See also the note following.

181. García-Inchaustegui's speech, with the several paragraphs from Dorticós's, is reproduced in Larson, ed., *"Cuban Crisis" of 1962,* 2d ed., pp. 102–10,
esp. p. 103. Whether for his performance during the crisis or otherwise, García-
Inchaustegui was suddenly recalled on October 31 and replaced by Carlos M.
Lechuga Hevia.

182. This point was omitted in Hilsman's and most other accounts of the
Fomin-Scali conversation but is in Scali's original notes of the meeting and in
his memoir account. See *Family Weekly,* October 25, 1964, pp. 4–5. Scali is,
however, in error in saying there was no such reference by the Cuban delegate.
The reference cited above was promptly located by State Department analysts
on October 26—it had, however, not previously been noted.

was adamantly against the idea of international inspection of any kind in Cuba. The Soviets nonetheless dismantled the sites, destroying what could not be removed, and cooperatively displayed the missiles as they were removed on the decks of Soviet cargo ships to facilitate American observation. This outcome, while satisfactory for the time, did not provide ironclad assurances for the future, and led the United States to hold back from a firm noninvasion commitment of the kind envisaged on October 28, as will be further discussed below.

The major issue holding up an end to the quarantine and to the military alert was the U.S. insistence that the "offensive weapons" mentioned by President Kennedy in his September warnings and October 23 quarantine proclamation included bomber aircraft, and Soviet and Cuban objection to removal of the forty-two IL-28 jet light bombers.[183] At first the Soviet negotiators believed this to be a minor matter, but they soon realized that the United States was serious in insisting on inclusion of the bombers. The fact that Khrushchev himself had referred to "the weapons that you [the United States] consider 'offensive,' " rather than mentioning missiles, weakened the Soviet case.[184]

There were divided views among American policymakers and

183. The Ilyushin-28 jet light bomber was already more than a dozen years old at the time. It had been virtually removed from active service in the Soviet Air Force in 1960. Still, it could carry 6,000 pounds of bombload 600 nautical miles (or less weight to 750 nautical miles) operational radius, and it could be a step toward increasing offensive capabilities. Even when it was a Soviet bomber, during the 1950s, it was not actually given a nuclear delivery role, although that fact was not appreciated by most American military analysts in 1962, since it had always been credited as having a "potential" for nuclear delivery—as, of course, do civilian airliners.

Khrushchev in his memoirs commented that "even though these bombers were obsolete, they would be useful against an enemy landing force. The IL-28 was too slow to fly over enemy territory because it could easily be shot down, but was well suited for coastal defense." See Talbott, ed. and trans., *Khrushchev Remembers* (1970), p. 495. It would have been useful to counter a new Bay of Pigs attack.

184. Some Soviets, in particular Sergo Mikoyan, have assumed the United States merely sought to take advantage of this loose language. See Mikoyan, *Latinskaya Amerika* (January 1988), pp. 77–78. As the discussion below shows, there was much more to it than that.

advisers over how strongly to stand on this issue. Some believed the missiles had been our real concern, and it was unwise and imprudent to appear to be pushing our advantage by raising objections to the IL-28s or any other weapon system. Some wished to press our advantage and to demand the removal of *all* Soviet military forces. Still others believed we should seek removal of at least the IL-28 bombers.[185]

While the administration had been prepared until October 16 to accept some jet light bombers in Cuba, as indicated implicitly in McGeorge Bundy's earlier-cited statement of October 14, once the Soviets were known to be introducing nuclear-armed medium-range ballistic missiles, it had been considered necessary to draw more tightly the definition of unacceptable offensive arms in Cuba.[186]

185. The following discussion draws heavily on my article "American Reaction to Soviet Aircraft in Cuba, 1962 and 1978," *Political Science Quarterly,* vol. 95 (Fall 1980), pp. 427–39.

186. When on Sunday, October 14, McGeorge Bundy had appeared on ABC's "Issues and Answers" and been asked about charges by Senator Keating that the Soviets were installing strategic missiles in Cuba, he expressed strong doubt that the Soviets and Cubans would "attempt to install a major offensive capability" in Cuba, and stated flatly that "I *know* there is no present evidence" that they are doing so. He also addressed in some detail the matter of aircraft. "It is true," he said, "that the MiG fighters which have been put in Cuba for more than a year now, and any possible additions in the form of aircraft, might have a certain marginal capability for moving against the United States. But I think we have to bear in mind the relative magnitudes. . . . So far, everything that has been delivered in Cuba falls within the categories of aid which the Soviet Union has provided, for example, to neutral states like Egypt or Indonesia, and I should not be surprised to see additional military assistance of this sort." See Hilsman, *To Move a Nation,* p. 180. Almost literally at the same time Bundy was speaking, the U-2 was overflying Cuba and obtaining the first clear evidence of the construction of medium-range ballistic missiles in Cuba. The same flight also confirmed that crates observed arriving in Cuba on September 28 did indeed, as suspected, contain IL-28 jet light bombers.

On October 10 U.S. Navy reconnaissance photos of Soviet ships approaching Cuba—photos actually taken on September 28, but unaccountably only circulated in Washington on October 9–10—showed topside storage of crates that intelligence analysts quickly identified as probably containing disassembled IL-28 light bombers. This was the first indication that the bombers were being provided to Cuba. The suspect IL-28 crates, together with the unconfirmed reports and suspicions of offensive missiles and the continuing SAM deployments, had led

On October 22 the president had applied the quarantine to "all offensive military equipment" going to Cuba. After describing the MRBM and IRBM missile sites, he stated: "In addition, jet bombers, capable of carrying nuclear weapons, are now being uncrated and assembled in Cuba, while the necessary air bases are being prepared." The quarantine order itself, of October 23, included "bomber aircraft" among the offensive arms prohibited from entering Cuba.

During the six days of confrontation, from October 22 to 28, there were no other references to the IL-28s or more generally to aircraft, although President Kennedy did refer in his letter to Khrushchev of October 22 to removing both "long-range missile bases" and "other offensive weapon systems in Cuba" (not specified), and in his letter of October 27 he referred to "all weapon systems in Cuba capable of offensive use." Khrushchev, for his part, referred on October 28 to "the weapons you describe as offensive," in agreeing to their removal.

On October 28, at the tenth Ex Comm meeting, the issue arose. The president stated that offensive weapons "in our view" included the IL-28 bombers, but that "we should not get 'hung up' on the IL-28 bombers."[187] The president was prepared for the U.S. side to argue to the Soviets that the IL-28s were among the weapons *we* viewed as "offensive," and therefore were covered by the convenient circumlocution used by Khrushchev. But he was not com-

---

to scheduling the October 14 U-2 photo reconnaissance mission, which observed the crates and the beginning of aircraft assembly at two airfields. (The intelligence community promptly dubbed this technique "cratology.")

Bundy had anticipated the IL-28s, and his statement on October 14 clearly signaled that a modest number of these bombers for conventional bomb delivery— as earlier supplied both to Egypt and Indonesia—would not, alone, be regarded by the administration as representing a "major offensive capability." But of course after October 16 it was not Ilyushins alone—the MRBMs and IRBMs had *not* been expected and they *did* represent a major offensive capability. The line was redrawn to seek the exclusion of all surface-to-surface missiles and all bombers.

187. As early as October 20, in an unusual early reference to the bombers, President Kennedy privately had said that the IL-28s didn't really "affect the balance of power" and didn't "bother" him. See Schlesinger, *Robert Kennedy*, pp. 510–11.

fortable with the fact that virtually the whole crisis exchange had focused on the missiles; in the record of the meeting the president's words were paraphrased as stating that "he did not want to get into a position where we would appear to be going back on our part of the deal. The IL-28 bombers were less important than the strategic missiles."[188] This somewhat equivocal stand was, of course, known only to those few most directly involved in the crisis management. And the decision did not specify how far to press the issue, if the Soviets were adamant, before deciding we were stymied.

Following the Ex Comm meeting, I was tasked at the State Department with preparing a paper on the subject. I submitted a memorandum titled "Considerations in Defining Weapons Which Must Be Removed from Cuba," to Deputy Undersecretary U. Alexis Johnson on October 29, and he in turn cabled it to Under Secretary Ball in New York. In the memorandum, I noted that "we would like to see the maximum military withdrawal from Cuba, but we must balance against this a reasonable interpretation of what is intolerable to us." For example, the president had clearly indicated on September 4 that the weapons then in Cuba—including the MiG fighters, coastal defense cruise missiles, and missile-armed patrol boats—were not then regarded as "offensive." On the other hand, the quarantine had included bombers. I concluded that as a bottom-line "the weapons systems which must be removed are the 1,000 n.m. and 2,200 n.m. surface-to-surface missiles, IL-28 jet light bombers, and the warheads and support equipment for these systems."[189]

188. "Summary Record of NSC Executive Committee Meeting No. 10, October 28, 1962, 11:10 A.M.," p. 2 (Top Secret; now declassified).

189. Telegram no. 1133, State Department to the U.S. Mission to the United Nations (hereafter, State to USUN), Eyes Only Under Secretary Ball from Alexis Johnson, October 29, 1962, pp. 1–2 (Secret; now declassified). This telegram, via State Department "backchannel," transmitted the full text of the memorandum I had prepared on "Considerations in Defining Weapons Which Must Be Removed from Cuba." It is reproduced as Appendix document F.

At the time of the first edition of this book, I had available on an unclassified basis only an emasculated version of my memorandum, sharply cut up in "sanitizing" a declassified version in 1980 because of sensitivity at the time to the then-current issue of MiG-23s recently brought into Cuba. I had written, "In

Direct negotiations with the Soviets, apart from the Kennedy-Khrushchev correspondence, were centered in New York, where Stevenson and McCloy had begun meeting with Mikoyan and Kuznetsov on October 29. Following the Ex Comm meeting on October 28 and the discussion drawing on my memorandum of October 29, Stevenson on October 31 was instructed to provide to the Soviets the list of weapons deemed offensive by the United States, including "bomber aircraft" and "bombs, air-to-surface rockets and guided missiles."[190]

In a dinner meeting of Stevenson and McCloy with Mikoyan and Kuznetsov on November 1, dealing with many matters including Mikoyan's attempts to raise Castro's five points, the Americans *forgot* to give the Soviets the list! Stevenson remedied this by a letter to Mikoyan the next day, November 2. Apart from thanking Mikoyan for the dinner, the letter read, in full: "One thing that Mr. McCloy and I neglected to discuss with you last night was the list of items that the United States considers in the category of offensive weapons within the meaning of the exchange between President Kennedy and Chairman Khrushchev. Such a list is appended to this letter. We trust that the weapons you plan to remove include all those on this list."[191]

Mikoyan, we now know, only received this letter with the broad list of what the United States considered "offensive weapons" literally as he was entering a taxicab for the airport to fly to Havana. He was incensed by it and declared it should be returned as unacceptable. Although it was not returned, Kuznetsov immediately registered an objection. And on November 5 Khrushchev sent a message to Kennedy strongly complaining: "I have studied the list and, I must confess, the approach of the American side to

---

addition to the MRBMs and IRBMs, the IL-28s should definitely be included, but the MIG fighters should not be." (P. 2.) This sentence, and indeed much of the discussion in the memorandum, had been excised in declassification. The full text of the memorandum incorporated in the telegram had, however, been declassified and released in 1976, before the MiG-23 issue arose, and I recently acquired it and now include it as an appended document.

190. Telegram no. 1147, State to USUN, October 31, 1962, pp. 2–3 (Secret; now declassified).

191. Letter, Adlai Stevenson to Anastas Mikoyan, November 2, 1962.

this matter has seriously worried me. . . . It is hard for us to understand what aim is being pursued by the introduction of that list . . . at a moment when we have already agreed with you on the main questions and when we on our part have already fulfilled what we agreed upon—have dismantled the rocket weapons, are loading them now on ships and these weapons will be soon shipped from Cuba." He asked Kennedy "to meet our anxiety with understanding," and pleaded: "We should understand the position each side is in and take it into consideration but not overburden, not complicate our relations, especially at such an important moment when measures are being taken to eliminate the acute tension and bring these relations to a normal state."[192]

Mikoyan, when Castro finally agreed to receive him, was treated to a tirade including a characterization of the new American demands as just what Castro had predicted—make one concession to the Americans and they'll demand ten more.[193]

On November 1 the president authorized immediate low-level reconnaissance flights both over the missile sites, to check on the dismantling, and over the IL-28 airfields. "The major reason for overflying the IL-28s," as stated in the record of the Ex Comm meeting, "is to make clear that we consider these planes 'offensive weapons' to be removed by the Russians, and, therefore, we must know whether they are being dismantled."[194] On November 2 reconnaissance photos taken the previous day showed continued assembly of the IL-28s, as well as continued dismantling of the MRBM and IRBM sites.[195]

On November 2 the matter was considered at an Ex Comm meeting, and the president made his decision: the IL-28s must be

192. Letter, Chairman Nikita Khrushchev to President John Kennedy, November 5, 1962.

193. Sergo Mikoyan, in interviews with me in 1987 and 1988, and cited by Blight and Welch, *On the Brink,* p. 268.

194. "NSC Executive Committee Record of Action, November 1, 1962, 10:00 A.M., Meeting No. 16," p. 1 (Top Secret; now declassified).

195. Assembly of IL-28s continued after October 28. During the first half of November a curious discrepancy was observed: at one of the two airfields where crated IL-28s were located, Holguín, assembly of aircraft soon stopped, while at the other, San Julian, it continued up until the final decision on November 19.

removed. The other short-range tactical systems, and Soviet military personnel, were not included. The president on November 3 issued further instructions, including a "requirement" for removal of "all bombers and their equipment," as well as all offensive missiles and equipment. He stated, "All Americans should stick firmly to this position."[196]

Reinforced by the president's firm instructions of November 3, Stevenson raised the issue of the IL-28s with Kuznetsov on that same day, noting the continued assembly of the bombers and stating that they should be removed.[197] On November 5 UN Secretary General U Thant also raised the issue of the IL-28s with Kuznetsov, who argued that the question of the bombers was "a new issue" and had not been "covered" in the Kennedy-Khrushchev correspondence.[198] That same day Robert Kennedy met with Ambassador Dobrynin and told him that "it was very clear that the bombers, the IL-28s, had to go."[199] On November 6 the president in his reply to Khrushchev insisted again that the bombers be removed, coupled, however, with an indication of readiness to drop the other items on the list.[200] On November 7, Secretary Rusk cabled Stevenson: "Our primary purpose is to get the MRBM's and IL-28 bombers out and we would be prepared to go far in reducing the list of offensive weapons in order to achieve this purpose."[201] He was authorized to fall back to the MRBMs and

196. Telegram no. 1177, State to USUN, November 2, 1962, p. 1 (Confidential; now declassified); and Telegram no. 1189, State to USUN, November 3, 1962, p. 2 (Top Secret; now declassified).

197. Telegram no. 1625, USUN to State, November 3, 1962, p. 1 (Secret; now declassified).

198. Telegram no. 1635, USUN to State, November 5, 1962, p. 3 (Secret; now declassified).

199. Robert Kennedy, memorandum of conversation with Ambassador Anatoly Dobrynin, November 5, 1962.

200. Letter, Kennedy to Khrushchev, November 6, 1962.

201. Telegram no. 1223, State to USUN, November 7, 1962, pp. 1–2. It was time to winnow down the list to the essentials. In retrospect, I am sure that the president's decision was the correct one; I regret to acknowledge that at the time I had recommended to Johnson that we still try a little longer to include some of the other weapons.

IRBMs, bombers, and nuclear weapons, and to drop the Komar patrol boats and other short-range land-based or sea-based missiles.[202] On November 8 and 13, Stevenson and McCloy met again with Kuznetsov and Zorin in continued argument over the IL-28s (as well as over the establishment of adequate inspection in Cuba and verification of withdrawal of the missile systems, which had been at issue since the negotiations in New York had begun), while on November 8 dropping the other items from our list of offensive weapons.

This was the situation Mikoyan faced in Cuba. The IL-28s posed a special difficulty for the Soviets because they were not part of their nuclear deterrent (offensive) forces. They naturally did not wish to renege on their earlier commitment to provide them as part of the Soviet contingent of forces for defense of Cuba. The United States, however, was determined and pressed the issue.

The status of the IL-28s presented something of a problem for the United States, too, although it was not given much weight except in terms of recognizing a possible difficulty in marshaling support of world opinion if the Cubans and Soviets were adamant and we continued to press the issue. Most, if not all, members of the Ex Comm considered our position justified. At the same time, as Bundy had alluded to publicly on October 14, IL-28s had been transferred to Egypt and Indonesia, and the United States and world community had not regarded that as other than normal and acceptable military assistance.

Strong feelings were generated and expressed among those involved in advising the Ex Comm and the president on what to do about the IL-28 bombers (and the other issues still unresolved, including verification).

There tended to be replays of the debates that had taken place in the first week of the crisis, and again in the second, between the three schools: to resort if necessary to military action to eliminate

202. Almost precisely five years later, on October 21, 1967, an Egyptian navy Komar missile patrol boat of the same class sank the Israeli destroyer *Eilat*—drawing at least fleeting world attention to this weapon system. But there was no real concern in the U.S. government in 1962 (except possibly in some quarters in the Navy) over the Komar boats in Cuba.

the bombers, to tighten the quarantine to include petroleum, or to concede on the issue. By and large the same people held to the same positions. The main difference was a much stronger readiness to consider conceding on this issue. Some believed that we had won on the main issue, the Soviet withdrawal of the missiles, and should not press our luck in forcing Moscow to back down again.

I recall an argument I had with a senior State Department official in early November, in which he challenged me as to the difference between IL-28s in Cuba and, say, in Indonesia. My first reply was that from Cuba they could strike Oak Ridge, which they could not from Java; but that was only a debater's argument. The real point was, as I argued, that the president had publicly committed the United States to regard the IL-28s as part and parcel of a dangerous offensive arms buildup in Cuba in his quarantine speech of October 22, and that was why the IL-28s as well as the missiles must come out. While the MiG-21s might be at least as dangerous in potential, and while both the Ilyushins and MiGs in fact represented no real threat so long as not armed with nuclear weapons, nonetheless the United States had committed itself to regard the Ilyushin "bombers" as dangerous offensive weapons, and had not so committed itself with respect to MiG fighters or fighter-bombers. I felt that difference was crucial, as I had argued in my memorandum of October 29, and as the president had decided on November 2.

Probably the most effective and important advice in persuading the president to stand firm on removal of the IL-28s was that of Ambassador Thompson, who counseled that since Khrushchev had made the much more difficult decision to withdraw the missiles, he would also agree to take out the bombers.

At several meetings in mid-November, in particular on November 12 and 16, the Ex Comm debated this subject. Sentiment was strong for threatening Khrushchev privately with a stiffer blockade if he would not agree. McNamara and Bundy favored a stiffer blockade. General Taylor, speaking for the Joint Chiefs of Staff, recommended tightening the blockade to include petroleum and, if that did not lead the Soviets to capitulate on the bombers, bombing the Cuban airfields. He was supported by Treasury Secretary Douglas Dillon. The extent of hardening resolve was reflected in a State Department contingency paper of November 14, based on the preceding Ex Comm discussion, proposing a range of action including not only "tightening of the blockade" (we did not in internal papers always bother with the euphemism "quarantine"), but also such measures as "'harassing surveillance' from the air," going beyond necessary reconnaissance. The paper suggested: "Up to a point this surveillance can be intensified as a measure of psychological warfare. But using aerial reconnaissance as a means of provoking attack on our planes, which would in turn justify retaliation from the air on Cuban targets (including the IL-28's on the ground), is not regarded as an appropriate form of action, *at least until all of the above steps have been played out.*"[203]

An "IL-28 crisis" thus threatened to follow hard on the heels of the missile crisis. From indications at the time, I personally believe that if the Soviets had said they would not remove the aircraft, President Kennedy would have expanded the "quarantine"; I am sure that he would not have taken the Joint Chiefs' recommendation in that contingency "to take them [the IL-28s] out by air attack."

The Soviet negotiators in New York finally offered to remove the planes quietly *after* the United States ended the blockade and made its "no-invasion" pledge; presumably Moscow felt that with this much of an American concession they could manage Castro's acquiescence and save face for the USSR.[204] But the American negotiators insisted on withdrawal of the bombers before ending

203. The Ex Comm meeting summaries do not review the discussion. General Taylor's position was, however, spelled out in his written "talking points" for the meeting, which have been preserved and now declassified. See [Joint Chiefs of Staff], "Chairman's Talking Paper for Meeting with the President," November 16, 1962 (Top Secret; now declassified), p. 1.

For the hard-line State Department paper see Memorandum, Deputy Undersecretary of State U. Alexis Johnson to McGeorge Bundy, with copies to all Ex Comm members, "Cuban Contingency Paper: Next Steps on the IL-28s," November 14, 1962, pp. 2–3 (Top Secret, Eyes Only; now declassified); emphasis added.

I participated in drafting this paper for the Ex Comm. I believed we should press hard for removal of the IL-28s and I was confident the Soviets would eventually accede. I did not, however, believe we should resort to an air attack on the airfields, or to deliberately provoking one.

204. Telegram no. 1856, USUN to State, November 19, 1962, p. 7 (Top Secret; now declassified).

the quarantine, and noted that the no-invasion pledge involved other unsettled issues as well, mainly on-site verification in Cuba that no offensive weapons remained or would be reintroduced.

On November 18, McCloy told Kuznetsov (who had complained that the United States was "stalling" in the negotiations) that the president was scheduling a press conference for 6:00 p.m. on November 20, and that the Soviets must promise before that time to withdraw the IL-28 bombers, or "it will put in question whether in fact we have an agreement with [the] Soviet Union in regard to removal of offensive weapons from Cuba."[205] On November 19 the United States informed its NATO and OAS allies at the head of government or foreign minister level that the Soviets had not yet agreed to remove the bombers and that unspecified further measures, by implication a tightened quarantine, might be required. In addition, the president sent personal messages to President Charles de Gaulle, Chancellor Konrad Adenauer, and Prime Minister Harold Macmillan advising them that the United States might have to resort to "renewed action" and expressing appreciation for their "firm support."[206]

On November 19 Castro gave in on the Ilyushins (although not on inspection issues). Early on November 20 Khrushchev informed the president and promised that the IL-28s would be removed within thirty days. He still objected that in the October exchange of key letters Kennedy had not made "a single mention of bomber aircraft," and that the IL-28s were obsolete and "at present cannot be classified as offensive types of weapons." But he agreed to withdraw them in exchange for American lifting of the quarantine.[207]

In his press conference on November 20, the president announced that the Soviets had agreed to remove the bombers, and that the quarantine would be lifted. All the missiles had by then been withdrawn. The SAC alert was canceled. On November 21 the USSR and Warsaw Pact nominal alerts were, in turn, canceled.

205. Ibid., p. 4. This message reported on the discussion of November 18.

206. Telegram no. 939, State circular, November 19, 1962, pp. 3–4 (Secret; now declassified).

207. Letter, Khrushchev to Kennedy, November 20, 1962.

The bombers were all removed by December 6. On December 12 Khrushchev informed the Supreme Soviet that the missiles and the IL-28s had been withdrawn in exchange for an American promise not to invade Cuba.

Once the missiles were being taken out, American attention had focused principally on the IL-28s. There were, however, three other elements in the American position with respect to weapons to be dealt with. One was the removal of nuclear warheads (if any) in Cuba; another was assurance against a Soviet submarine base; and third was a less clear-cut but growing interest in seeking Soviet withdrawal of their ground combat forces.

There was no real issue over the withdrawal of nuclear warheads. The United States had included "warheads" for missiles and bombers in the list Stevenson had given to Mikoyan on November 2. On November 5 a message sent to Stevenson and McCloy in the name of the president, mainly on the IL-28s, also stated that "we need assurances on warheads as much as on missiles themselves. Moreover, we need to know about possible warheads for IL-28s and even MiG 21s."[208] The later, pared-down listing given to the Soviet negotiators on November 8 specified missiles, bombers, and "any nuclear warheads for missiles, nuclear bombs for aircraft, or any type nuclear weapon."[209] Even before that renewed instruction, however, Kuznetsov on November 6 had said the question of removal of nuclear warheads was "a detail," that without doubt warheads would be removed "if indeed any warheads are in Cuba"; the Soviet Union was removing "everything" associated with the so-called offensive missiles. Later the Soviets gave categorical assurances to that effect. On November 18 Kuznetsov told McCloy that "he was now authorized to say that no nuclear weapons whatsoever were any longer on the territory of Cuba," and that the Soviet government reaffirmed that "all nuclear weapons had been removed and that they were not going to reintroduce them."[210]

Assuming that the recent Soviet acknowledgment that some of

208. Telegram no. 1194, State to USUN, November 5, 1962, p. 1 (Top Secret; now declassified).

209. Telegram no. 1223, State to USUN, November 7, 1962, p. 2 (Top Secret; now declassified).

210. Telegram no. 1856, USUN to State, November 19, 1962, p. 8.

the nuclear missile warheads had been in Cuba is correct, the record of Soviet statements in November 1962 is entirely consistent with the known facts. As earlier described, the Soviets now say the nuclear warheads were removed on "November 2–5," and as earlier discussed the United States had always regarded the *Aleksandrovsk,* which departed Cuba on November 5, as the most likely carrier if there were warheads.[211]

While couched in terms that implied there had been warheads in Cuba, the Soviet purpose was to reassure the United States—which had raised the issue as though warheads were there. Thus even if no warheads had ever reached Cuba, the Soviets would not have wanted to stimulate American suspicions or a new issue by stating so. For its part the United States did not want to admit that it did not know if there were any nuclear warheads in Cuba. On the other hand, it could not seek to inspect the removal of something it did not know was there. It did not wish to acknowledge doubt as to the presence of nuclear warheads and possibly stimulate any Soviet temptation to conceal and keep in Cuba any warheads it might have there. In real terms, the Soviet leaders would almost certainly have been every bit as interested as the American leaders in promptly returning to the Soviet Union any nuclear warheads sent to Cuba. But worst-case military calculations, and domestic political realities, ruled out an explicit American judgment to that effect.

The result was agreement that "any [nuclear] warheads" for the missiles and bombs for the bombers were being returned. Although American surveillance and intelligence did not conclusively detect the return of any nuclear warheads to the Soviet Union, that very fact tended (except for the most suspicious) to confirm the estimate that none had been there. That judgment may have been in error. Assuming nuclear warheads had been there, the available evidence tends to corroborate the Soviet account of their removal. Most significant, in the subsequent quarter of a century there have been no indications that any nuclear weapons were in Cuba.

211. See the discussion in "Stage 3: Confrontation."

The negotiations with respect to submarine basing—years later to become very important—tended to be "lost" in the concentration on the IL-28s. When on November 2 Stevenson had sent Mikoyan the list of offensive weapons, it included naval missiles in a category together with medium-range land-based missiles: "surface-to-surface missiles including those designed for use at sea."[212] By the time of the scaled-back instructions with the November 8 list, and throughout in the actual discussions, sea-based missiles (never in Cuba, except for the short-range missiles on patrol boats) were given little attention.

On November 3 President Kennedy clarified his instructions in a message to Stevenson and McCloy. Again, the main thrust was to reaffirm the importance of removing the IL-28s, but the president also sought to clarify "our policy and purpose": "In blunt summary, we want no offensive weapons and no Soviet military base in Cuba, and that is how we understand the agreements of October 27 and October 28." Moreover, the instruction noted that "there is some evidence of an intent to establish a submarine-tending facility," and it was explicit on the American position with respect to a submarine base: "All the offensive weapon systems, including anything related to a submarine base, must be removed, or we shall have to consider further action of our own to remove them."[213] Following this strong and explicit statement of the American position, the very next day (November 4) McCloy raised the matter with Kuznetsov, and also stressed more generally that the United States would object to establishment of a Soviet military base in Cuba. Kuznetsov denied that the Soviet Union was building a submarine base, referring to Khrushchev's assurances to Ambas-

212. Letter, Stevenson to Mikoyan, November 2, 1962. The negotiating history makes clear that while the short-range missiles on naval patrol craft in Cuba were raised by the United States, although not vigorously pursued, the fact that the broad language was intended to cover submarine-launched missiles as well may never have been made clear. The "forgotten" list was not really discussed or clarified with the Soviet negotiators; discussion concentrated almost exclusively on the IL-28 bombers. There was some discussion of submarine bases, as indicated in the paragraphs following.

213. Telegram no. 1189, pp. 1, 2, 4. The "evidence" on the submarine-basing facility did not prove to be valid.

sador Kohler concerning Mariel on October 16. On the general subject of objecting to bases, he said he understood that point of view—and how about U.S. bases in Turkey?

Following receipt of the report on the McCloy conversation with Kuznetsov, the Ex Comm in its next meeting, on November 5, considered the exchange unsatisfactory and again instructed the negotiators in New York to tie down a commitment against construction of a submarine base. The fishing port at Mariel was no longer of concern, but the Ex Comm did want to obtain a Soviet commitment as to the future. The matter was not, however, raised in the next meeting of the negotiators in New York on November 6. Another instruction was then sent on November 7, but the matter was not again addressed in the New York negotiations, which remained focused on the removal of the IL-28 bombers and on the issue of verification arrangements in Cuba. The president, however, raised the matter in his letter to Khrushchev on November 6. He stated, "I hope you will understand that we must attach the greatest importance to the personal assurances you have given that submarine bases will not be established in Cuba."[214] Khrushchev did not comment further on this subject.

Ultimately, the Ex Comm in its twenty-eighth meeting, on November 20, approved a settlement of the issues and lifting of the quarantine, *without* further consideration of the question of submarine bases. The resolution of the existing problems had simply taken precedence over potential longer-term issues.

Beginning as early as President Kennedy's letter of November 6,

214. Letter, Kennedy to Khrushchev, November 6, 1962. Even drafts of President Kennedy's letter of November 6, 1962, have now been declassified, although to my knowledge never discussed in print. From the drafts, it is now known that the language on submarine basing replaced the following more categorical draft statement on the subject: "We would be bound to regard any move to establish a submarine base in Cuba just as seriously as we regarded the installation of missile bases and bombers."

President Kennedy's continuing interest in this subject is evident from a brief memorandum he sent Director of Central Intelligence McCone in mid-December, which, in its entirety, read: "I am sure that we are watching for any developments by the Soviet Union of a submarine base in Cuba. Will you keep me informed periodically as to whether or not anything of a suspicious nature has turned up in this regard." [John F. Kennedy], "Memorandum for Director McCone," unsigned, December 15, 1962.

but most pointedly in a statement by McCloy to Kuznetsov on November 18, the United States also raised the matter of withdrawal of the four reinforced ground force regiments, the existence and extent of which had been belatedly discovered by American surveillance during the first half of November.[215] But the United States did not insist on more than the Soviet assurance that military personnel associated with offensive systems, including their protection, would be withdrawn. President Kennedy did pursue the matter privately with Khrushchev in early 1963, and in early February Khrushchev agreed to withdraw several thousand more Soviet military personnel from Cuba.[216] Secretary Rusk repeatedly stated publicly in the first half of 1963 that the continued presence of Soviet troops in Cuba was "not acceptable" to the United States.[217] But there was no Soviet commitment to withdraw all

215. Telegram no. 1856, pp. 5–6. An "eyes only" instruction to Under Secretary Ball on November 1 had conveyed the president's interest in making the point to Kuznetsov and Mikoyan that if the Soviets were removing the missiles and bombers, "there seems [to be] no need for [the] Soviets to leave in Cuba equipment and military technicians brought to Cuba primarily to protect the offensive weapons"—meaning the ground troops (then estimated at only a few thousand men), and the air defense missiles as well. See Telegram no. 1159, State to USUN, Eyes Only for Under Secretary Ball, November 1, 1962, p. 2 (Confidential; now declassified).

The JCS in particular drew attention to these forces. General Taylor's talking points for the November 16 Ex Comm meeting had stated, after noting the MiGs, SAMs, and large stocks of army equipment: "But more important than this equipment are the thousands of Soviet military personnel who remain in Cuba to man it. The Soviet presence in Cuba poses a particularly sensitive problem to the United States." [JCS], "Chairman's Talking Paper for Meeting with the President," November 16, 1962, p. 1. Unlike the issue of the IL-28s, however, there is no indication in the Ex Comm records that General Taylor actually addressed the troop issue in the meeting.

216. These presidential messages have not been declassified. The Soviet government did, on February 18, 1963, provide a written aide-mémoire to the United States alluding to these and other discussions of the issue and advising that it had "taken a decision to withdraw from Cuba Soviet military personnel connected with the protection of the types of weapons withdrawn from Cuba and likewise *some* of the military specialists involved in the training of Cuban troops." [USSR government], Aide Memoire (Informal Translation), [USSR Embassy], Washington, February 18, 1963, p. 2; emphasis added.

217. Rusk either raised the subject of Soviet troops in Cuba, or responded to questions of news correspondents, on January 27, February 1, 13, 26, March 12, April 18, 28, and May 29, 1963. See *State Bulletin,* vol. 48 (January–June 1963),

Soviet military personnel. The United States government believed that the four regimental combat teams were withdrawn, although it was considered possible that some of the troops remained in a training unit, as well as the air defense personnel manning the SAM antiaircraft missile sites, and other training specialists. The continuing Soviet military presence was a source of agitation to some American politicians for months thereafter, but did not become a major public issue.[218]

We now know, from recent disclosures by Soviet and Cuban officials, that in fact one of the regiments remained, at Cuban insistence. At first the Soviets resisted, and Khrushchev—being pressed by the United States—wanted to bring all four regiments home. Finally, he acceded to Castro's urgings, and the one regiment remained as a symbol of Soviet solidarity, a thin "plate glass" against American attack, and a training unit.[219]

If the United States had known in October and November 1962 that the Soviet military presence in Cuba was not merely ancillary to the missile deployments and for training, but also involved a substantial contingent of Soviet combat forces, the troop issue would have been much more serious. President Kennedy, whose own warning on September 4 had laid down a marker against "any organized combat force in Cuba" from the Soviet Union or any

---

pp. 238, 245, 313, 388, 470, 686, 733, 934. While he said the presence of Soviet troops in Cuba was not "normal" or "acceptable," it was reluctantly accepted.

218. In particular, Senator Keating in a speech on January 31, 1963, began a new campaign on the Soviet troops remaining in Cuba, but it failed to attract wide popular interest. Speeches continued for some months. On September 23, 1963, the Senate voted on an amendment proposed by Senator Goldwater to the Limited Nuclear Test Ban Treaty that would have postponed implementation of the treaty provisions until all Soviet troops had left Cuba. The amendment was defeated by a vote of 75 to 17. That, in effect, ended the issue until its rebirth in 1979.

At the time of the 1979 "mini-crisis" over the Soviet brigade in Cuba, McGeorge Bundy wrote an article accepting responsibility for letting the issue fade away in 1963–64. See McGeorge Bundy, "The Brigade's My Fault," *New York Times,* October 23, 1979.

219. Sergo Mikoyan first disclosed at the 1987 Cambridge conference that the Cubans had asked for one regiment to remain (see Blight and Welch, *On the Brink,* p. 267). The Cubans, and other Soviet officials, later made known Khrushchev's initial resistance.

other Soviet bloc country, would have had to press at least as hard for their withdrawal as he did for the IL-28s. The Soviets might have agreed to remove the Soviet military personnel as Cubans were trained to take over the arms there, but the issue would have stretched tension still tighter.

Khrushchev had made the Soviets vulnerable on this point. In his letter of October 26, he had said that the American assurances he was seeking would obviate not only the need for Soviet missiles in Cuba, but also "the necessity for the presence of our military specialists in Cuba"—using the euphemistic term he had consistently employed to refer to *all* Soviet military personnel in Cuba.[220] And indeed President Kennedy, in his reply of November 6, had referred to that statement in support of a call for removal of a Soviet military presence. He also argued that while the United States had "limited our action at present to the problem of offensive weapons," Khrushchev should "consider whether a real normalization of the Cuba problem can be envisaged while there remains in Cuba large numbers of Soviet military technicians, and major weapons systems and communications complexes under Soviet control."[221]

Evidently, a year or two after the crisis Khrushchev decided to phase out Soviet air defense and coastal defense forces, training Cubans and turning over to them the MiG-21s, radar and SAM systems, coastal defense cruise missiles, and Komar missile patrol boats. But that had not been the Soviet plan in the summer of 1962, nor—owing to a gap in American information—was it made part of the direct crisis settlement.

One incident that occurred in the midst of these negotiations from October 28 to November 20 may have affected the American position favorably, although it was not planned by or even known to the Ex Comm. By November 8 the United States had begun perceptibly to stiffen its insistence on the IL-28s and other issues at dispute, including what the Soviets could only see as an effort to backpedal on what was, for them, the key question remaining:

220. Letter, Khrushchev to Kennedy, October 26, 1962 (see Pope, ed., *Soviet Views on the Cuban Missile Crisis,* p. 48).

221. Letter, Kennedy to Khrushchev, November 6, 1962.

American assurances not to attack Cuba. On that date, a Cuban emigré covert action sabotage team dispatched from the United States successfully blew up a Cuban industrial facility.[222] To the Soviets and the Cubans, this act was probably seen as a subtle American reminder of its ability to harass and perhaps subvert the Castro regime.[223]

In fact, on October 30, after the peak of the crisis, the United States had belatedly suspended its Mongoose covert operations in Cuba—once Robert Kennedy had by chance learned that they were still going on! At the end of October, a new mission was about to be dispatched by Task Force W operating out of Miami. One of the operatives was sufficiently uneasy about such an operation just after the great Kennedy-Khrushchev agreement to end the crisis that he got a message to Robert Kennedy to verify that the mission was in order. As noted, the Mongoose infiltration and sabotage operations had been reinvigorated earlier in the month. But the operation had been forgotten when the crisis was resolved. The new mission was hastily called off, and all infiltration and attack operations against Cuban soil suspended. General Lansdale was sent to Miami to ensure that operations were closed down. But three of ten six-man sabotage teams planned earlier in October to be sent into Cuba had already been dispatched and were beyond recall. One of them, on November 8, had carried out its mission.[224]

While this incident was never raised in the U.S.-Soviet talks, and was unknown to most if not all members of the Ex Comm, it may have reinforced Soviet interest in a settlement. It surely must

222. This incident was first publicly disclosed in the original edition of this book. On November 13 the Cubans publicly claimed they had smashed a CIA sabotage team, but did not publicize the actual action five days earlier. Another of the teams had been prevented on October 25 from destroying facilities at the Matahambre copper mine. I do not know if that was publicly disclosed by the Cuban authorities.

223. A senior Cuban official has recently (January 1989) confirmed to me that the incident on November 8 was assumed in Havana to be related to the continuing diplomatic confrontation.

224. For this account of the October 30 standdown of operations, see Schlesinger, *Robert Kennedy*, pp. 533–34; and Prados, *Presidents' Secret Wars*, p. 214; and see *Alleged Assassination Plots*, pp. 147–48.

have reinforced Castro's doubts that the United States had really agreed to anything.[225]

The final item on the agenda, so far as American interests were concerned, was the commitment in Khrushchev's letter of October 28 to inspection under UN auspices in Cuba to verify the removal of the offensive arms. With the impasse in Havana soon apparent, on November 4 the Soviets proposed, and the Americans agreed to, procedures whereby the Soviets made it easier for U.S. reconnaissance aircraft to observe the missile withdrawal on Soviet ships and the Soviet dismantling and bulldozing of the missile sites. Apart from minor problems of notification, these procedures worked satisfactorily and by November 9 had been completed. On December 3–5 the same procedures were used to monitor the removal of the IL-28s on three ships. The United States had no real doubt that the offensive weapons had been removed. But it tied the question of verification against reintroduction of offensive arms to the question of American assurances against invasion.[226]

Castro, in addition to refusing to permit any foreign inspections on Cuban soil to verify the dismantling and removal, did offer his own terms for on-site inspection and verification. On November 25 he offered to allow inspection in Cuba, but only if there were also inspection of the dismantling of emigré Cuban "training camps

225. On November 15, in a letter to the UN secretary general, Castro referred directly to this incident as buttressing his objection to the continued U.S. reconnaissance overflights. He stated: "The capture of the leader of a group of spies trained by the CIA and directed by it, here in Cuba, has shown us how the photographs taken by spying planes serve for guidance in sabotage and in their operations and has also revealed, amongst other things, a desire to cause chaos by provoking the deaths of 400 workers in one of our industries." The letter was passed to the United States by the United Nations, in unofficial UN translation, and was cabled to Washington in Telegram no. 1802, USUN to State, November 15, 1962, p. 3 (Secret; now declassified).

226. President Kennedy, in his letter of October 27, had called upon the Soviet government to remove the offensive weapons in Cuba and to "undertake, with suitable safeguards, to halt the further introduction of such weapons systems into Cuba." In his reply of October 28 accepting this general deal, Khrushchev wrote only of dismantling and removing the weapons there and said, "We are prepared to come to an agreement with you to enable representatives of the UN to verify the dismantling of these systems." He said nothing about safeguards against future reintroduction of such systems.

for mercenaries, spies, saboteurs and terrorists; of the centers where subversion is prepared; and the bases from which pirate vessels set out for our coasts" in the United States and in Puerto Rico.[227]

There was a great deal of attention devoted to the inspection and verification issue, both within the U.S. government and in the negotiations in New York, both bilateral with the Soviets and multilateral in the UN framework. As reflected in a memorandum I wrote early in this process, on October 30, the United States approached the problem with two criteria: to "provide reasonable assurance against clandestine introduction of nuclear delivery systems into Cuba" and to "limit our freedom of action as little as possible." In particular, we did not wish to constrain movement of U.S. nuclear weapons through any denuclearized zone that might be established in the Latin American region (a suggestion on the table owing to a Brazilian draft resolution and widespread Latin American interest). We also foresaw possible contingent use of conventional forces in local crisis situations in the region.[228] Initially, positions were drawn up for the alternatives of Cuban acceptance, or nonacceptance, of inspection. The United States also sought to use the Organization of American States as much as possible, but principal reliance remained on unilateral U.S. intelligence.[229] Ultimately, when no agreed arrangements could be reached, that was our only recourse, but not a weak one.

All the matters I have been discussing here in the negotiations

227. Letter, Osvaldo Dorticós and Fidel Castro to U Thant, UN Security Council Document S/5280, November 26, 1962, pp. 1–6; reprinted in Larson, ed., *"Cuban Crisis" of 1962,* 2d ed., pp. 214–19; quotation on p. 218.

228. Garthoff Memorandum, "Comments on Items III and IV of the Agreed Agenda for the State-Defense Meeting of October 30," October 30, 1962, p. 1 (Top Secret; now declassified), appended as document G.

229. See appended document H, "Draft Instruction to USUN for Consideration by the Executive Committee," November 3, 1962 (Secret–Eyes Only; now declassified), of which I was a codrafter; and document I, Memorandum from Garthoff to Messrs. Wallner, Fisher, Martin, Barber, and Chayes, "Draft Instruction on Long Term Verification Arrangements Concerning Cuba," October 31, 1962 (Secret; now declassified). These three documents are only part of the flow of paper on this subject, not necessarily the most important, but illustrative, available, and declassified.

from October 28 to November 20—the IL-28s, nuclear weapons, submarine bases, army combat teams, and verification arrangements—have concerned American interests. The other major issue discussed throughout this period was the Soviet endeavor to obtain as formal, binding, and far-reaching an American commitment on noninvasion of Cuba as possible. Without reviewing the long series of exchanges on that subject, one can move to its conclusion. With the absence of agreement on verification in Cuba, the United States considered there was no basis to give more of a commitment than already implied by the exchange of letters on October 27–28. The undertaking offered by President Kennedy in his message of October 27 had been "to give assurances against an invasion of Cuba," but explicitly conditioned on "the establishment of adequate arrangements through the United Nations to ensure the carrying out and continuation of these commitments."[230]

President Kennedy's press conference statement of November 20 clearly spelled out the American position: " *If* all offensive weapons systems are removed from Cuba and kept out of the hemisphere in the future, under adequate verification and safeguards . . . we shall neither initiate nor permit aggression in this hemisphere." In this same statement the president made clear that while it had been promised that the IL-28s would be withdrawn, and the missile sites had been dismantled and the missiles withdrawn under our surveillance, "important parts of the understanding of October 27 and 28 remain to be carried out. The Cuban Government has not yet permitted the United Nations to verify whether all offensive weapons have been removed, and no lasting safeguards have yet been established against the future introduction of offensive weapons back into Cuba."[231]

These conditions were not met.

The Soviets had been pressing for an American commitment ever since the exchange of messages on October 28. Two days later Gromyko had received Ambassador Kohler and sought to "codify"

230. Letter, Kennedy to Khrushchev, October 27, 1962; reprinted in Larson, ed., "Cuban Crisis" of 1962, 2d ed., pp. 187–88.

231. "The President's News Conference of November 20, 1962," *Public Papers: Kennedy, 1962*, p. 831.

the undertakings of both sides. Draft statements of assurances, including a Soviet-Cuban draft formal protocol that looked like a treaty (proposed on November 15), were all discussed in numerous meetings in New York, and in at least six of the ten or more exchanges of letters between President Kennedy and Khrushchev in November and December.

In addition to stressing conditions that had not been met by the other side, the United States also interpreted the assurances we would give as conditional in another sense: depending upon changes in the situation, and above all in Cuban behavior. The U.S. negotiators insisted that any assurances must be stated in terms that made clear that they did not diminish American obligations (and rights) under any other existing treaty, thereby including the Rio Treaty and the Platt Amendment granting the United States its base in Guantánamo Bay in Cuba. The Cubans and Soviets balked at acknowledging and reaffirming even indirectly U.S. rights to Guantánamo Bay, and for that matter our interpretation of the Rio Treaty—which the United States had invoked in declaring the quarantine. The United States also gave as examples of Cuban behavior that would void any U.S. assurance the shooting down of a U.S. aircraft or Cuban support for subversion in another country in the hemisphere. Again, the Cubans and Soviets were unwilling to underwrite continuing U.S. aerial surveillance of Cuba, or American interpretations of limits to Cuban assistance to popular revolutionary movements elsewhere. We also told the Soviets that if the Cuban people revolted against the communist regime and Soviet troops in Cuba attempted to oppose them, as the Soviet Army had done in Budapest in 1956, any United States assurance against invading Cuba would be inapplicable. Overall, the United States "assurances" really boiled down to a declaration of present intent not to invade, but did little if anything to constrain any future U.S. decision to do so.

The most authoritative exchange on future commitments occurred in a meeting of First Deputy Prime Minister Mikoyan with President Kennedy on November 29, 1962. Mikoyan repeatedly pressed for clarification and confirmation that the U.S. accepted a commitment not to invade Cuba. President Kennedy reassured him that the United States had no intention of invading Cuba, but stressed that the conditions called for in the exchange of letters in late October (international verification in Cuba and safeguards) had not been met. Without making the unequivocal future commitment the Soviets wanted, Kennedy did state that if the Soviet Union abided by the exchange of correspondence, so would the United States.[232]

In executive hearings held before the Senate Foreign Relations Committee on January 11, 1963, declassified and made public only in December 1986, Secretary Rusk testified at length on the outcome of the missile crisis. He stressed that "we never made an unadorned commitment not to invade Cuba in the first place," and besides, "a crucial element on the conditions that we then talked about specifically have not been performed." He confirmed that, even as proffered, our assurances "certainly didn't mean no invasion under any circumstances"—for example, "if Castro committed aggressive acts" against others, or "an attack on Guantánamo," or "if, as a result of our necessity for over-flying, the situation moves into a point where we have to invade," in sum, "if Castro were to do the kind of things which would *from our point of view* justify invasion," or "if Russian troops in Cuba start shooting at Cubans a la Hungary [1956]." In these or other changed circumstances, the United States would be free to invade notwithstanding the assurances given in the Kennedy-Khrushchev exchange.[233] While this testimony was not publicly known at the time, the substance of the American position was known to the Soviet side. They had no recourse but to quietly fold up the negotiations. The United States administration, while determined not to preclude possible future intervention in Cuba, had no *intention* of invading and was content to let the public record rest as it stood.

232. While no official American or Soviet account of this exchange has to date been published, this discussion is based on my familiarity with the U.S. record of the meeting.

233. "Briefing on the World Situation, January 11, 1963," in *Executive Sessions of the Senate Foreign Relations Committee* (Historical Series), vol. 15, 88 Cong. 1 sess., 1963 (GPO, 1987), pp. 17–26, quotations from pp. 23, 17, 25, 23, 25, 23; emphasis added.

On January 7, 1963, Stevenson for the United States and Kuznetsov for the Soviet Union sent a joint letter to UN Secretary General U Thant stating that "while it has not been possible for our Governments to resolve all the problems that have arisen in connection with this affair, they believe that, in view of the degree of understanding reached between them on the settlement of the crisis and the extent of progress in the implementation of this understanding, it is not necessary for this item to occupy further the attention of the Security Council at this time."[234] The United States had made no pledge against invasion, and in the absence of verification measures on the ground in Cuba, it continued its unilateral air reconnaissance. The Soviets made one final attempt to get American assurances when, on January 15, Soviet special envoy First Deputy Foreign Minister Kuznetsov had a meeting with the president before he returned to Moscow. He, too, tried unsuccessfully to obtain a more binding U.S. commitment.

Seeking to put the best gloss possible on the outcome of the crisis, Khrushchev (on December 12 and other occasions) and other Soviet spokesmen later publicly claimed that there was an American "pledge" not to invade—a claim not supported by any official American statement. But as late as Khrushchev's speech to the Supreme Soviet on December 12, in which he laid down the official line on the whole crisis, he was evidently still expecting to be able to obtain a formal American commitment. He and his colleagues wished by his report to the Supreme Soviet to put the whole matter behind them, but he could not avoid implicitly admitting that the American commitment was not all that they had sought. Thus on the one hand Khrushchev claimed: "The president declared quite definitely, and the whole world knows, that the United States would not attack Cuba and would also restrain its allies from such actions," thereby permitting the Soviet Union to withdraw the missiles, since they had sent the missiles to prevent an attack.

On the other hand, Khrushchev was still seeking more of a

234. Letter, Adlai Stevenson and Vasily Kuznetsov to U Thant, UN Security Council Document S/5227, January 7, 1963, p. 1; reprinted in Larson, ed., *"Cuban Crisis" of 1962*, 2d ed., p. 230.

commitment, so at a time when Americans, and the world, considered the crisis long settled, he was saying only that "at present favorable conditions have been created for liquidating the dangerous crisis that arose in the Caribbean. Now it is necessary to bring the negotiations to completion, to put on record the agreement reached as a result of the exchange of messages between the government of the Soviet Union and the U.S. government, and to seal this agreement with the authority of the United Nations."[235] Yet this was never done, and as noted, on January 7 the two governments closed the issue with their joint note to the secretary general removing the item from the UN Security Council agenda. Soviet commentaries never refer to this inconclusive outcome or even to the extended negotiation.

American commentaries, too, have tended to overlook the inconclusive tailing off of negotiations seeking "clarification" in Cuba and American assurances. The general understanding has, quite reasonably, taken as an assumption of political realities that the United States did not intend to invade Cuba. Moreover, criticisms from the right that the Kennedy administration had "sold out" a right to invasion were dismissed without public rebuttal that we had retained full rights. Nonetheless, the United States did not in 1962–63 formalize a commitment assuring against possible invasion of Cuba.[236]

235. "The Present International Situation and the Foreign Policy of the Soviet Union, Report by Comrade N.S. Khrushchev at the Session of the U.S.S.R. Supreme Soviet, December 12, 1962," *Pravda,* December 13, 1962; and in Pope, *Soviet Views on the Cuban Missile Crisis,* pp. 71–107.

236. McGeorge Bundy also notes this in his recent account: "Formally those assurances never took effect, because they were conditional . . ." and the conditions not met. Bundy, *Danger and Survival,* p. 407.

At the Moscow conference on the missile crisis in January 1989, after several Soviet and Cuban speakers had referred to the U.S. "commitment" against invasion given in 1962, and no American had addressed the matter, I registered a categorical dissent for the record, without going into the matter given the pressing agenda. No one reopened discussion of the issue. The two senior Soviet Foreign Ministry officials present, both acquaintances and one a friend for twenty-five years, separately came up to me later and chided me, *not* for misstating the situation, although they did not necessarily agree, but for raising the issue with the Cubans there.

The Aftermath

THE CUBAN missile crisis has had important long-term effects. Even during the crisis itself, some of us in the U.S. government, and I presume in the Soviet government as well, were thinking ahead to the future. For example, I had argued for a tough stand on the removal of the missiles and the bombers, but also for movement toward a reduction in tensions after resolution of the crisis. In the memoranda of October 25 and 27, I suggested that the United States should, "while solving the Cuban base question with determination, forcefully reaffirm its readiness to reach agreements on arms control and disarmament" and other broader diplomatic arrangements (Appendix documents B and C). Those doves who argued most strongly for seeking to resolve the crisis through diplomatic means sought not only to find matching concessions, but also to use the occasion to advance a more far-reaching political agenda. By contrast, most hawks opposed any move toward a détente. There were, however, also those, including myself, who favored a tough stand on the question of removal of the offensive weapons, but also hoped that in the aftermath there could be movement toward a détente in U.S.-Soviet relations. Thus in another memorandum to Alexis Johnson, on October 29, on the "Significance of the Soviet Backdown for Future U.S. Policy," while calling for strength, I also stated "it is vitally important that the U.S. take the initiative in offering to negotiate on major issues between East and West" (Appendix document F).

President Kennedy included in his key letter of October 27, as an incentive to Khrushchev, a statement that once the crisis was settled, the effect on easing tensions would make possible broader negotiations. And in his reply to Khrushchev's letter of October 28 he reiterated his agreement with Khrushchev that increased attention should be given to disarmament. There had not, however, been any consideration in the Ex Comm or decision by the president on specific disarmament or other negotiating positions beyond the terms of settlement of the immediate crisis.

The main work on possible future negotiations with the Soviet Union was carried out by a group under the guidance of Walt Rostow, in which I participated. On November 9, after the crisis had passed its peak, a paper on "Post-Cuba [Crisis] Negotiations with the USSR" was circulated to the Ex Comm.[237] It foreshadowed negotiations for a hot line, nuclear nonproliferation, curbing space weapons, and other arms control measures. Khrushchev on October 27 had specifically called for renewed nuclear test ban negotiations, and President Kennedy had agreed in his letter of October 28 acknowledging Khrushchev's acceptance of the settlement offered. In the private exchanges between the two leaders in November and December, not published with the October crisis correspondence, as the more immediate issues of IL-28s and U.S. noninvasion assurances faded, the nuclear testing question became more central.[238]

While I do not know what parallel planning for arms control and other negotiations may have been under way in the Soviet Union, there must have been some at an early date.

237. I do not recall and available declassified records do not show whether the memorandum was in fact discussed in the Ex Comm. In any case, it did enter into the train of policy thinking in the government.

238. On December 19 Khrushchev devoted an entire message to the president to the test ban issue and indicated that—on the basis of what Ambassador Arthur Dean had told Kuznetsov on October 30—the Soviet Union was prepared for a comprehensive test ban providing two or three on-site inspections. Unfortunately, there had been a misunderstanding as to the American position, as Kennedy indicated in his response on December 28. Expert talks were agreed on but soon foundered over this issue. It did, however, prove possible to negotiate a ban on nuclear weapons testing in the atmosphere, oceans, and outer space. The Limited Nuclear Test Ban Treaty was signed in Moscow on August 5, 1963. The most complete and accurate account of these developments is in Glenn T. Seaborg, *Kennedy, Khrushchev, and the Test Ban* (Berkeley: University of California Press, 1981), pp. 178–262.

In the United States, there was general (though not universal) approbation for President Kennedy's handling of the crisis, and renewed—although sobered—confidence within the administration.

President Kennedy's remarkable speech at American University on June 10, 1963, set a new tone in U.S. relations with the Soviet Union, and contributed to the emergence of a limited détente. It stemmed directly from a new awareness by Kennedy of the need for improving relations and a new recognition of the possibility of doing so. He reiterated his desire for improved relations in an address to the UN General Assembly on November 20, only two days before his untimely death. While affected by the death of the president and a transition in leadership, the new policy continued in effect another year until it fell victim to intensified commitment to the war in Vietnam.

In the Soviet Union, Khrushchev to some extent benefited from an initial rallying of the leadership to show solidarity in the first months after the crisis, but in the longer run the outcome of the affair undoubtedly contributed to his fall from power two years later. Indeed, on a number of issues he was under attack within the leadership from late 1962 until the sudden incapacitating illness of his chief challenger, Frol Kozlov, in April 1963. Save for that fortuitous event, Khrushchev might well have been ousted earlier. Kennedy's preparedness to give Khrushchev a confidential unilateral assurance that the U.S. Jupiter missiles would be withdrawn from Turkey and Italy within months may well have made the settlement deal sufficiently satisfactory from the standpoint of conservative Party leaders and the military leadership to have contributed to his ability to recoup his own political position.[239]

239. The Kennedy administration was on the horns of a dilemma in terms of not acknowledging to Congress what it had done. While properly denying that removal of U.S. missiles from Turkey was a quid pro quo for the withdrawal of the Soviet missiles from Cuba, it was forced also to cover up the actual role played in resolving the crisis by the authoritative presidential statement of that intention. Secretary Rusk, in testimony in an executive session of the Senate Foreign Relations Committee in January 1963, was pressed into denying any connection with the settlement of the crisis. While generally reassuring senators that the United States had long been planning to remove the Jupiters, and

Some of the events set in train by the limited détente of 1963–64 in Soviet-U.S. relations probably helped him for a time, but the long-term negative impact of the missile crisis on his standing remained.

There was a perceptible, if not complete, turn in Soviet policy toward the West after the crisis. One cannot be sure to what extent the experience of the crisis was responsible for the shift, but it very likely tempered Soviet ambitions, curbing their inclination to press some challenges, as over Berlin. It is also likely that the crisis opened up a degree of greater belief in the possibility of mutual accommodation. Soviet pronouncements after the crisis will be examined in the last chapter in the context of its long-term influence. They suggest a certain interest in moving beyond the cold war, and a belief that the experience of the missile crisis would lead in that direction. But many other factors were at play, including the impact on Soviet policy of shifts of influence within the Soviet leadership, and the range of opportunities and challenges and Soviet calculations about them. Suffice it here to repeat the general conclusion that the experience of the crisis probably did contribute to a degree of shift in Soviet policy toward détente.

It is often contended in the West that the missile crisis led the Soviet Union to build up its military power. A remark Kuznetsov made to McCloy is frequently cited as evidence. Having had to accede to American demands and failing to get from the United States the kind of noninvasion commitment the Soviets had sought, Kuznetsov was painfully aware of the weak bargaining position of the Soviet Union, and of the humiliating defeat the Soviet Union had suffered. Kuznetsov is reported to have said to McCloy, as the Soviet missiles were being withdrawn: "You Americans will never

correctly stating that the action was "not the basis of any deal or agreement," when Senator Bourke Hickenlooper asked whether the secretary meant that the removal of the missiles from Turkey "was in no way, shape or form, directly or indirectly, connected with the settlement, the discussion or the manipulation of the Cuban situation," Rusk replied, "That is correct, sir." Senator Stuart Symington then expressed gratification that it had "no relationship with the Cuban situation." The decision in late October 1962 to remove the missiles from Turkey and Italy within six months *was*, however, explicit in the discussions and "connected with the settlement" of the Cuban crisis. See "Briefing on Cuban Developments," January 25, 1963, in *Executive Sessions of the Senate Foreign Relations Committee* (Historical Series), vol. 15, pp. 105, 106, 111.

be able to do this to us again."[240] It is, however, attributing too much to that statement to assert—as many who cite it do—that he was signaling that the Soviet Union would as a consequence of its defeat build up its military power in ways or to a degree it would not otherwise have done. In the first place, the Soviet Union did *not* enter on a "crash" program of accelerated buildup of its strategic military power. Moreover, while they did later build up to rough parity with the United States (some would say to more than parity), that was not due to the missile crisis. That buildup would have occurred in any case and was stimulated not only by the missile crisis in late 1962, but by the rapid Kennedy administration military buildup set in motion in 1961.[241]

The record clearly shows the turn toward détente and arms control. Within a year, three important arms control agreements were reached: in June it was agreed to establish a "hot line" direct communications link between Washington and Moscow, in August the Limited Nuclear Test Ban Treaty was signed, and in September U.S.-Soviet agreement was reached to support a UN General Assembly resolution banning the placing of nuclear weapons or other weapons of mass destruction into space (codified in 1967 in the space treaty).[242]

240. Charles E. Bohlen, *Witness to History, 1929–1960* (New York: W.W. Norton, 1973), pp. 495–96. When I discussed the missile crisis with McCloy some years later he recalled Kuznetsov as having said: "We will fulfill our agreement, but never again will we let ourselves be put in such a position." Garthoff, "Memorandum for the Record: Conversation with John J. McCloy on the Cuban Missile Crisis," January 9, 1984. His statement implies an obligation on the Soviet Union to tailor its actions to the limits of its power, for example, by not being so rash as in placing missiles in Cuba, as well as implying a Soviet desire to become stronger.

241. General Volkogonov has confirmed that the Soviet military buildup toward strategic parity had been established earlier and was not generated by the Cuban missile crisis. Interview in Moscow, February 1989.

242. The agreements on the hot line and the Limited Test Ban Treaty are widely known; the 1963 U.S.-Soviet agreement to jointly support a UN General Assembly resolution banning weapons of mass destruction in space is not. Indeed, the Soviet Union was even prepared in 1963 to conclude a treaty banning nuclear weapons in space; President Kennedy decided not to go that far so soon after the controversial test ban treaty, but this fact was not publicly known. The fullest account is available in my article "Banning the Bomb in Outer Space," *International Security*, vol. 5 (Winter 1980–81), pp. 25–40.

The experience of the missile crisis, in addition to stimulating these three agreements in 1963, also contributed to the resolve of both sides to agree on the Treaty on the Non-Proliferation of Nuclear Weapons (NPT), even though agreement was not reached until 1969. Similarly, it contributed to efforts to reach agreement on strategic arms limitations, although it was not until 1969 that the SALT negotiations began and not until 1972 that the first arms limitation agreements were reached.[243]

Also, there was no new Berlin crisis. While the precise relationship of this fact to the October 1962 crisis can only be conjectured, I believe the absence of a new flare-up over Berlin in 1963 to be an important consequence of the outcome of the Cuban crisis. Indeed, there was no renewed Berlin crisis in the years following, and in 1971 the Quadripartite Berlin Agreement effectively defused that longstanding point of contention.

Within NATO, there was relief over the resolution of the crisis and satisfaction with its favorable outcome. The only indirect specific consequence was the prompt alliance decision, announced in January 1963, to remove the Jupiters from Turkey and Italy and to replace them with a commitment to the alliance of ten American Polaris submarines. In the discussion the idea of a multilaterally manned naval nuclear missile force was also introduced, an idea earlier suggested by Ambassador Thomas Finletter, the U.S. representative to NATO. In the very first memorandum on planning for the removal of the Jupiters from Turkey, on October 30, Walt Rostow raised this possibility.[244] Such a force, later termed the Multilateral Force (MLF), was discussed from 1963 to 1966 but never created.

Nor was there any renewed threat of an American invasion of Cuba. The United States did, however, continue to conduct an active policy of seeking to undermine and displace the Castro regime, including continued covert operations against Cuba.

243. Efforts undertaken from 1964 to 1968 to launch strategic arms talks were hampered by the disparity in U.S. and Soviet strategic forces, and only with the advent of strategic parity was negotiation on a basis of equality possible in the Strategic Arms Limitation Talks (SALT) that began in November 1969.

244. See Memorandum, W. W. Rostow for Mr. [McGeorge] Bundy, "Turkish IRBM's," October 30, 1962, p. 2 (Secret; now declassified).

In the aftermath of the crisis, American policy toward Cuba badly needed redefinition. Policy papers began to be written even before the crisis ended, and on December 4 the Ex Comm discussed "Future Policy toward Cuba."

One step was taken in the conclusion of semiofficial exchanges that had begun months earlier to arrange release of the survivors of the Bay of Pigs. On December 22, 1962, the 1,113 prisoners, veterans of the ill-fated "Brigade 2506" (and twenty Cuban CIA agents also separately captured), were freed and turned over to the United States in exchange for nearly $54 million worth of medical supplies and baby food. The arrangement was negotiated by James B. Donovan, who had also arranged the swap of spies that obtained the release of Francis Gary Powers, the U-2 pilot shot down over Sverdlovsk on May Day 1960. In a bizarre twist the CIA decided to use this opportunity to send as a gift from Donovan to Castro, an avid scuba diver, a diving outfit impregnated with bacteriological agents. Donovan, for whatever reason, discarded it and gave another diving suit to Castro.[245]

The veterans of the Bay of Pigs brigade were personally welcomed by President Kennedy on December 29, against the advice of both Dean Rusk and McGeorge Bundy; it was essentially a domestic political and personal decision. Kennedy extemporaneously injected in his speech to them a promise to see their brigade flag fly in "a free Havana."[246] The brigade veterans then went on to other things.[247]

The covert action program Mongoose, as noted earlier, had

245. Prados, *Presidents' Secret Wars,* p. 215; and Schlesinger, *Robert Kennedy,* pp. 534–37; Larson, ed., *"Cuban Crisis" of 1962,* 2d ed., p. 358. Donovan had seen Castro as late as October 20, just before the crisis broke.

246. Schlesinger, *Robert Kennedy,* p. 358.

247. Many entered a new special military training program set up by the United States that lasted until late 1965, involving in all some 2,700 men. Sixty-one of these, mostly Brigade 2506 veterans, were eventually granted American citizenship and entered the U.S. Army. (One, originally a military cadet under Batista, was by the mid-1980s a full colonel and the U.S. Army action officer for Central American and Caribbean affairs, actively boosting the Contras and still eager to see Castro overthrown.) Others entered the service of the CIA, some being sent to the Congo in 1964 (the first introduction of armed Cubans into African civil wars), others breaking into Watergate in 1972, and still others mining ports in Nicaragua in 1984.

been suspended on October 30. The future of Mongoose was on the Ex Comm agenda for the thirty-first meeting, on November 29, but it is not clear if it was discussed then. There was also a problem of what to do with *another* Cuban brigade, trained in 1961–62, not committed at the Bay of Pigs. On January 25, 1963, the Ex Comm considered what to do with this other brigade and with Mongoose.[248]

In January–February 1963 the Ex Comm and the Special Group (Augmented) were replaced by a "Standing Group" of the NSC; Mongoose was abolished; and the CIA Task Force W was merged into its Miami station (which remained, with Desmond FitzGerald replacing William K. Harvey).[249]

On November 29 at the Ex Comm meeting President Kennedy had requested the State Department to develop a long-range plan to "keep pressure on Castro." Yet as early as January 4, 1963, McGeorge Bundy proposed exploring the possibility of communicating with Castro.[250] The Ex Comm, later the Standing Group, at their January 25 meeting and others subsequently, developed a plan for several somewhat disparate paths of action to meet divergent aims. The United States wanted to see Castro removed, but if that were not to be, then it wanted him to be as independent of the Soviet Union as possible. Policy papers therefore posed as objectives both "encouraging and supporting any developments within Cuba that offer the possibility of *divorcing* the Cuban Government from its support of Sino-Soviet Communist purposes," and simultaneously "encouraging and supporting any developments within Cuba that offer the possibility of *replacing* the Cuban Government with a regime that would break with the Sino-Soviet Bloc, it being understood that our ultimate objective is replacement of the regime by one fully compatible with the goals of the United States."[251] These objectives, in practice, were

248. See Prados, *Presidents' Secret Wars,* p. 215; and Coordinator of Cuban Affairs, Department of State, "Memorandum for the National Security Council's Executive Committee—United States Policy toward Cuba," January 25, 1963, pp. 1–8 (Confidential; declassified with considerable deletion).

249. See *Alleged Assassination Plots,* p. 170.

250. See Schlesinger, *Robert Kennedy,* p. 538.

251. Coordinator of Cuban Affairs, "Memorandum . . . United States Policy toward Cuba," p. 2; emphasis in original. Note that an initial successor "regime"

contradictory and clashed. Even to attempt to divorce Cuba from the Soviet Union would require contacts and incentives, which ran against the idea of replacing Castro's rule.

And American policy, in practice, was contradictory. In March and April 1963, covert sabotage operations were discontinued and attempts were made to crack down on similar unauthorized Cuban emigré operations by such groups as Alpha 66. But on June 19, a new sabotage program was launched. Similarly, while covert CIA assassination attempts against Castro (not discussed in the Standing Group, in the 303 Committee, which controlled covert activities, or in any other interagency body) through the Mafia were abandoned, a new channel was opened. This renewed assassination attempt, through former Castro comrade-in-arms Major Rolando Cubela Secades (who had been recruited by the CIA in 1961), led to a tragic irony. On November 22, 1963, the very day that President John F. Kennedy was assassinated, the CIA in Paris supplied Cubela with a poison pen to give Castro. Covert American-directed operations, raids, and assassination plots did not end until 1965.[252]

At the same time, steps were taken through two authorized semiofficial channels from September to December 1963 to develop a contact with Castro and sound out ways of ameliorating relations.[253]

The aftermath of the missile crisis, in sum, left American policy toward Cuba hostile, but with some beginnings of a belief that the United States should accept the Castro communist regime as a fact of life.

Soviet relations with Cuba were also left in need of redefinition in the aftermath of the crisis. Castro's anger and disenchantment remained, but so did his dependence on the Soviet Union—if anything, it was greater than before. The equivocal American "promise" not to invade was not taken as a real assurance.

---

could be of any stripe; ultimately the United States wanted a government in Cuba compatible with both our democratic ideals and our own national interest.

252. See *Alleged Assassination Plots,* pp. 170–75; Schlesinger, *Robert Kennedy,* pp. 533–49; and Prados, *Presidents' Secret Wars,* p. 216. Cubela is referred to in some of these references under his CIA code designation, AM/LASH.

253. See Schlesinger, *Robert Kennedy,* pp. 551–58; and *Alleged Assassination Plots,* pp. 173–74.

In April–May 1963 Castro visited Moscow, for the first time and for more than a month. He and the Soviet leaders worked out a modus vivendi, despite continuing differences. At the close of the visit, Castro overcame his resentment enough to pay a glowing tribute to his hosts and benefactors. After recalling that in World War II the Soviet Union had lost more lives than the entire population of Cuba, he praised the Soviet Union because it "did not hesitate to assume the risks of a severe war in defense of our little country. History has never known such an example of solidarity. *That* is internationalism! *That* is communism!"[254]

During the mid-1960s, Cuban and Soviet foreign policy nonetheless continued to diverge in several respects. Cuba sought to develop a more independent line in the nonaligned world, one that placed a greater stress than did the Soviets on revolutionary action. While in some respects his inclinations coincided with Chinese criticisms of the Soviet Union, Castro in no way became a "Maoist." Rather, he sought to champion a genuinely third-world Cuban communism, though with little success.

The divergence with Soviet policy reached a climax in 1968, when Castro toyed with echoing Eurocommunist criticism of the Soviet-led invasion of Czechoslovakia. The Soviets privately let Castro know in no uncertain terms that they would cut off all economic assistance if such criticism persisted. He capitulated. Thereafter Cuban foreign policy increasingly came into line with Soviet policy.

If there was an opportunity for the United States in the years 1963–68 to develop a relationship that could have weaned Castro away from the Soviet Union, it was missed. One cannot be certain that there was a real possibility, but one also cannot be certain that there was not at least the chance for a partial change in Cuban alignment.

254. "Speech by Prime Minister Fidel Castro of Cuba," *Pravda,* May 24, 1963.

The Afterlife

THE MISSILE crisis not only had an aftermath in its effects on subsequent U.S.-Soviet relations (and Soviet-Cuban relations, and indirectly other developments not reviewed here), but also had a series of resurrected aftershocks or an "afterlife."

In the years following the missile crisis the Soviet Union was not disposed to attempt again to deploy elements of its strategic nuclear power in Cuba, and the United States was not disposed to invade Cuba. In that fundamental respect the settlement was solid. It was not, however, until 1970 that it became clear that there *was* a 1962 Soviet-American "understanding" of continuing, or newly activated, validity. As earlier noted, the United States had never issued any public or official statement of a commitment not to invade Cuba after the highly conditional statement by President Kennedy of November 20, 1962—the conditions of which (an international inspection in Cuba to verify the continuing absence of offensive arms) had not been met. This studied silence on a U.S. commitment was a considered position maintained throughout the Kennedy and Johnson administrations.[255]

255. As the action officer in the Department of State on such matters during most of the 1960s, I drafted or cleared several later letters replying to congressional inquiries, provided press guidance, and in other ways ensured that the United States government did *not* state that it had accepted a formal noninvasion commitment.

The Soviet position holds that not only did President Kennedy accept a formal commitment, but so did President Lyndon Johnson. Anastas Mikoyan attended Kennedy's funeral and had a conversation with the new president on November 29, 1963. In Mikoyan's view, Johnson at that time reaffirmed the 1962 agreement; see Blight and Welch, *On the Brink,* p. 270. According to the American record,

The matter was unexpectedly raised for clarification by the Soviet side in August 1970—shortly *before* the United States became aware of the start of construction of a Soviet submarine base at Cienfuegos in Cuba. Chargé Yuli M. Vorontsov met with national security adviser Henry Kissinger on August 4, 1970, seeking assurances of American acceptance of the "understanding" of 1962. After reviewing the 1962 record, Kissinger became aware and advised the president that "there was no formal understanding in the sense of an agreement, either oral or in writing." Nixon and Kissinger nonetheless decided (without consulting the secretaries of state and defense) that it would be useful to tie Moscow down by taking the opportunity the Soviets had unaccountably proffered to "reaffirm" and activate the spongy 1962 understanding. So Kissinger assured Vorontsov on August 7 that the United States regarded the understanding as in effect, and "noted with satisfaction" that the Soviet Union also regarded it as "still in full force."[256]

The reason for the Soviet initiative in raising the 1962 Cuban understanding in August 1970 was unclear and perplexing. Kissinger, writing years later in his memoir, still found it "hard to imagine" why the Soviets had raised the matter in view of their own actions then under way to test and weaken the constraint. Did the Soviet leaders seek to reassure the United States that the submarine base they were preparing to build was not a step toward the placing of land-based missiles again in Cuba in the hope that the United States would then acquiesce to the submarine base?

Kissinger had, as it turned out, jumped to a conclusion with respect to Vorontsov's message. "What he had come to convey," states Kissinger, "was his government's desire to reaffirm the

---

Johnson gave renewed assurances that the United States did not intend to attack Cuba, but did not reconfirm a commitment that had never been formalized. See Telegram no. 1714, State to American Embassy Moscow, December 2, 1963 (Secret, Limited Distribution; now declassified), pp. 1–2.

256. See Henry A. Kissinger, *White House Years* (Boston: Little, Brown, 1979), pp. 632–35. The first time that even key officials in the U.S. government who were involved in the Cienfuegos incident a month later learned of this prior August exchange of assurances was this revelation by Kissinger in his memoir nine years later.

Kennedy-Khrushchev understanding of 1962 with respect to Cuba.''
This way of putting the matter suggests unaccountable Soviet
interest to reaffirm their acceptance of the constraints imposed.
Fortunately, Kissinger accompanies his own interpretation with a
verbatim quotation from Vorontsov's démarche: "We would like
to stress that in the Cuban question we proceed as before from the
understanding on this question reached in the past and we expect
that the American side will also strictly adhere to this understanding.''[257] It is clear from this statement that the Soviet purpose was
to elicit an *American* reaffirmation of the understanding, rather
than to stress their own desire to reaffirm it, although of course
their reaffirmation was also entailed.

A senior Soviet official directly involved in the matter at the
time informed me some years later that the Soviet Union had raised
the matter because of Cuban concern over a possible American
attack. While Soviet intelligence did not confirm that possibility,
he said, Moscow still concluded it should elicit American reaffirmation of the understanding. It could then reassure Castro that it
had taken the matter up with the Americans and that there would
be no American intervention. The Soviets had a strong incentive
to avoid precipitating a new crisis centered on Cuba. Only two
years earlier Castro had agreed to return to the Soviet fold, and
then because of Soviet economic pressures, and the Soviets did
not wish again to arouse Cuban fears at being endangered by the
budding Soviet rapprochement with the United States.

The 1962 understanding was thus *consummated* only on August
7, 1970, when for the first time American leaders unequivocally
accepted continuing mutual commitments.[258] The Soviet commit-

257. Ibid., p. 632.

258. The texts of the Soviet note of August 4 and the American reply of
August 7, 1970, have not been made public, but as stated in Kissinger's memoir
account the United States reiterated the understanding "as prohibiting the
emplacement of any offensive weapon of any kind or any offensive delivery
system on Cuban territory"—without redefining those terms carried over from
1962. Ibid., p. 634. President Nixon, more loosely, thought there was a 1962
understanding and described the existing understanding as barring the Soviets
from putting *nuclear weapons* on Cuban territory; see Richard Nixon, *RN: The
Memoirs of Richard Nixon* (New York: Grosset and Dunlap, 1978), p. 486.

ment, in addition to being affirmed in the note delivered by Vorontsov, was soon thereafter publicly reaffirmed in an "authorized" TASS statement on October 13, 1970, which declared that the Soviet Union was not doing and would not do anything that would "contradict the understanding reached between the Governments of the USSR and the United States in 1962."[259] And on November 13, 1970, there followed the first public American confirmation of an understanding, when a State Department spokesman awkwardly noted President Kennedy's statement of November 20, 1962, and the TASS statement of October 13, 1970, as the basis for a conclusion that "we are confident that there is an understanding by the two Governments of the respective positions on the limits of their actions with regard to Cuba."[260] Thus, the "understanding" projected in November of 1962 was not really consummated until August of 1970, and not confirmed publicly until October of that year. Both governments, however, preferred to gloss over the past uncertainties and differences and to attribute the understanding to their predecessors of 1962.

While the Soviet activation of the 1962 understanding in August 1970 was prompted by renewed Cuban concerns, it was followed almost immediately by a near-crisis precipitated by a Soviet action probing the edge of the constraints on its actions and the American reaction. There is no need to review the issue in detail, as it goes beyond the subject of this study and has been done elsewhere.[261] It is, however, useful to consider how it related to the Cuban missile crisis, not only in terms of defining the formal obligations of the 1962/1970 settlement, but more basically how it reflected the longer-term impact of the 1962 crisis.

In the late summer of 1970, as the leaders of the United States and the Soviet Union were moving tentatively toward what became the détente of the 1970s, a significant incident occurred. No sharp

259. TASS, in *Pravda,* and on Radio Moscow, October 13, 1970.

260. Robert McCloskey, Department of State press briefing, November 13, 1970. Note the unusual character of the statement, indicating the lack of previous "confidence" in the existence of such an understanding.

261. See my article "Handling the Cienfuegos Crisis," *International Security,* vol. 8 (Summer 1983), pp. 46–66.

public clash or crisis arose, and the issue was resolved by quiet diplomacy. Nonetheless it was significant because of what it represented to the leaders on both sides with respect to conflict management in a new era of political relations and under an emerging new strategic relationship. The Soviet leaders were seeking to test the relationship of the two powers in a dawning age of strategic, and they hoped political, parity. And the American leaders were seeking to contain what they regarded as Soviet expansionist impulses and to "manage" the emergence of Soviet power under the new conditions of parity.

The incident was precipitated by the Soviet construction of a submarine base in Cienfuegos Bay on the southern coast of Cuba, clearly with the intention of using this base to support its own expanding naval presence on the world ocean, if the United States were to acquiesce. One reason for the special significance of the probe was the unusual neuralgia over Cuba in the United States from the time Castro took power, especially after the resounding defeat for the United States at the Bay of Pigs in 1961, which was only partly offset by the American success in the Cuban missile crisis confrontation.[262] The other reason was the neuralgia of the Soviet leaders over the constraints imposed in the settlement of the Cuban missile crisis. Thus, apart from the intrinsic significance of Soviet submarine basing—providing certain measurable advantages to the Soviet Union and corresponding disadvantages for the United States—the establishment of a base for Soviet missile-carrying submarines would have marked a symbolic repeal of the American imposition of limits on Soviet freedom of action in 1962.

From the American perspective, the missile crisis had resulted from a surreptitious Soviet deployment of medium- and intermediate-range strategic·missiles in Cuba, despite earlier clear public

262. President Nixon had a special sensitivity, and hostility, to Cuba, dating from the time of Castro's rise to power (on which John Kennedy had capitalized in narrowly defeating Nixon in the 1960 electoral campaign). One of Nixon's first acts in office in 1969 was to direct the CIA to intensify covert operations against Cuba—just as the CIA was winding down such actions through Miami-based exile groups. See Tad Szulc, *The Illusion of Peace: Foreign Policy in the Nixon Years* (New York: Viking, 1978), p. 175, although Szulc attributes the pressure to Kissinger, who in fact was acting at Nixon's insistent behest.

warning against such an action by the American president, and despite false denials and assurances from the Soviet leadership. The United States had successfully deterred a provocative Soviet deployment that would have altered the balance (that is, diluted the American preponderance) of strategic military power, and restored the political and military *status quo ante*. And we had reasserted the Monroe Doctrine and rebuffed a Soviet political as well as military encroachment on our vital interests in our own backyard, so to speak. The outcome was widely regarded as an outstanding American victory in the cold war.

From the Soviet standpoint, the Soviet Union in 1962 had been under no obligation to obey American unilateral injunctions against deploying weapons on the territory of an ally—precisely as the United States itself had done in a number of states immediately around the Soviet Union—nor to inform the Americans of their intention to do so. They were doing nothing illegal or improper under international law, nor indeed other than the United States itself had done. Then the United States had used its superior military power to compel their withdrawal of the missiles, humiliating them (despite such face-saving elements as an equivocal American promise not to invade Cuba and the informal secret statement of intention to withdraw American IRBMs from Turkey). The American action had been an offensive use of military power—compellence, not deterrence—and spurred Soviet resolve to acquire countervailing strategic military power. And while they would never admit it openly, they deeply nursed resentment that they had been compelled to give up a prerogative of great power status. The outcome of the Cuban missile crisis had been a rankling defeat in the cold war.

Hence in 1970, as the Soviet Union was acquiring strategic parity, the Soviet leaders sought to circumscribe the limitations imposed in 1962 on their military presence in Cuba, to erase that legacy from a time of American superiority and cold war, an imposed constraint not in keeping with "parity" with the United States as a global power, to which they now aspired.

The "mini-crisis" of 1970 arose in September and was resolved by October. Briefly, the facts were these: on September 16, a U-2 reconnaissance plane photographed construction of a naval facility at Cay Alcatraz in the Bay of Cienfuegos that suggested preparation of a submarine-servicing facility. On September 9 a Soviet flotilla including a submarine tanker, an ocean-going tug, and a ship carrying two special-purpose barges (recognized as a type used to support nuclear-powered submarines) had just arrived at Cienfuegos. The U-2 mission had in fact been prompted both by the arrival of the flotilla, and by observation in an August flight of then-still-unidentified early construction.

President Nixon wanted to respond sharply but he also wanted to delay his response until after a scheduled European visit. The Pentagon favored a strong diplomatic action to evict the Soviets; the State Department favored more deliberate diplomatic clarification of the question. Kissinger did not want to delay, but the president decided to wait until after his trip. Then a press leak on September 25 (possibly inspired by Kissinger) led to a Pentagon press briefing on the details of the construction and the naval visit— a briefing made by mistake! Kissinger next entered the picture with a background briefing to the press by a "White House source" (all on that same day), recalling President Kennedy's statement of November 1962 in which he had outlined the understanding on nonstationing of Soviet offensive weapons in Cuba that resolved the Cuban missile crisis. Kissinger warned: "The Soviet Union can be under no doubt that we would view the establishment of a strategic base in the Caribbean with the utmost seriousness." That same day Dobrynin saw Kissinger, and was reported "ashen" (again!) from shock when Kissinger had spelled out the full basis for, and extent of, American concern.[263]

By early October the "crisis" was resolved. There would be no Soviet naval base in Cuba, and the understanding on nonstationing of offensive weapons was reaffirmed and made more explicit. On October 13 TASS publicly denied that the Soviet Union was

---

263. See Kissinger, *White House Years*, pp. 632–52. For background on the Cienfuegos episode, see also Garthoff, "Handling the Cienfuegos Crisis," *International Security*, pp. 46–66; and *Soviet Naval Activities in Cuba*, Hearings before the Subcommittee on Inter-American Affairs of the House Committee on Foreign Affairs, 91 Cong. 2 sess. (GPO, 1971).

building a submarine base in Cuba and confirmed that the Soviet Union would continue to adhere to the understanding. Moscow thus clearly accepted a Soviet commitment under the 1962 understanding not to establish a missile submarine base in Cuba. The Soviet attempt to reduce the constraints imposed in 1962 had not succeeded, but there had been no public confrontation and no public backing-down.

The Soviet Union did not want to jeopardize what they had treated since 1962 as an American commitment not to act militarily against Cuba, even though the American side conspicuously had never confirmed such a commitment. Hence the successful Soviet effort in August to reinforce the overall 1962 "understanding," with its American commitment, before their probe of the American position on submarine basing. This history also explains why the American administration also wished to date the U.S. commitment to 1962, and to state that the 1970 understanding merely "reaffirmed," "clarified," and "amplified" the 1962 understanding to cover Soviet submarine missile systems. Overall, in 1970 the United States got a greater degree of Soviet commitment against permanent missile submarine basing in Cuba, while the Soviet Union finally got an American commitment to the 1962 understanding and the pledge not to invade Cuba.

In May 1972, on the eve of the first summit meeting between President Nixon and General Secretary Brezhnev, the Soviets again probed the limits of the 1962/1970 constraint by sending a diesel-powered nuclear ballistic missile Golf-II class submarine to visit Cuba (not, however, Cienfuegos). While Nixon and Kissinger did not raise this missile submarine visit during the summit, the Soviet leaders had received a powerful signal of American displeasure. As the Soviet flotilla left Bahia de Nipe on May 6 (where a U.S. surveillance patrol had remained throughout its six-day stay, just six—not twelve—miles off the harbor entrance), the submarine submerged immediately outside the harbor entrance. The U.S. surveillance ships, aided by P-3 patrol aircraft (based at Guantánamo Bay in Cuba), made sonar contact and forced the submarine to surface. Several times at night this was repeated, with the Soviets even firing flares to discourage the P-3 aircraft, and with high-speed maneuvers by the Soviet and American ships; the submarine was repeatedly forced to surface until the Soviet formation was well into the Atlantic.[264]

All this was undoubtedly known to the Soviet leaders in Moscow during the summit. But incredible as it may seem to those not familiar with the workings of government bureaucracies, from all available evidence (including interviews with a number of the American participants), it appears that this entire incident was not known to President Nixon, or to Dr. Kissinger, in orchestrating policy then or even long after the event![265]

The Soviet leaders also tested the 1962 and 1970 "understandings" in another way. Shortly before the Cienfuegos confrontation in 1970, but not involved with it, the Soviet Union had begun occasional flights of Tu-95 Bear turbo-prop reconnaissance aircraft from Murmansk to Cuba over the North Atlantic. Then in September 1972, soon after the summit, a new pattern began. Operational reconnaissance flights from Havana, returning to Cuba, began to occur, unlike the earlier flights where reconnaissance was incidental to transit from the USSR to Cuba and return flights. These flights all involved the naval reconnaissance version of the Bear (the Bear D), not the air force bomber version.[266] The case of the Soviet reconnaissance Bears never became an issue between the United States and the Soviet Union. Of course, the American *non-*reaction *was* a response to Moscow, and the appropriate one since there was no good basis for a challenge.[267]

264. This entire incident became known only when revealed in 1980 by the retired former commander of the U.S. surveillance patrol; see Captain Leslie K. Fenlon, Jr., USN (ret.), "The Umpteenth Cuban Confrontation," *U.S. Naval Institute Proceedings,* vol. 106 (July 1980), p. 44.

265. For a more detailed account of this episode, see Garthoff, "Handling the Cienfuegos Crisis," *International Security,* pp. 58–60.

266. The two versions of the aircraft are visually distinguishable, the reconnaissance version having a large observation bubble and no bomb bay.

267. Secretary of Defense Melvin Laird wrote to Secretary of State William P. Rogers in September 1972, after the first such reconnaissance mission along the U.S. East Coast, urging an immediate protest, and again in January 1973, after the first letter was not acted upon. In fact, at the State Department action level we had found no basis for charging the Soviets with violating the under-

A decade later, in 1983, the Soviets began also to send flights of two Tu-142 antisubmarine warfare (ASW) versions of the Bear (the Bear F). This was accepted. They have never sent the bomber or air-launched cruise missile versions of the Bear aircraft, which would undoubtedly be challenged as not compatible with the 1962 and 1970 understandings.

In 1978, a brief alarm arose over the Soviet transfer of MiG-23 fighter-bombers to Cuba. The administration was able, after monitoring closely the situation in Cuba and after consulting the Soviet leadership, to reassure the public that there was no evidence that a nuclear attack capability was being provided, and that the Soviet authorities had given assurances that no nuclear capability would be provided—and, moreover, that the 1962 understanding would continue to be adhered to. The matter soon faded as a public issue, but not before again raising the question of what the 1962 understanding covered—clearly strategic offensive ballistic missiles, ballistic missile submarine bases, and Soviet strategic bombers. But what about MiG-23 fighter-bombers?[268]

Crated MiG-23 fighter-bombers had begun to arrive in Cuba in late April 1978. The first public reference to their introduction into Cuba was on October 30, and the first real attention was drawn to

standings of 1962 or 1970, so far as the latter were known, but could only note that the White House was the only party that knew the full content of the earlier exchanges. The State Department at a senior level was orally instructed by Dr. Kissinger to "sit" on the Defense requests, and nothing was ever done.

This account is based on my direct involvement as deputy director of the Bureau of Politico-Military Affairs of the Department of State, 1970–73.

Kissinger had, in fact, raised the matter of the Bear flights with Dobrynin in 1972, seeking to curb Soviet expansion of such flights or their extension to include bombers, without challenging the Soviet right to occasional reconnaissance flights. He did not, however, report this fact to the Department of State or the Department of Defense at the time, nor cite it as a reason for non-action in 1973. (Information from a member of Kissinger's NSC staff.)

268. Some who in 1978 most vigorously challenged the compatibility of MiG-23s in Cuba with the 1962 understanding did so for other reasons—chiefly in order to raise doubts both as to Soviet trustworthiness and intentions, and as to the strength and steadfastness of the Carter administration. In particular, some opponents of a SALT II agreement sought to use the issue to brand the Soviets as "hard" and the administration as "soft" on a security question, and thereby to discredit both. Others wondered whether the Soviets were probing or "testing" the mettle of the United States.

them by a syndicated article by Rowland Evans and Robert Novak on November 15, 1978. That article referred to a secret memorandum on the subject sent by Secretary of Defense Harold Brown to President Jimmy Carter on October 23.[269] A considerable brouhaha developed in the press over the next two weeks. At a press conference on November 30, President Carter stated that the Soviet government had provided assurances that no shipments of arms to Cuba had or would violate the terms of "the 1962 agreement," and that we had no evidence of nuclear weapons in Cuba.[270] While not silencing all critics, this quieted most concerns.[271] The matter was laid to rest by a State Department statement on January 17, 1979, concluding that the MiG-23s in Cuba did not constitute a violation of "the 1962 agreement," that they were not configured for nuclear weapons delivery, and that there were not any nuclear weapons in Cuba.[272] Again in 1982, when a second squadron of MiG-23s was sent to Cuba, there was a flurry in the new administration, but no issue was made of the matter.

Based on the record of 1962, it is clear that the introduction of limited numbers of MiG-23 fighter-bombers into the Cuban air force beginning in 1978 was not inconsistent with or in violation of any understanding between the U.S. and Soviet governments, so long as these aircraft were not given a substantial offensive capability by being armed with nuclear weapons.

269. Rowland Evans and Robert Novak, "Cuba's Mig 23s," *Washington Post,* November 15, 1978; and see Fred Hoffman, AP release, October 30, 1978, for the first public reference. Ironically, the purpose of the memorandum from Secretary of Defense Brown was precisely to alert the president to the *political* sensitivity of the new findings about the brigade—a danger activated by the leak about the memorandum itself in the sensationalistic Evans and Novak article.

270. "The President's News Conference of November 30, 1978," *Weekly Compilation of Presidential Documents,* vol. 14 (December 4, 1978), p. 2101.

271. By December 8, even Evans and Novak had shifted targets and reported that "concern over Soviet shipments of Mig 23 attack aircraft to Cuba now centers not on possible Soviet violations of the 1962 Kennedy agreement so much as on Moscow's future targets for its all-purpose economy-sized Cuban mercenary force." See Rowland Evans and Robert Novak, "Those Cuban Migs," *Washington Post,* December 8, 1978.

272. Department of State, "Questions and Answers," press release, January 17, 1979.

In 1979 another mini-crisis of even greater moment arose over the belated discovery of the presence of a Soviet "combat brigade" in Cuba, probably the descendant of one of the four introduced in 1962.[273] A question was again initially raised by some as to whether that presence violated "the 1962 understanding"; it was soon generally acknowledged that it did not, although other concerns and objections remained. In 1962 the Soviets had informed us they would withdraw the military personnel associated with the missile systems, and they did—but they did not promise, nor as earlier noted did we consistently press them, to remove all Soviet military personnel and refrain from introducing others in the future.

Some American advocates of a more hard-line policy toward Cuba and the Soviet Union have, over the years, suggested that the 1962 understanding included a ban on Cuban support of or assistance to communist revolutionaries in other countries. That was not a part of the 1962 exchanges or negotiations settling the missile crisis. It is true that President Kennedy, in stating American policy, asserted that Cuba, and the Soviet Union through Cuba, should not export revolution. In his statement on November 20 marking the close of the crisis, President Kennedy stated that "if all offensive weapons systems are removed from Cuba and kept out of the hemisphere in the future, under adequate verification and safeguards, and if Cuba is not used for the export of aggressive Communist purposes, there will be peace in the Caribbean."[274] But those who have interpreted this to mean that the understanding of 1962 included a ban on Cuban support for communist revolutions in other countries have failed to recognize that there was no such undertaking by Khrushchev (to say nothing of Castro).[275] Equally important, they have misconstrued the reason that the president added that reference. He was under no illusion that his statement would add any Soviet or Cuban commitment; his reason for stating

273. For a detailed review of that crisis, see Raymond L. Garthoff, *Détente and Confrontation: American-Soviet Relations from Nixon to Reagan* (Brookings, 1985), pp. 828–48.

274. *Public Papers: Kennedy, 1962*, p. 831.

275. See, for example, Jeane Kirkpatrick, "Our Cuban Misadventures," *Washington Post*, April 21, 1986.

it was to loosen the *American* commitment not to invade Cuba. If there were a serious change in Cuba's role, he did not want the statement of U.S. intention not to initiate or permit aggression against Cuba to free Cuban hands to initiate aggression against any of its neighbors. In addition, of course, the proviso on "adequate verification and safeguards" was, at least in part, in the Khrushchev message, and the failure to implement it (to be sure, owing to recalcitrance by Castro, not Khrushchev) meant that the whole understanding was one that the United States could escape it if wished. The Soviet Union and Cuba never accepted any commitment on nonsupport to revolutions in other countries, and were not even asked to do so, as part of the settlement of the missile crisis in 1962.

The United States government, at least until the Reagan administration, never claimed such a broad interpretation of the 1962 understanding. And in the confirmation of an understanding in 1970, this matter was not included.

The Reagan administration never formally charged a violation of the 1962/70 understanding with the Soviet Union, nor asserted formally its interpretation of that understanding. There was no charge of a violation made to the Soviet Union, nor cause to do so. The penchant of President Ronald Reagan and members of his administration to state their personal feelings publicly did, however, becloud the matter somewhat. For example, on September 14, 1983, he stated to a group of reporters that "as far as I'm concerned, that agreement has been abrogated many times by the Soviet Union and Cuba in the bringing in of what can only be considered offensive weapons, not defensive, there."[276] The While House press spokesman, Larry Speakes, later explained that the president was referring to violations of the "spirit of the agreement, . . . in the light of all the Soviet military equipment that's been shipped into Cuba over the years." He also said that the United States did not intend to abrogate its commitment under the agree-

276. Francis X. Clines, "President Accuses Soviet on '62 Pact," *New York Times,* September 15, 1983. At a press conference on February 18, 1982, Reagan had evaded a question as to whether the Soviet Union was abiding by the 1962 understanding in its supply of MiGs to Cuba.

ment.[277] In 1985 Reagan again referred casually to what he termed "Cuba's willful disregard of the 1962 Kennedy-Khrushchev understanding," although Cuba was never party to an understanding, and the incomplete U.S.-Soviet 1962 understanding did not cover the matter to which Reagan was referring ("export of aggressive communist purposes").[278]

277. Clines, *New York Times*, September 15, 1983.

278. Address by President Reagan, White House Press Release, December 14, 1985. Other members of the Reagan administration also made casual and unwarranted charges of Soviet violation of the 1962 understanding by supplying arms to Cuba. Most notably, see the interview with CIA Director William J. Casey, "The Real Threat in El Salvador—and Beyond," *U.S. News and World Report*, vol. 92 (March 8, 1982), pp. 23–24.

CONCLUSIONS

The Long-Term Legacy

OVER A QUARTER of a century has now passed since the Cuban missile crisis, and despite serious international frictions there has not been another incident like it. Nonetheless the risks from any direct confrontation, even if small in probability, are enormous in potential consequence.

The United States and the Soviet Union are great powers with global interests, and sometimes those interests clash. *Crisis management* is necessary if crises arise; but *crisis prevention* and *crisis avoidance* based on political restraint and accommodation of differences are much to be preferred. Arms control limitations and reductions are important in their own right and because they can favorably affect political relations. Prevention of nuclear war, and hence prevention of any war involving the United States and the Soviet Union, are of the highest priority. Nonetheless, since political efforts to resolve disputes peacefully are not always successful, we must be prepared to deal with and defuse any crises that may, despite our best efforts, occur. This includes the need to de-escalate crises, and still more any armed hostilities that might break out. Studying the experience and learning the lessons of the 1962 missile crisis, and to the extent possible doing so together, can help both the United States and the Soviet Union to ensure not only that such a crisis never recurs, but also that a greater catastrophe never occurs.

In the United States greatest attention has been given to crisis management and more broadly to conflict management. This tendency is true in general, and with respect to study of the Cuban missile crisis. In the Soviet Union, on the other hand, the general inclination and most attention given to the Caribbean crisis of 1962 has been directed to developing political accommodation and crisis prevention, rather than crisis management. Curiously reversing the usual stereotypes, the Americans have been sober, pessimistic realists, assuming that, regrettably, crises will occur and must be safely managed, while the Soviets have appeared to be optimistic, if not hopelessly idealistic, in arguing that crises can and must be prevented by political collaboration. Under the surface, however, the American "realism" may spring from an idealistic faith that with a will anything can be managed, and the apparent Soviet belief in political accommodation may shield a deep pessimism over the ability of the two sides reliably to manage a crisis. The Soviet concentration on seeking political regulation of differences so as to preclude crises may be generated more by that concern than by any conviction that the task of political settlement will be easy or necessarily successful.

Both Kennedy and Khrushchev were highly aware of the dangers of uncontrolled occurrences and of the situation acquiring a momentum that might escape their control. As the record shows, those concerns were well founded. Many events were interpreted by the other side as planned and controlled actions when in fact they were neither. Actions were undertaken on what one might term "inertial guidance"—something moving by its own momentum but no longer controlled or even remembered. Only when a U-2 accidentally overflew Soviet territory at the height of the crisis did anyone recall there were still U-2s flying near the Soviet Union. The Soviet shooting down of another U-2 over Cuba the same day, October 27, we now know, was the result of an action taken by a local Soviet commander without authorization, stretching if not breaking his instructions. When a CIA-dispatched sabotage team blew up a Cuban plant on November 8 it was almost certainly seen in Moscow (and certainly in Havana) as an intended signal, yet it was the result of an inadequately monitored covert action program that had been stimulated at the start of the crisis in mid-October but then forgotten about while the crisis was being resolved (and not thought of again until October 30, when it was too late to recall three teams already sent in).

As for actions by third parties, what if Colonel Penkovsky's farewell signal had been taken seriously? The United States might well have then undertaken some further action (such as DEFCON 1) that Moscow could have construed as preparation for immediate hostilities. The president's speech on Cuba might then have been seen, in suspicious Moscow intelligence, military, and even political circles, as a feint to cover American mobilization for a first strike. Soviet military doctrine in 1962 called for *Soviet* preemption if there was positive indication that the United States was preparing imminently and irrevocably for a first strike. SAC doctrine also called for preemption if a Soviet attack was imminent. In both cases, to be sure, an ultimate political decision was predicated. But was it absolutely assured? One need not predict the outcome to say that the risk and danger to both sides could have been extreme, and catastrophe not excluded.

Other deliberate and intended actions had unanticipated and uncontrolled dimensions. The DEFCON 2 SAC alert was ordered, but a flourish of open communication was neither authorized by nor even subsequently known to the American leaders. Nor was the American leadership aware that the Jupiter missiles in Turkey were being turned over to Turkish control on October 22, although there is good reason to believe the fact had registered with Khrushchev.

Certainly President Kennedy and his principal advisers, and by all indications Chairman Khrushchev and his colleagues in the Soviet leadership, sensed at first hand that no other objective can be of greater importance than avoiding nuclear war. That judgment, by those leaders at that time and by their successors, does not of course mean that other objectives will not be pursued simultaneously. What it does mean is that in critical situations with a high risk of leading to war, leaders will seek solutions that involve compromise of their various conflicting objectives and interests.

A readiness to seek a compromise resolution of a crisis is, alone, no assurance agreement will be reached, but such readiness on both sides is probably a necessary condition. The nature of the compromise will vary with the case, depending on such factors as the nature of the issues, the perceived stakes, the resolve of the parties, and their respective relevant power.

One reason for the Soviet miscalculation of the American reaction to the missile deployment in Cuba was an incorrect assessment of the American stakes—as they would be weighed by the American leadership. The planned delay in disclosing the missiles to the United States until after the U.S. congressional elections was expected by the Soviet leaders to take care of any domestic political problem that President Kennedy might have in accepting the modest deployment. Evidently they greatly underestimated the complex of political considerations that would enter into the American decision. The Soviets also undoubtedly misjudged the solidarity the other Latin American countries would show in support of the United States' position under the circumstances that their own secret action had created. They also misjudged the general world reaction.

The United States, for its part, did not deter the Soviet Union from making its decision to deploy its missiles in Cuba and embarking on deployment. Several Ex Comm members, in retrospect, and later American analysts of the crisis have concluded that the United States should have given stronger and clearer warnings earlier. Above all, earlier. Yet it is not easy to see how the Soviet course of action could have been predicted. (One of the principal authors of the national intelligence estimates in 1962, overstating this point, later argued that the *estimates* had not been wrong—Khrushchev had!) Quite simply it is hard to predict an irrational, or unsound, or simply unique initiative by another party.

Direct communication between the leaders, and secrecy of that and other diplomatic intercourse, were at least valuable and may have been essential to the working out of a mutually acceptable resolution of the crisis. This was the virtually unanimous judgment of those actually engaged on both sides and of later analysts of the missile crisis.

In President Kennedy's later continuing confidential exchange of letters with Khrushchev, after the latter had referred to the value of other confidential channels as well, Kennedy assured him that he too valued these contacts. But he also used the occasion to say: "I have not concealed from you that it was a serious disappointment to me that dangerously misleading information should have come through these channels before the recent crisis," referring to the message through Georgi Bol'shakov.[279]

The Kennedy-Khrushchev exchanges did not of course lead either side to change its policy positions, but they did help to identify a basis for a compromise. Normal diplomatic channels were, in fact, essentially set aside, or at least adapted (for example, Robert Kennedy became the chief interlocutor with Ambassador Dobrynin). The unorthodox Fomin-Scali channel did contribute to the president's belief that Khrushchev's October 26 message (which was less explicit than Fomin's) would provide an acceptable basis. Kennedy nonetheless later cautioned Khrushchev about new, unofficial (and especially press) intermediaries, and this caution was appropriate. It was a desperate makeshift move because the Soviet leaders had "burned" their established informal channel—Georgi Bol'shakov to Robert Kennedy. Not only had it been unwise to engage in a direct deception of the president; it also made the channel no longer credible.

Khrushchev and his colleagues no doubt believed in October as they had in May that they were justified in placing the missiles in Cuba. They discovered that their earlier judgment that the Americans would, reluctantly, accept the deployment, and the related belief that they could install such weaponry in secret and announce a fait accompli in their own time and way, were wrong. They did then recognize that the initiative in precipitating the crisis, if not the responsibility and blame, resided in their decision on deploying the missiles. This acknowledgment contributed to their readiness to make the larger share of concessions in order to resolve the

279. Letter, John F. Kennedy to Nikita S. Khrushchev, December 14, 1962, p. 2 (now declassified). Kennedy also used this occasion to criticize Soviet use of the Fomin-Scali channel, presenting it as something presumably not authorized by Khrushchev, a caution he did not extend to Bol'shakov's disinformation. He mentioned in particular the hazards of using a member of the American media owing to the fierce competition of the press, their unaccountability to the U.S. government for what they report, and their penchant for later publicizing what they may learn privately. Ibid.

crisis. The initiative is a factor both sides weigh in evaluating the stakes and deciding on elements of a compromise. The responsibility for the precipitating move, in other words, is an element in the balance of resolve.

The element that looms largest in most peoples' minds, and in many analyses, is the relative power of the two sides. This is undoubtedly a bedrock factor, but it is not the only one and often not even the one that determines the resolution of a crisis.

The United States had both local conventional and global nuclear superiority in 1962. The ability to effect the quarantine, and to pose credible threats of air strike and invasion, could not be countered by the Soviet Union. It would, however, be unwise to draw conclusions from the outcome of the Cuban missile crisis based on simple correlation with the balance of military forces.

The most basic element in one sense was the strategic nuclear balance. While neither side ever contemplated a resort to nuclear weapons, the American superiority undoubtedly contributed to Soviet caution against matching the American local conventional superiority around Cuba by a countermove at a place of Soviet local superiority such as Berlin. Contrary to a widely expressed view, I believe the outcome today under strategic nuclear parity would be the same. The Soviet failure to attempt to repeal the constraints of the 1962/1970 understanding about Cuba in the 1980s, or to test a comparable move in Nicaragua, I believe, bears strong witness to that fact. The reasons why they do not seek to test the U.S.-imposed constraint in Nicaragua are probably mixed, but that only underlines the fact that many considerations other than the strategic balance are involved and indeed usually determining.

Deterrence of moves that may precipitate a crisis is directly related to the matters of initiative, stakes, resolve, and relative power. If the United States leadership had known that the Soviet leaders were contemplating a missile deployment in the spring of 1962, they might have been able to convince the Soviet leaders not to do it. In that circumstance, with respect to the Cuban case in 1962, a strong private warning might have been enough. But mere warnings and other indications of strong feeling about something are usually not enough to deter a diplomatic political-military move, even a hostile one, that does not present a clear and present danger. For example, an American warning to the Soviet Union not to intervene in Hungary in 1956 would not have been heeded, despite the clear American strategic superiority. The Soviet stake in Hungary was great if not vital; the American was not. For the same reason, *not* because of changes in the strategic balance, the Soviet leaders ignored repeated warnings from the United States not to intervene in Afghanistan in 1979, and not to build a base in Vietnam in the same year. Yet they did heed a private American warning in 1982 not to introduce MiG fighter-bombers into Nicaragua, because the stakes were recognized to be different. The United States could and did invade Grenada, and could invade Nicaragua today, without a crisis confrontation with the Soviet Union. (It should not do so, but for other reasons.)

In the Cuban missile crisis the American strategic nuclear superiority was overwhelming. I recall a three-star U.S. Air Force military planner saying with great confidence that we could destroy at least 90 percent, and possibly 100 percent, of the Soviet strategic nuclear forces before they could reach the United States. Yet the president was inclined against an air strike on the missiles in Cuba, among other reasons, because the U.S. Air Force could not guarantee even that all the missiles there would be destroyed. Even a surviving 10 percent of the small Soviet intercontinental striking force in 1962 could mean perhaps twenty or thirty American cities incinerated by thermonuclear weapons. The president did not want, in any case, to strike the Soviet Union, but in the crisis he was "deterred" in a sense by the possibility that matters would spiral out of control, and a nuclear war could mean millions of American casualties. That the United States could launch 3,000 strategic weapons against the Soviet Union and possibly be hit by only 30 (or at most a few dozen more than that) was no consolation. The mere possibility of nuclear war was the deterrent. While Khrushchev had a statistically much stronger reason for being determined to avoid nuclear war, his own thinking, and that of his successors under conditions of rough parity, strongly supports the conclusion that they, too, are determined that there must never be a nuclear war.

The global strategic balance is much less important in deterring or resolving crises than many have assumed, because the prospect of nuclear war deters even leaders who command an overwhelming superiority, as shown in 1962, and all the more so leaders on both sides with larger but more equal forces, as demonstrated ever since.

Similarly, as President Kennedy understood in 1962, particularly in dealings between the two nuclear powers, the side with greater power should not press its advantage too far. As Kennedy put it in his key speech at American University seven months later: "Above all, while defending our own vital interests, nuclear powers must avert those confrontations which bring an adversary to a choice of either a humiliating retreat or a nuclear war."[280]

Some critics of the outcome of the crisis resolution argue that the United States could and should have "done better," driven a harder bargain. Specifically, they contend the United States should have been able to constrain further any Soviet military presence, and arms supply, to Cuba. I would argue that one lesson of the crisis is that it is important to do what you have committed yourself to doing, but a mistake to escalate demands. I think it was important to obtain the removal of the IL-28s because we had, from October 22, defined them as "offensive weapons." But I think it would have been a mistake, after the Soviets had accepted our central demands, to have suddenly raised new ones such as removal of all Soviet military personnel. Certainly with an eye to the future, it was important that the Soviet leaders understand that we always mean what we say; when we said "offensive weapons" we meant it—not less, but also not more.

The Soviet deployment of combat forces in Cuba also raises interesting questions. If the fact had become known to the United States, as it did not, it would certainly have posed a difficult issue for the administration. Undoubtedly some within it (in loose terms, the hawks) would have urged pressure to compel the withdrawal of the Soviet "organized combat forces"—deployment of which,

---

280. "Commencement Address at American University in Washington, June 10, 1963," *Public Papers: Kennedy, 1963*, p. 462.

along with offensive arms such as missiles, had been declared in effect unacceptable by President Kennedy on September 4.[281] Although the president might have decided not to press the matter, it would then very likely have leaked and become a domestic political issue. Two pertinent points emerge: should the United States have considered *any* Soviet deployment of defensive combat forces unacceptable? And if so, how could the United States have more effectively conveyed its warnings? There is one sign that the Soviets recognized the American sensitivity: the dispatch of Soviet combat forces was kept secret—and successfully.

One doubts if an administration today could successfully conceal for six years something as important as President Kennedy's indication to the Soviet ambassador, through his brother, of his intention to remove the Jupiter missiles from Turkey and Italy. It was not a direct element of a deal, a quid pro quo, but it was raised in the negotiation and, from the Soviet standpoint, was a consideration in making the deal. It is understandable, and was politically sensible in terms of alliance sensitivities (to say nothing of domestic political reactions), that the discussion of the matter not be made public. Yet Secretary Rusk was pressed into an untrue statement to the Senate in executive session that there was no direct or indirect connection between the removal of the Jupiters from Turkey within six months and the settlement of the Cuban missile crisis.

Another interesting question that has not received much attention is whether we should have *asked* for more in exchange for *giving* more. Restoring the *status quo ante* September 1962, removing the offensive arms from Cuba but leaving others, met our main interest. Part of that interest was to establish that the status quo should not be upset by a surreptitious unilateral Soviet military shift affecting the global U.S.-Soviet relationship. But the U.S. leadership did not really consider a more radical alternative: agreement to alter the status quo in a mutually acceptable way. A Brazilian proposal of October 25 may have offered such an alternative. The Brazilian proposal called basically for denuclearization

281. *State Bulletin* (September 24, 1962), p. 450.

of Latin America and a guarantee of the territorial integrity of all countries in the area. This would have involved, at a minimum, withdrawal of all Soviet nuclear systems from Cuba (and American ones from Guantánamo Bay and Puerto Rico), in exchange for no more than an implied renewal of commitments by all countries, including the United States, not to invade Cuba—and for Cuba not to invade any country in the region.

There were also informal discussions in New York of a possible broader deal under which the United States would have had to give up its base at Guantánamo Bay and return that territory to Cuba as part of a military neutralization of the island. The deal would have involved multilateral assurances against invasion of Cuba in exchange for a complete removal of both the Soviet and American military presence from the island, an end to external arms supply to Cuba, and Cuban nonalignment (still with its Communist government under Castro, but with a commitment not to join any military alliance or alignment).

If such an arrangement had been pursued, the United States would have been acceding, not to any Soviet demand, but to a Latin American proposal. It would have had the broader effect of removing any Soviet military presence from the hemisphere. Though the United States would have given up something, it would also have gained much more than the status quo of September 1962. Moreover, and preferably, the deal could have been pursued *after* the resolution of the U.S.–USSR crisis on the same basis on which it was in fact ended. As a subsequent step, under Latin American initiative and auspices, the United States *and Cuba* could have entered into the agreement, with the Soviet Union an affected but only peripheral participant.

Under such an arrangement, the United States would have been able to seek a much more satisfactory relationship with Cuba. Future Cuban military involvements in Angola and Ethiopia would have been precluded because the Cubans would not have had the necessary military establishment. And the United States would have benefited by disembarrassing itself earlier of its lingering covert operations against Cuba (whether as part of the deal, or through better recognition of its own interests vis-à-vis a militarily neutralized Cuba). Numerous frictions with the Soviet Union in the 1970s over constraints on allowed Soviet military activities in Cuba would also have been avoided. In the case of the 1979 Soviet brigade in Cuba, in particular, the cost of the episode in delaying and prejudicing the prospects for ratification of the SALT II Treaty may have been very high.

If nothing more, this brief excursion into an alternative outcome suggests a connection between crisis resolution and broader political accommodation. That in turn raises the question of "preemptive" crisis resolution, or crisis avoidance, through political accommodation, a subject in which the Soviets have shown interest.

Despite efforts to avoid them, crises do arise. And crises do involve a clash of aims and wills, and of the applications of power. One of the lessons drawn from the Cuban missile crisis by many of its participants and later analysts is the virtue of limited and graduated application of force. The quarantine, with the potential of being tightened, and with more direct military actions in reserve for possible use, worked. Perhaps it worked more as a tourniquet than as a step on an escalator, but it did stop a further buildup. Still, the quarantine by itself did not get the missiles removed; that took diplomacy and, as the Soviets stress, "mutual concessions."

It is not the Cuban missile crisis, though, that is usually seen as the test case for limited and graduated application of force. It is Vietnam. If, as many critics allege, the veterans of the missile crisis such as McNamara, Bundy, and Rostow later were tempted into an unsuccessful graduated escalation in the use of military power in Vietnam because of a lesson learned in October 1962, it was the wrong application of the lesson. I doubt, however, that the experience of the Cuban missile crisis had much to do with Vietnam policymaking.

What the Cuban missile crisis really demonstrated was that direct use of military force should not be resorted to when there are still diplomatic options for resolving a crisis satisfactorily. Military power may brace a diplomatic stand, and it may be required in some cases. But its direct use should not be one's first resort or resort of choice, if for no other reason than the inherent risks of losing control of the situation (and there are other reasons also). In the first days of the crisis deliberations in Washington, October 16 to 18, the case for an air strike seemed compelling to most members of the Ex Comm. Only on October 19–20, after many hours of discussion, did the disadvantages of that course and the feasibility of an alternative become the consensus. And only after interaction with the Soviet leadership in the second week did the possibility of a mutually acceptable compromise become clear. For only then could a missile withdrawal for a noninvasion pledge be taken seriously, when it was learned that those were acceptable Soviet terms. Yet that deal was not even envisaged in the early Ex Comm deliberations.

This leads to another general conclusion: a crisis is an interaction, and it should be resolved through diplomatic interaction. Naturally it is necessary to clarify one's own priorities before entering a negotiation, but there should be enough flexibility in the positions one advances to allow movement in more than one direction, depending on the priority interests of the other side. It is sound to leave bargaining room, and to start well above one's "bottom line," but not to the extent of ruling out serious possibilities for negotiation by signaling a hard position on lines that may lead the other party to judge incorrectly that a line of interest to him has been ruled out. For example, an authoritative American statement in the first four days of the confrontation (October 22–25) suggesting a noninvasion pledge was absolutely out of the question might have cut off that productive line of negotiation. The United States did not advance a noninvasion pledge, not because it was unacceptable, but because its importance to the other side was unrecognized at first. That was found only through diplomatic interaction.

Just as it is important in a crisis to determine the views of the adversary, so too is it useful in a consideration of the legacy and lessons of this crisis to seek and articulate not only American views, but also those of the Soviet adversary-partners in the experience.

For the Soviet view of the crisis experience, its significance, and its lessons, one must begin with the few key official statements made immediately after the event. Given the paucity of later Soviet information and analysis on the crisis, these early official explanations not only set the line for 1962–63 but provided the basis for the historical image of the crisis as understood in the Soviet Union for a quarter of a century, until the late 1980s.

Until October 28, 1962, the Soviet public record held that the United States had stirred up a crisis because of its designs on Cuba and denied that there were any Soviet missiles there. Then, suddenly, Khrushchev's letter of that date was published, setting forth the agreement to remove the missiles because of an American pledge not to invade the island. Next, on November 6, before the crisis was fully resolved, First Deputy Chairman of the Council of Ministers and senior Presidium member Kosygin commented on the situation in his leadership address on the anniversary of the revolution. Kosygin naturally stressed support for Cuba and blamed the crisis on "aggressive U.S. imperialism." He noted the U.S. president's pledge not to invade Cuba and to lift the blockade. "Now that, through compromise and mutual concessions, the conflict has lost its acuteness and talks are under way toward its complete liquidation," he said, "some people may ask: was it worthwhile to yield? In our view it was right to yield, for both sides, because this was a case of mutual concessions, of a reasonable compromise." He spoke also of "concessions on both sides, concessions to reason and peace."[282]

Kosygin had to acknowledge that there had been a major Soviet concession, and it was natural and appropriate that he would put it in terms of "mutual concessions." Moreover, the Chinese had already sharply criticized Khrushchev and the Soviet leadership for "adventurism" in deploying the missiles in Cuba in the first place, and then "capitulationism" for taking them out. But Kosygin went further than a mere defense of the Soviet action as justified expedience. He reaffirmed, but also redefined, peaceful coexist-

---

282. "Forty-fifth Anniversary of the Great October Socialist Revolution, Report by Comrade A. N. Kosygin," *Pravda,* November 7, 1962. Kosygin's very raising of the question "was it worthwhile to yield" strongly implies that some Soviet officials and citizens were asking that question. Soviet officials do not even rhetorically raise questions implying criticism or doubt as to the soundness of the leadership's decisions unless it is necessary to deal with them publicly.

ence. "The Leninist policy of peaceful coexistence," he said, "implies admission by the two antagonistic systems on our planet, the socialist and the capitalist, that they live without war, that is, can coexist. This itself is a compromise, this itself is a mutual concession. It postulates that disputed issues will be settled not by war, but by negotiations based on the principle of peaceful coexistence, of peaceful competition."[283]

Khrushchev did not speak out on the crisis until he virtually had to do so at the meeting of the Supreme Soviet on December 12. (There is nothing in the publicly released record as to what he might have said at the Central Committee plenum meeting November 19–23.) The November 20 settlement of course had resulted in the raising of the American quarantine, but that occurred only in exchange for a further Soviet concession to remove the IL-28 bombers, while the basic American concession for the October 28 deal, a firm commitment not to invade Cuba, had still not been made. On December 12 that remained the situation, but Khrushchev could hold back no longer. He needed to make his case to the public.

Khrushchev's speech reiterated what was to become the standard explanation. "Our purpose was only the defense of Cuba," the missiles were placed in Cuba only to deter an American attack. And they had succeeded: "The attack on Cuba prepared by aggressive imperialist circles of the United States of America has been prevented." Further, "had there not been a threat of invasion . . . there would have been no need to place our missiles in Cuba." He also attempted to bolster confidence in Soviet strength by stating there was no other reason to place missiles in Cuba, because the Soviet Union possessed "sufficient intercontinental missiles of the necessary range and power" on "our own territory."[284]

283. Ibid. This point was picked up at the time by the U.S. Embassy in Moscow; see Telegram no. 1227, Moscow to State, November 7, 1962, p. 1 (Secret; now declassified).

284. "The Present International Situation and the Foreign Policy of the Soviet Union, Report by Comrade N. S. Khrushchev at the Session of the U.S.S.R. Supreme Soviet, December 12, 1962," *Pravda,* December 13, 1962. Quotations in the following four paragraphs are from the same source.

Khrushchev did not rest his case on the success of warding off an American invasion. He admitted that the Soviet leadership had "received information from Cuban comrades and from other sources on the morning of October 27 directly stating that this attack would be carried out in the next two or three days. We interpreted these cables as an extremely alarming warning signal. And the alarm was justified. Immediate action was necessary to prevent the attack on Cuba and to preserve peace. A message was sent to the U.S. president prompting a mutually acceptable solution."

He stressed the need "to bring the negotiations to completion; to put the agreement on record," while also claiming that the U.S. president had already, "as the whole world knows," pledged not to invade Cuba. He said they were "pleased with the outcome."

Khrushchev was on the defensive. He admitted that "some allege that the United States forced us to make concessions." But, he claimed, "if one employs such a standard, these persons should have said that the United States, too, was obliged to concede something." He also invited his audience to "imagine for a moment what might have happened had we acted like diehard politicians and refused to make mutual concessions. . . . If we had taken an uncompromising stand we would only have helped the 'lunatic' camp to use the situation to strike at Cuba and unleash a world war." But, fortunately, "among the ruling circles of the United States there are also persons who appraise the situation more soberly" and realize the futility of war.

In sum, Khrushchev concluded that "a mutually acceptable settlement was reached that signified a victory for reason." Who won? "Reason won, the cause of peace and of the security of nations won." He said that both sides "displayed a sober approach," and reiterating what Kosygin had said, "agreement was reached as a result of mutual concessions and compromise"; it was "a reasonable compromise."

Soviet leaders rarely commented on the crisis in the months that followed, and Soviet historians have generally given it rather brief attention, although this may now change.

One other contemporary public statement should, however, be

noted, and also a particularly interesting discussion appearing in a confidential journal. Both are especially significant because they concern the Soviet military.

Marshal Malinovsky, the minister of defense, published a booklet that happened to go to press just as the crisis broke. The manuscript had been submitted for publication on October 9, but it was not "signed to press" until November 28, permitting a brief passage to be inserted after the crisis was essentially resolved, although before Khrushchev's speech. As he had in his November 7 anniversary of the revolution parade speech, Malinovsky credited Khrushchev personally for his "wise proposals" that "showed the way to a reasonable compromise." Apart from these genuflections to the leader and to the official line, Malinovsky credited a "severe warning to the American aggressors and the taking of measures to increase [Soviet] combat readiness" as contributory. He did, however, also credit the fact that "the Soviet Union in those days exhibited a maximum of restraint and circumspection." Looking clearly with an eye to the interests of the military establishment, he said that "overcoming the crisis in the Caribbean is a great victory of the forces of peace. But it must not arouse a sense of complacency among us or dull our vigilance. . . . Our answer to any provocations of the imperialist aggressors must be the firmly established defense power of the Soviet Union, the constant combat readiness of its armed forces."[285] Malinovsky did not speak about the withdrawal of the missiles, "mutual concessions," sober forces in the U.S. leadership, or new prospects for negotiation.

The other contemporary Soviet discussion also went to press before Khrushchev's speech laying down the official line. It is contained in an article by an unidentified civilian writing in the confidential General Staff organ *Military Thought*. Clearly, the Central Committee believed it important that an explanation and the line be given quickly, authoritatively, and confidentially to the leadership of the military establishment. Editorials on current

285. Marshal R. Ya. Malinovsky, *Bditel'no stoyat' na strazhe mira* (Vigilantly Stand Guard over the Peace) (Moscow: Voyenizdat, 1962), p. 14.

foreign political situations in that journal are rare. In some ways, this article is the most interesting Soviet account of the crisis in all the literature. It has only recently become available.

The title of the article, "Be on Guard, Keep Your Powder Dry!" and its closing paragraphs are strikingly different from the rest of the article, enough so to suggest that they may have been additions of the military editors. The line they took was standard: "The brazen provocation of the United States against Cuba once again shows that we do not have the right in the slightest degree to weaken our vigilance, our combat readiness." And: "The Soviet Union unswervingly pursues a policy of peaceful coexistence of states with different social systems. But if the imperialists, despite the will of the peoples, unleash a new world war, they will receive a crushing retaliatory strike."[286]

Those are the concluding words of the article, but they are strangely irrelevant to its thrust and implied conclusions. The article begins by describing the crisis in the last ten days of October as "the most severe trial [for the world] since World War II." Matters, it seemed, "would reach a direct armed clash between the two most powerful world powers, the United States and the USSR, a clash that would inevitably have grown into a world thermonuclear war." The cause was simple: "Aggressive actions of the United States against Cuba led to a most serious crisis in international relations."[287] It is, by the way, the *only* Soviet discussion to refer throughout to the "Cuban crisis"—the standard line of the "Caribbean crisis" had not yet been set.

The Soviet argument that the whole crisis emerged from long-standing aggressive American military designs on Cuba is made forcefully, not pro forma. The idea that a "new situation" had arisen in Cuba in mid-October (meaning, unstated, the American discovery of the Soviet missiles), catching the United States unawares, is strongly rebutted. "An analysis of just the military dimension of American actions against the Cuban Republic permits

286. L. Sedin, "Be on Guard, Keep Your Powder Dry!" *Voyennaya mysl'* (Military Thought), no. 12 (December 1962) [issue signed to press November 21, 1962], p. 21. It should be noted that while retaliation is said to be assured, there is no claim of victory.

287. Ibid., p. 16.

no doubts that the Cuban crisis was prepared gradually, planned, like a long-thought-through operation is planned, and in no way was it a simple improvization." The article cited the immediate marshalling of forty-five warships and 20,000 soldiers, including 6,000–8,000 Marines, and stated, "Even with the modern equipment of the army and navy such a mobilization of forces cannot be accomplished in a few hours."[288]

Finally, in that context, there is a curious description of the American military reaction. "Indeed, the spectacle of contemporary America, scattering its military bases all around the world, and at the same time quivering from fear over a handful of missile launchers which were installed in Cuba, created at least a strong impression. But it was clearly not a matter of a mood of panic in the Pentagon, although the American military in general didn't distinguish themselves by strong nerves. Cries of a Cuban 'threat' were sounded to cover preparation for an open aggression against Cuba. . . . A fear of Soviet missiles, although perhaps genuine, in this case served only as an excuse."[289]

The article also has some observations, perhaps wishful or biased, reporting that the Latin American countries in practical terms gave only grudging support to the United States, and that in Western Europe "the unilateral actions of the United States, taken without concern for consultation with its partners on matters of life and death for some of them, will not facilitate growth in the popularity of the aggressive NATO bloc."[290]

While these observations on the American reaction (and other Western reactions) represent a curious explanation to be given to the Soviet military in 1962, the discussion of the resolution of the crisis, and its meaning for the future, are far more important in judging the legacy of the crisis in Soviet thinking.

Settlement of the crisis is described as a "reasonable compro-

288. Ibid., p. 19. This refers to the long-planned U.S. Caribbean exercise *Phibriglex*.

289. Ibid., p. 17.

290. Ibid., p. 21. This expresses more of a Soviet hope than an actual picture of the European reaction. As earlier noted, the United States prudently exempted its forces in Europe from the full DEFCON 3 alert imposed in the rest of the world.

mise," resulting from "negotiations on the basis of mutual concessions," and "that outcome of the Cuban crisis cannot be evaluated
other than as a victory for reason." Kosygin's statements on
mutual concessions in his speech of November 6 are cited. The
result is also described as "the only correct approach under the
contemporary situation." Thus, the Soviet leaders (and the position
taken is attributed to "the Soviet Government and Comrade N. S.
Khrushchev personally") were said to have displayed "Leninist
firmness and flexibility," and "cool, restrained, and statesmanlike
wisdom."[291]

The American role in reaching a reasonable compromise with
mutual concessions is mainly implied, but it is there. And there is
a reference to "sound-thinking" Americans. "Sound-thinking
elements in the whole world, including those in American society,
draw from the Cuban crisis above all the conclusion that in our day
no question in international affairs must be permitted to go to the
brink of war." "The whole world" clearly includes the Soviet
Union, although in the Soviet view the most likely source of
carrying things to the brink is the United States. Hence a prime
"capitalist" source is also cited as evidence. "Not by chance the
influential organ of American big business, the journal *Business
Week,* at the beginning of November has warned its government
'We must not give way to illusions that we can unilaterally repeat
a balancing on the brink of war in the future.' "[292]

In terms of the impact on *Soviet* thinking the article declares
that "a new, deep meaning has been given to the concept of
'peaceful coexistence of the two systems.' "[293]

Finally, the article includes a remarkable statement raising the
question of a far-reaching basis for détente. "Will this crisis remain
only an incident in the 'cold war,' or can it open a new and better
page in the postwar history of international relations? There are
serious grounds for putting the question that way."[294]

It is only by considering subsequent Soviet actions and reactions

291. Ibid., pp. 16–17.
292. Ibid., pp. 20–21.
293. Ibid., p. 21.
294. Ibid., p. 17.

in international politics that one can weigh the practical impact of this early indication of what today in the Soviet Union is called "new thinking."

Until now most Soviet histories have given the crisis no more than brief mention. Dr. Anatoly Gromyko, son of the 1962 foreign minister, wrote most of the more detailed Soviet accounts that appeared in the 1970s and early 1980s.[295] These accounts, which benefited from his access to the Soviet Foreign Ministry archives, as well as to early published American reports, presented a strong defense of the Soviet political and especially diplomatic handling of the crisis. His and all other Soviet accounts until very recently, however, have been limited by several factors. First, the Soviets have exhibited an understandable reserve about delving into the history of the whole affair because of its continuing sensitivity for Soviet-Cuban relations. Second, besides the usual Soviet reticence to address political and diplomatic decisionmaking by the leadership, there was a ban on discussing Khrushchev's role; virtually no account written between 1965 and 1985 even cites his name. There is very recently an opening up in the study of Soviet political history. Third, the Soviets have barely begun to publish accounts based on recently declassified U.S. records and renewed study.[296]

---

295. See Anatoly A. Gromyko, "The Caribbean Crisis, Part 1: The U.S. Government's Preparation of the Caribbean Crisis," *Voprosy istorii* (Questions of History), no. 7 (July 1971), pp. 135–44; Gromyko, "The Caribbean Crisis, Part 2: Diplomatic Efforts of the U.S.S.R. to Eliminate the Crisis," *Voprosy istorii*, no. 8 (August 1971), pp. 121–29; Gromyko, *Vneshnyaya politika SShA: uroki i deystvitel'nost', 60–70-e gody* (U.S. Foreign Policy: Lessons and Reality, the 1960s and 70s) (Moscow: Mezhdunarodnyye Otnosheniya, 1978), 301 pp.; Gromyko, *1036 dney prezidenta Kennedi* (President Kennedy's 1,036 Days) (Moscow: Politizdat, 1971), 279 pp.; Gromyko, "The Caribbean Crisis," in V. V. Zhurkin and Ye. M. Primakov, eds., *Mezhdunarodnyye konflikty* (International Conflicts) (Moscow: Mezhdunarodnyye Otnosheniya, 1972), pp. 70–95; Anatoly Gromyko and Andrei Kokoshin, *Brat'ya Kennedi* (The Kennedy Brothers) (Moscow: Mysl', 1985), 480 pp.

One other source deserves note. Individual authorship is not known, but the chapter on the crisis in the standard official diplomatic history bears all signs of authorship by one of the Gromykos. See "The Caribbean Crisis 1962," in A. A. Gromyko and others, eds., *Istoriya diplomatii* (History of Diplomacy) (Moscow: Politizdat, 1974), vol. 5, bk. 1, pp. 616–45.

296. A. A. Kokoshin and S. M. Rogov, *Seryye kardinaly Belogo doma* (Gray Cardinals of the White House) (Moscow: Novosti, 1986), p. 350.

In time, however, they probably will, and they are even beginning to make available additional Soviet source materials.

The Soviet political scientist, commentator, and Communist Party intellectual Fedor Burlatsky published a striking article on the crisis in November 1983, and a play based on it in 1986.[297] His account is a fictional pseudo-documentary on the *American* decisionmaking, based mainly on a Soviet interpretation of and extrapolation from the American literature. It is not very accurate as history, but that is not its primary purpose.

Burlatsky had several objectives in writing these pieces. One was a desire to capitalize on renewed interest in the Soviet Union in both the Kennedys and the Caribbean crisis.[298] But there were two more profound reasons. He wished to make the point, indirectly yet clearly, that it was both necessary and possible for the Soviets to deal with the United States, to negotiate and reach agreements, even in times of crisis. As Burlatsky has commented, it is dialectically possible to collaborate even when there are sharp tensions. At the time he first wrote, in November 1983, there was a much stronger mood of tension and pessimism in Moscow than in the United States. (It was after the KAL 007 shootdown, the start of deployment of intermediate-range nuclear forces (INF) missiles in Europe, and the like.)

His second reason was an interest in crisis management. Burlatsky concluded that it is important to realize that crises *can* be managed, if they occur; but it is also important to recognize that crises *may* not be managed, so they should not be permitted to occur. Burlatsky's lessons on crisis management, from studying the Caribbean crisis, are these: (1) close control over escalation; (2) direct communication between the leaders; (3) secret diplomacy; (4) readiness to compromise; and (5) never placing the

297. Fedor Burlatsky, "Black Saturday," *Literaturnaya gazeta* (Literary Gazette), November 23, 1983, pp. 9–10. It was reprinted in Fedor Burlatsky, *Voyennyye igry* (War Games) (Moscow: Sovetskaya Rossiya, 1984), pp. 21–45. The play is called "Bremya reshenii" (The Burden of Decision), and it premiered in Moscow in February 1986.

298. A letter to the editor commenting on Burlatsky's article indicated that many Soviet citizens only now realized how dangerous the Caribbean crisis of 1962 really was. See A. Kurganov, in Fedor Burlatsky, "1984: What Does It Hold in Store for Mankind?" *Literaturnaya gazeta*, January 4, 1984, p. 15.

adversary in a corner, always letting him have a line of withdrawal.[299]

Burlatsky's writings in the mid-1980s, and those of a few others,
drew modest attention to the Cuban missile crisis in the course of
a reawakening interest in American politics and Soviet-American
relations of the 1960s.[300] Two events in the late 1980s, however,
stimulated a burst of new attention, a new level of information, and
a new breadth of interpretation. The first of these was the occasion
of the twenty-fifth anniversary of the crisis, a spate of new American
analyses (including the first edition of this book), and the beginnings
of an unprecedented interchange between Soviet and American
scholars and others interested in the subject. The second new
element was the advent of the Gorbachev leadership and encour-
agement of "new thinking" on political affairs and history, including Soviet foreign policy and international politics. The first of
these was a vehicle, the second the motor, for change.

Reawakened American interest in the Cuban missile crisis led
to a conference held in Hawk's Cay, Florida, in March 1987 under
the sponsorship of Harvard University's John F. Kennedy School
of Government. Bringing together for the first time a number of
American participants in the crisis and scholars of it, this conference drew attention to the large gaps in our knowledge and
uncertainties still remaining in our understanding of the Soviet side
of the crisis. The sponsors decided not only that a follow-through
conference would be useful, but also that knowledgeable Soviet
participation, if it could be arranged, would add greatly to the value
of the meeting.[301] At the second conference, held in Cambridge,

299. My interpretation of Burlatsky's meaning and intentions has been greatly
aided by two long discussions of these works with him.

300. See the aforecited works by Gromyko and Kokoshin, *Brat'ya Kennedi*,
and by Kokoshin and Rogov, *Seryye kardinali*, and one writer's memoir, T. A.
Gaidar, *Grozy na yuge: Reportazhi o revolyutsii* (Threats to the South: Reportage
on Revolution) (Moscow: Voyenizdat, 1984), pp. 3–194. Timur Gaidar, a writer
and rear admiral in the reserve, was in Havana in October–November 1962 as a
journalist and describes his recollections.

301. Even earlier, I had discussed the Cuban missile crisis with Burlatsky,
and with Sergo Mikoyan, and had struck an agreement with Mikoyan that I
would contribute an article on the crisis to his journal, *Latin America*, if he would
also write one drawing on his father's unpublished notes and memoir. He agreed,

Massachusetts, in October 1987 on the twenty-fifth anniversary, three Soviet scholars participated: Fedor Burlatsky, Sergo Mikoyan, and Georgi Shakhnazarov.[302]

The success of that conference, in turn, led the Soviet participants and others to recommend a third conference, in Moscow, including Cuban as well as Soviet and American participation. The decision to sponsor the Moscow conference (or symposium, as the Soviets termed it), held in January 1989, was made by the Politburo. Among the Soviet participants were Andrei A. Gromyko, the retired chairman of the Presidium of the Supreme Soviet who had been foreign minister in 1962, Anatoly F. Dobrynin, a retired Party Secretary who had been Soviet ambassador to Washington in 1962, and Aleksandr I. Alekseyev, in 1962 the Soviet ambassador to Havana (as well as many others, again including Shakhnazarov, Mikoyan, and Burlatsky).[303] Cuba was represented by a delegation including Politburo member Jorge Risquet Valdes and General Sergio del Valle Jiménez, both senior military commanders in 1962, and Emilio Aragonés Navarro, a close political associate of Castro's active in the 1962 Cuban-Soviet negotiations on the missiles in Cuba. They met with Fidel Castro before the conference and were filled in on many details of the crisis by Castro himself.[304]

---

and also commissioned a Cuban contribution; the three articles were published in *Latinskaya Amerika* in January 1988.

302. Burlatsky had not only written on the crisis in the mid-1980s, he had been peripherally involved as a consultant to the Central Committee and occasional speechwriter for Khrushchev in 1962. Mikoyan had accompanied his father to Cuba in November 1962 as his secretary and had later assisted his father in compiling his memoir. Shakhnazarov had not been directly involved in 1962, although he too had then been a consultant to the Central Committee, and in 1987 was senior deputy head of the Central Committee department handling relations with Cuba as well as the socialist countries of Eastern Europe. By 1989 he had become an adviser to General Secretary Gorbachev, on his personal staff.

303. The Moscow conference also included active participation by Sergei Khrushchev, son of the late Soviet leader; two senior officials of the Foreign Ministry; the heads of the Academy of Sciences Institutes for international relations, general history, United States and Canada, and Europe; the chief of the Institute of Military History of the Ministry of Defense; and other influential members of the Soviet political establishment. Several other veterans of the missile crisis also participated, including two senior KGB operatives, Aleksandr Fomin and Georgi Bol'shakov.

304. Castro had personally shown an interest in the Cambridge conference

American participants included three influential members of President Kennedy's Ex Comm: former Secretary of Defense McNamara, Special Assistant to the President for National Security Affairs Bundy, and presidential counselor Sorensen, as well as several other veterans of the 1962 crisis and scholars of it. The U.S. government played no official role in the conference, though President George Bush, as well as President Mikhail Gorbachev, sent messages of greeting.

I have dwelt to this extent with the development of cooperation between American and Soviet officials and scholars, including the conferences of 1987 and 1989, because this experience has represented a remarkable breakthrough in collaborative reexamination of the history of the cold war, and may serve as the pilot boat for similar ventures.

In turning to examine the renaissance of interest in the crisis in Soviet writing, spurred by these conferences, one finds a mixed picture. There has still not been a single serious Soviet book-length study. Most articles have been brief commentaries, along with a few memoir articles. Moreover, discussions in the late 1980s divide distinctly into unreconstructed examples of the "old thinking," little different from those of ten or twenty years ago, and revisionist accounts, usually keyed to lessons for the present and future based on the "new thinking." Virtually all of the old thinking appears in military writings; most of the new in articles by political proponents of Gorbachev's policies.[305]

The old thinking is thin on facts and thick with selective bias. For example, some brief references in military writings make no mention at all of the presence of Soviet missiles in Cuba in 1962, or at least no mention of their role in generating the crisis.[306] An

---

and in Cuban participation in the follow-through in Moscow. Only two years earlier, one of the Soviet officials with whom I had explored the possibility of a joint American-Soviet discussion had, while expressing interest, shown concern over the possible Cuban reaction and reopening of old Cuban-Soviet wounds.

305. Two recent memoirs do not fall into these categories, but are predominantly old thinking. One is the very brief discussion in a two-volume memoir by Andrei A. Gromyko, *Pamyatnoye* (Memoir) (Moscow: Politizdat, 1988), bk. 1, pp. 389–98; and Aleksandr I. Alekseyev, the aforecited article in *Ekho planety* (November 1988), pp. 26–37. Alekseyev is writing a book-length memoir.

306. For examples of the former, see [General of the Army] Ye. F. Ivanovsky,

extreme example of distortion is an account published at the end of 1987 that, among other things, claims that the CIA and Bundy "cooked up" the data presented to President Kennedy on the morning of October 16 in order to create a crisis and pretext for invasion—claiming that the data on the U-2 photographs was "nothing new," that Bundy went to see the president "only after careful instruction by the CIA," and answered the president on the significance of the allegedly new data on offensive missiles with a reply "prepared in the inner depths of the CIA." Moreover, the meeting McNamara had with the Joint Chiefs on October 1 (about which the president probably was unaware) is described darkly as having been "kept secret from the president." As for the U-2 that strayed into Soviet airspace in the Arctic during the crisis, the U.S. Air Force is said to have sent it deliberately, "ignoring Kennedy's order to suspend for the duration of the crisis reconnaissance flights over the territory of the USSR"—flights that had been stopped by President Eisenhower in May 1960 and were never again authorized.[307]

The main lessons of the crisis for the Soviet school of old thinking are (1) if the Soviet Union stands firm in a confrontation, the United States will back down; (2) Soviet military power is needed to compel the United States to back down in a crisis confrontation; and (3) the Soviet Union fulfills its internationalist duty by defending other socialist states from U.S. threats. Some works with these

---

Na strazhe Rodiny (In Defense of the Motherland) (Moscow: DOSAAF, 1986), p. 82; [Col.] A. A. Babakov, *Vooruzhennyye sily SSSR posle voyny (1945–1986 gg.): Istoriya stroitel'stva* (The Armed Forces of the USSR after the War, 1945–1986: A History of Their Development) (Moscow: Voyenizdat, 1987), pp. 147, 168; and Lt. Gen. of Aviation V. Serebryannikov, "The Correlation of Political and Military Means in the Defense of Socialism," *Kommunist vooruzhennykh sil*, no. 18 (September 1987), p. 12. For the latter, see Dr. A. Borisov, "At the Fateful Brink: What the Lessons of the 'Caribbean Crisis' Teach Us," *Krasnaya zvezda*, October 21, 1987.

307. I. V. Nechayev, *Po stupenyam yadernogo bezumiya* (Through Stages of Nuclear Insanity) (Moscow: Voyenizdat, 1987), pp. 79–80, 82, 96. This book is one in a Military Publishing House series called "Imperialism: Events, Facts, Documents" that has been published since the latter 1970s, and remains distinguished by a cold war propaganda approach that plays fast and loose with events, facts, and documents.

themes do also add a moderating comment on "compromise" crisis resolutions, and some suggest that a successful Soviet stand can induce the United States subsequently to turn in the direction of détente. But the overriding lesson is political and military strength and determination.

This line of thinking was, of course, the orthodox interpretation for a quarter of a century. The official *History of the Communist Party of the Soviet Union* in its brief treatment of the crisis held that "the United States abandoned its planned aggression in view of the firm determination of the Soviet Union to defend Cuba by all [necessary] means."[308] This is still the line for most military commentaries.[309] Both the Soviet decision to place missiles in Cuba and the withdrawal are seen as justified and correct decisions. The United States is alleged to have been preparing an attack on Cuba before the Soviet missiles were deployed. The Soviet dispatch of arms, "military specialists" (the combat contingent), and the missiles, together with Cuban determination, frustrated American plans for an invasion. Soviet military mobilization during the crisis also played its role. Soviet military actions, while "not provocative," indeed reflecting an "exceptional self-control, restraint and a sense of responsibility," in order "not to permit uncontrolled escalation," nonetheless were an effective deterrent, so that "Washington made a sufficiently sober evaluation of the military might of the Soviet Union, of the readiness of our country to meet any aggressor fully armed, and of our retaliatory missile strike potential."[310] As earlier remarked, the late General Statsenko in

308. *Istoriya kommunisticheskoy partii Sovetskogo Soyuza* (History of the Communist Party of the Soviet Union) (Moscow: Politizdat, 1985), 7th ed., p. 571. This 1985 edition continued the interpretation given in earlier editions in the 1960s and 1970s. A completely new history is in preparation.

309. For example, see Ivanovsky, *Na strazhe Rodiny,* p. 82; Babakov, *Vooruzhennyye sily SSSR,* p. 168; Serebryannikov, *Kommunist vooruzhennykh sil* (September 1987), p. 12; Statsenko, *Kommunist vooruzhennykh sil* (October 1987), pp. 82–85; and P. N. Bobylev and others, *Sovetskiye vooruzhennyye sily: Voprosy i otvety—Stranitsy istorii: 1918–1988* (The Soviet Armed Forces: Questions and Answers—Pages from History: 1918–1988) (Moscow: Politizdat, 1987), p. 380.

310. Borisov, *Krasnaya zvezda,* October 21, 1987. The author even refers to

his account even justified the shooting down of an American U-2 on October 27 as a "deserved rebuff" to the "American air pirates."[311]

These analyses usually conclude that the crisis "fully demonstrated that the [U.S.] policy of acting 'from a position of strength', conducted directly or indirectly, sooner or later inevitably damages American-Soviet relations, raising the danger of military confrontation and threatening international security."[312] Some go on to note that détente and some arms control agreements followed resolution of the crisis.[313] One, however, argued that "the [American] 'hawks' drew a different conclusion. In their opinion [the lesson] was that it is essential to gain uncontestable military superiority over the Soviet Union and then act from a position of diktat in situations like that in the Caribbean crisis."[314]

One of the most interesting recent discussions by a hard-line, if not old-line, Soviet military commentator occurs in an article directed at the new thinking on reliance on political means to achieve security. General Vladimir Serebryannikov chose to cite the experience of the 1962 Caribbean crisis to make his point that "a tense diplomatic struggle in combination with military means (sending arms, specialists [the Soviet combat forces], and warning the aggressor of a retaliatory strike in case of his attack) permitted finding a peaceful way out of the crisis."[315] He thus argued for the need to brace diplomacy with military measures.

---

declassified CIA reports from October 1962 (which reported no evidence of a real Soviet military alert) to document the claim that Soviet military actions were not provocative.

311. Statsenko, *Kommunist vooruzhennykh sil* (October 1987), p. 84. A unique reference of this kind, it takes special meaning because it was General Statsenko who was responsible for the action, unauthorized by Moscow and contrary to instructions.

312. V. L. Chernov, "The Crisis of the Policy of the 'Cold War' and the First Steps in the Normalization of Relations in the 1960s," in G. A. Trofimenko and P. T. Podlesny, eds., *Sovetsko-Amerikanskiye otnosheniya v sovremennom mire* (Soviet-American Relations in the Contemporary World) (Moscow: Nauka, 1987), p. 70.

313. For example, see ibid., p. 71.

314. Lt. Col. V. Markushin, "There Is No Right to Complacency," *Krasnaya zvezda*, November 21, 1988; in a review of Nechayev's book earlier cited.

315. Serebryannikov, *Kommunist vooruzhennykh sil* (September 1987), p. 12.

By contrast, the new thinking has sought to illuminate the actual crisis events in order to overcome the severely one-sided picture that has predominated and permit more balanced conclusions to be drawn. The main lessons for the school of new thinking are (1) political, not military, means must govern international politics and be used to prevent or resolve conflicts; (2) compromises based on mutual interests and mutual respect for the interests of both sides are the principal foundation for resolving crises; (3) military parity and abandonment of the quest for military superiority will help to prevent crises, as well as to resolve them if they do arise; and (4) political liberalization and openness can help prevent crises, both in terms of international relations and internal decisions.

In the view of those who take this approach, the Caribbean crisis in some respects showed the danger of the old thinking and in other respects foreshadowed elements of the new thinking. Some, though not all, new thinkers openly criticize the Soviet decision to place missiles in Cuba. They also strongly criticize the United States for its policy of hostility and pressure on Cuba, for conducting political, economic, psychological, and covert warfare, and for planning, even "contingently," an invasion of Cuba. Thus, while much of the new thinking involves revising Soviet history and acknowledging Soviet errors, it also finds lessons in perceived American actions as well. Shakhnazarov, for example, concludes that "one of the most important causes of the crisis was a firm confidence of the American leadership in its military superiority over the USSR."[316] (This superiority is readily conceded, and sometimes quantified as seventeen to one, with or without citing McNamara as the source.) The new thinkers less directly also sometimes recognize Soviet strategic inferiority as having contributed to their deployment of the missiles in Cuba to "take the first step to strategic parity," as Burlatsky has put it.[317] Another Soviet writer, Aleksandr Pumpyansky, puts it differently, seeing the Caribbean crisis as "a bold bid for parity. Moscow used a shock tactic to show that it would no longer be treated other than as an equal. The principle of parity

316. Georgi Shakhnazarov, "A Moment of Fear and Revelation," *Novoye vremya,* no. 49 (December 4, 1987), p. 27.

317. At the Cambridge conference, quoted in Blight and Welch, *On the Brink,* p. 229.

was however not accepted by Washington right away," but only years later.[318] Shakhnazarov also has argued that even if, in this case, there was a parity of assured retaliation, as McNamara argued at Cambridge, that was not sufficient—there had to be a recognition of parity and acceptance of the inadmissibility of nuclear war by both sides, and that at best such recognition on the American side only began at that time.[319] As Pumpyansky sees it, Americans are not inclined to accept propositions based on common sense, but "invariably require arguments relying on force. That logic underlay the Caribbean crisis. Only after the Soviet missiles made their long excursion to the New World did Washington somewhat cool its anti-Cuban, and anti-Soviet, ardor. But at that moment the matter reached incandescent danger. Can't such white-hot danger be avoided?"[320]

Burlatsky has been more inclined to see and agree with McNamara's point. As he put it at the Cambridge conference, "The Cuban missile crisis showed that numerical superiority is nothing"; the United States had a superiority of about seventeen to one "and despite this fact, you could not use it. This is a very good lesson for both sides."[321]

But it is also a lesson not really learned in 1962. Burlatsky himself has asked, "Why then has the nuclear arms race continued ceaselessly all the period since then?"[322] Colonel Markushin was earlier cited as suggesting—not very convincingly—that American hawks saw a need to seek greater military superiority.[323] More relevant is Stanislav Kondrashov's frank observation: "In the fall of 1962, under U.S. pressure, the Soviet Union withdrew the missiles from Cuba, but the Soviet leaders and military drew practical conclusions from America's clear nuclear missile supe-

318. Aleksandr Pumpyansky, "Before the Abyss," *Novoye vremya*, no. 44 (October 30, 1987), p. 27.

319. Shakhnazarov, *Novoye vremya* (December 4, 1987), p. 27.

320. Pumpyansky, *Novoye vremya* (October 30, 1987), p. 27.

321. Burlatsky, quoted in Blight and Welch, *On the Brink*, pp. 230, 283.

322. Fedor Burlatsky, "The Caribbean Crisis and Its Lessons," *Literaturnaya gazeta*, November 11, 1987.

323. Markushin, *Krasnaya zvezda*, November 21, 1988.

riority. . . . When Khrushchev was ousted two years later, our military were, judging by everything, given carte blanche."[324] "In the fifteen to twenty years after the Caribbean crisis, having mastered its lessons, the Soviet Union, especially after the removal of Khrushchev, made up for its lag in strategic nuclear weapons."[325]

Kondrashov has also stressed the importance of *glasnost,* openness, citing its absence on the Soviet side as contributing to the crisis in several ways. First, Soviet secrecy and deception under Khrushchev contributed to the American campaign claiming a "missile gap," providing support for Kennedy's real buildup and the weak position of the Soviet Union at the time of the 1962 crisis. Later, because of the post-Cuba buildup to parity under Brezhnev, Soviet secrecy permitted American opponents of détente to prevail both in U.S. public opinion and in the U.S. political-military establishment by playing on American fears of Soviet superiority, thus facilitating President Reagan's massive arms buildup in the first half of the 1980s, "a response not only to our [Soviet] military program, but also to our secrecy."[326]

Restraint in the use or even deployment of military forces is integral to the new thinking. As earlier noted, at the Cambridge and Moscow conferences several Soviet participants described the Soviet dispatch of missiles to Cuba as a mistake. Sergo Mikoyan openly conceded that "the missile crisis was a result of our adventurism."[327] Kondrashov has expanded this into a general

324. Stanislav Kondrashov, "Ends and Means, or a Digression into History Prompted by Current Events," *Izvestiya,* December 15, 1988.

325. Stanislav Kondrashov, "More on the Caribbean Crisis, in the Critical Light of Glasnost," *Izvestiya,* February 28, 1989. See also "Secret Plans of the Pentagon," *Mezhdunarodnaya zhizn'* (International Affairs), no. 4 (April 1989), p. 145.

326. Kondrashov, *Izvestiya,* December 15, 1988, and February 28, 1989.

327. Mikoyan at the Cambridge conference, quoted in Blight and Welch, *On the Brink,* p. 284. A number of other senior political analysts share this view, as the transcript of the Moscow conference will show. Some, however, take strong issue. Ambassador Alekseyev, when recently asked the main lessons of the crisis, replied: "Above all, I want to note that the installation of our missiles [in Cuba] under the prevailing circumstances was justified; it must not be considered, as some suggest, as an empty adventure. Precisely after that the United States was

lesson drawn by the Soviet leadership: never again to deploy nuclear missiles "across the ocean."[328] This they have never done, and despite extremist American alarms in the early 1980s the Soviet leadership has always given assurances that it would never place missiles in Cuba, Nicaragua, or elsewhere, including assurances made during the Soviet campaign against American intermediate-range missiles (INF) in Europe, in which they drew an analogy to the American reaction to medium-range missiles in Cuba.

The new thinking also stresses control of military forces and actions. Soviet commentators have thus noted some of the examples of less-than-complete control of American military actions in the Cuban crisis, and occasionally even of their own. Burlatsky, for example, in direct contradistinction to General Statsenko, argues that the unauthorized Soviet shooting down of an American U-2 at the height of the crisis, far from helping to restrain the United States, was the "culmination of escalation of the crisis. Conservative elements in the American administration used that incident to intensify psychological tension and attempted to push the president to extreme measures, even to bombing Cuba."[329]

Aside from seeking to hold military forces to parity or at a minimum level, and carefully controlling military forces in crisis, the new thinking stresses reliance on political rather than military means in resolving crises (as well as, preferably, in preventing them). Even the generally hard-line account of the Caribbean crisis in the armed forces newspaper *Red Star* cited above shifted to new thinking in the end. Concluding that the foremost lesson was that "in contemporary war there would be no winners," the Caribbean crisis was held to show that military-strategic parity prevailed at the time and that "it is only possible to find a way out of a crisis situation in the nuclear age on the basis of mutually acceptable compromises." The lessons of the crisis are said to constitute a "warning to imperialist political leaders not to have blind faith in

---

compelled to enter into a dialogue with the USSR on the basis of parity. . . ." See interview in *Argumenty i fakty* (March 11–17, 1989), p. 5.

328. Kondrashov, *Izvestiya*, February 28, 1989.

329. Burlatsky, *Literaturnaya gazeta*, November 11, 1987. He also cited my disclosure of Colonel Penkovsky's false war-alert signal as an example of an uncontrollable factor posing great risk.

the omnipotence of 'nuclear deterrence' or to harbor exaggerated hopes of obtaining political advantages through pressing the arms race." But the bottom line is that "force cannot be a rational means of resolving differences among states in the nuclear-space age, and that international security can only be ensured by political means."[330]

The final aspect of the new thinking that should be noted is the relationship drawn between internal Soviet "democratization" (or liberalization or *glasnost*) on the one hand, and more open and deliberative national policymaking on the other. Several Soviet participants in the Moscow conference drew attention to the fact that Khrushchev decided to emplace the missiles after consulting only a few members of the leadership, and suggested that had there been wider consultation the judgment might have gone the other way. This same point has been made about other foreign and defense policy choices of Soviet leaders from Stalin through Brezhnev, such as the Soviet decision to intervene militarily in Afghanistan in 1979, and to deploy the SS-20 intermediate-range ballistic missile.

From studying the Soviet literature, and still more from talking with many Soviet officials, diplomats, and academicians, as well as from the 1989 Moscow conference, I believe the Soviets drew some other lessons from the missile crisis, particularly from their own experience. One was not to bluff. Another was to become aware of the disadvantages of disinformation and deception. They gained nothing—and lost a great deal—by their deception of the American leaders about the missile deployment. Another lesson was not to challenge an adversary who is stronger, and its corollary, to become stronger oneself. But more broadly, I believe they drew the lesson that crisis avoidance was better than crisis management. Above all, political accommodation was possible, and preferable, from a basis of rough equality and on terms of rough equality. In any given case, perhaps in every given case, there might be greater advantage on one side or the other. But while short-term advantage would carry some weight, in most settlements the mutual desire for long-term stability would be a stronger counterweight.

The recent awakening of Soviet interest in the "Caribbean

---

330. Borisov, *Krasnaya zvezda*, October 21, 1987.

crisis'' of 1962, the reawakening here, and above all the beginnings of a dialogue are welcome as new sources of data and understanding on the crisis itself. The beginnings of a collaborative assessment is especially useful, even though differences among American, and among Soviet, historians and commentators ensure that no single school of interpretation is likely to dominate. And such collabora-tive efforts can, in fact, help to rectify one of the critical shortcom-ings that precipitated the crisis in 1962: a disjunction in perceptions of reality. There must and can be a greater meeting of minds interpreting reality, even though differences of interest will remain between the two powers.

The Chinese ideogram expressing ''crisis'' is composed of the two ideograms meaning ''danger'' and ''opportunity.'' The Cuban missile crisis bears out this combination. The danger was real, if probably not so great as many saw it. And it did yield opportunity. The successful resolution of the crisis did give some impetus toward a new political relationship between the United States and the Soviet Union, although not sufficient to overcome all existing and new obstacles.

The cardinal lesson of the crisis does seem to have been taken to heart: such crises must not be permitted to occur. No event of comparable intensity and danger has erupted in the more than quarter-century since that time. While this successful avoidance of sharp superpower crises cannot be entirely attributed to the lesson of the Cuban missile crisis, that experience did have a strong impact. The key element was a sense of the nuclear danger underlying the event. Of course the nuclear danger had been understood before, even well understood; but it had not been felt viscerally by the leaders whose decisions could unleash war.

Leaders in Washington and Moscow could weigh the responsi-bility for decisions on resort to nuclear war (a decision they never had to face during the Cuban crisis, but could imagine at several removes), and realize that no real political aim would justify a nuclear war (keeping missiles in Cuba? Getting them out?). But while of utmost importance, that was never really a question at issue. What the missile crisis brought home, in some ways under-stood by the leaders then (and, we now know, in many other ways they did not then realize), was the danger of a nuclear war generated by the crisis itself through events and political or military processes outpacing (or lagging) control by the leaders. Too many things happened that could have started a war by triggering an uncontrolled chain of circumstances without deliberated decision.

This was a danger both sides felt. And one of the principal lessons that derived from the crisis, if not understood by all, was that the common nuclear danger was a far more potent force in constraining the crisis than all the calculated criteria of the military balance and deterrence. The common nuclear danger indeed proved far more significant than the massive American nuclear superiority. President Kennedy knew that in a nuclear war the United States could with high confidence deliver ten to twenty times as many nuclear weapons on the Soviet Union as the Soviet Union could on the United States. But that was no comfort for the likelihood that the Soviet Union could destroy a number of American cities, and it made little difference if that number were 100 or 10. Some analysts have considered that he could have used the U.S. superiority to press for greater concessions, without real risk of war. But I doubt that another American president would under the circumstances have been any more inclined to risk nuclear war, above all not for political concessions on the margin of a settlement achieving our proclaimed objectives.

So one lesson of the crisis, even though not articulated for several years, was a recognition in the United States that strategic parity was, if not preferred, at least acceptable. Moreover, I agree completely with the view of McGeorge Bundy that "the result of the confrontation in 1962 would have been the same with strategic parity as it was with American superiority."[331] Indeed, as Robert McNamara, another key veteran of the Ex Comm, has somewhat provocatively argued, "Parity existed . . . at the time of the Cuban missile crisis . . . [d]espite an advantage of seventeen to one in our favor." And: "In 1962 it would have made no difference in our behavior whether the ratio had been seventeen to one, five to one,

331. Bundy, *Danger and Survival*, p. 450, and see his superb analysis of the primacy in crisis resolution of the common nuclear danger over superiority; ibid., pp. 446–53.

or two to one in our favor—or even two to one against us. In none of these cases would either we or the Soviets have felt we could use, or threaten to use, nuclear power to achieve a political end.''[332]

Some may argue over the circumstances under which strategic superiority by the *other* side might make a difference, but the robust state of essential parity in strategic retaliatory capabilities of the two superpowers since the early 1970s and for the foreseeable future makes that question moot. Parity is enough, and parity helps to prevent crises or to constrain action in crises if they occur.

The Cuban missile crisis also showed the disadvantages of a situation in which a massive superiority by one side, the United States, led the other to undertake the very action that precipitated the crisis. (I am here discounting, although not rejecting, the Soviet contention that the missile deployment was also designed to deter an American attack on Cuba. I believe the perceived Soviet vulnerability and disadvantage of American superiority were the most important motivations in the Soviet decision to place missiles in Cuba.)

The lessons of the Cuban missile crisis on the political utility of military power are more varied and complex. The first set of questions relates to the role of military instruments of policy (and other less-calculated military processes) in generating the crisis. American resort to a proxy military force at the Bay of Pigs, to continuing covert operations, and to military exercises testing elements of contingency war plans against Cuba clearly contributed to Cuban concerns and the desire for Soviet military support. The possibility, in some quarters read as a probability, of American military intervention in Cuba also contributed to the Soviet and Cuban decisions to introduce nuclear-armed Soviet missiles and conventionally armed Soviet military forces into Cuba. These acts in turn came close to precipitating in October the very attack and invasion that had been feared, but was not otherwise then planned. While neither the Soviet Union nor the United States later saw this sequence of events as a lesson on the negative consequences of military assistance to vulnerable allies, it did point up the risk of

---

332. Robert S. McNamara, *Blundering into Disaster: Surviving the First Century of the Nuclear Age* (New York: Pantheon Books, 1986), pp. 44–45.

stimulating a cycle of military measures and countermeasures that may have had some effect in both countries on later consideration of such measures.

The U.S. "quarantine" blockade successfully interdicted further Soviet shipment of offensive arms (in practice, of any arms) to Cuba. The blockade alone did not, however, compel the Soviet leaders to withdraw the missiles already in Cuba.

To deal with the missiles if diplomatic negotiation did not lead to their withdrawal, the United States amassed a large air strike and invasion force. Was that military step necessary? I believe that the American readiness to invade and occupy Cuba was the crucial factor that led Khrushchev to agree to withdraw the missiles. By October 26 he was faced with a credible threat of American invasion, and proposed the withdrawal; by October 27 he was faced with a probability of its imminent occurrence and decided to accept the terms offered. This reasoning is valid though it is now known that President Kennedy was still disposed to seek a negotiated solution rather than launch an attack as a next step even if Khrushchev had equivocated on October 28. If Khrushchev had remained adamant, an invasion remained possible, and under some circumstances probable.

Even American preparation for and threat of an air strike on the missile bases, without preparation for an invasion, might have failed to induce Khrushchev to capitulate. He (and Castro) might have accepted an air strike rather than give in on the missile withdrawal.[333] But an invasion would have been the end of socialist Cuba. I agree with McGeorge Bundy's retrospective judgment that the decisions after October 16 correctly weighed the need for both diplomacy and military readiness: "If diplomacy were to be successful, it must be diplomacy based on a persuasive readiness to use force if necessary."[334]

This lesson of the Cuban crisis is not that diplomacy must be

---

333. It should be borne in mind that until his message offering to withdraw the missiles, Khrushchev had never publicly acknowledged their presence in Cuba. An American air attack could have been denounced as a piratical attack on the Cuban people, without acknowledging the missiles (or Soviet casualties). What would have happened then?

334. Bundy, *Danger and Survival*, p. 394.

based on military force, but that in some situations diplomacy must
be braced by credible readiness to use military force if necessary.
Optimally such cases should not occur; realistically, they should
be made as rare as possible, never a preferred resort, but a reluctant last resort where the stakes and circumstances require and
justify it.

One of the disputed "lessons" of the Cuban crisis is whether
actual resort to military force by the United States would have
entailed escalation and war beyond Cuba. What would the Soviet
Union have done if the United States had launched an air strike
and invasion of Cuba in October–November 1962? There are signs,
cited in the discussion of Stage 3, that the Soviet leadership was
determined not to escalate even if the United States attacked Cuba,
but these indications are not conclusive. No Soviet official has
purported to know; privately, some have argued that they believe
Khrushchev would have had to do something, somewhere, to offset
the defeat; others have said they are sure that he would not have
undertaken military action anywhere. But no one knows.

American participants in the crisis and other analysts are split.
Some believe the Soviet leaders would have countered with a
forceful move somewhere; others are sure they would not.[335] What
options did Khrushchev have? None that promised a compensating
"victory"; all would have entailed heightened risks over the past
when by the record they had not been judged worth it.

Judgments on the degree of actual danger of war hinge in part
on the answer to that question: what chain of escalatory actions
and reactions might have propelled the two powers, neither wanting
war, into it? Here, too, the divide is present along similar lines,
and from what one can tell, in both countries.

Even though the risk of war was probably not great (say, at most
1 in 100, rather than ranging from even to 1 in 3, as President

---

335. "Hawks" in 1962 (for example, Nitze, Dillon, and McCone) for the most
part believed then, and now, that the Soviets would not have responded with
forceful action; "doves" (for example, McNamara and Sorensen) tended then
and now to believe they would have. Some "owls" (or hybrids) such as Bundy
do not believe they would have. I did not then and do not now believe they
would have responded with use of force anywhere.

Kennedy at the time remarked), it was palpable and led the leaders on both sides to resolve the crisis on the basis of a mutual compromise.[336]

There remains another source of danger and risk of war, perhaps the chief one: war as a consequence of *uncontrolled* actions and events beyond control, posing unpredicted and uncalculated risks. As this study has shown, in the Cuban missile crisis there were a great variety and range of such uncontrolled actions that were liable to be misconstrued by one or both sides. Studies of operational experience and crisis stability show that errors, accidents, and false alarms are more likely to occur when military forces leave normal routine and when tensions are high.[337] Moreover, these actions or reported actions are more likely to be misunderstood, and ominous interpretations more liable to be made. It is true that there is a countering caution, but on balance I believe that the risks are appreciably increased in crises.[338]

The Cuban crisis may also offer material (if not lessons) for a better understanding of how to reconcile competing or conflicting interests of potential adversaries politically. Could the United States have reduced Cuban and Soviet fears of an American invasion? Could Cuba have reduced American concerns that it was working against American interests? Could political means have obviated the perceived need for resort to military measures by any or all of the three countries directly involved? In short, if we accept the major lesson that crisis *prevention* is greatly to be preferred to crisis *resolution,* can the events of 1962 help us identify ways that the crisis might have been averted?

For example, most analysts agree that it is important to see more clearly the perspectives of the other side or sides. It is not difficult

336. For a similar conclusion, see Bundy, *Danger and Survival,* pp. 455–58, 461.

337. See Scott Sagan's forthcoming study on the operational dimension of crisis stability, which draws in particular on a detailed study of events during the Cuban missile crisis based on declassified U.S. military operational data.

338. In this case, I disagree with the net judgment of McGeorge Bundy, who gives more weight to the countering caution than I do; see *Danger and Survival,* p. 455.

to see ways in which that would clarify the process of crisis resolution, but it is more difficult to apply to crisis prevention. The aims and interests of the United States and Cuba, and of the United States and the Soviet Union, differed sharply and clashed in many respects. Perhaps one or all of the powers should have had other objectives, but crisis prevention and resolution must deal with the hard cases where there *are* clashing aims, ambitions, and interests.

The careful and thoughtful study of past experience reveals not only transferable "lessons," but the interrelationships of events and broad foundations on which current and future political decisions rest. The Cuban missile crisis offers a rich example of crisis interaction. Despite the recency of the event, an unusually wide range of data is now available. As a recent episode in diplomatic history, it is unique in the extent and scope of original documentation already available (on the U.S. side, literally thousands of documents) and in going beyond mere memoirs or oral histories into active dialogues between scholars and veterans of the crisis itself, and now between the two sides and three countries involved. This process includes political figures, diplomats, military men, and even intelligence officers.

Finally, if this unique experiment with the Cuban missile crisis can be extended to other cases of recent diplomatic history, in particular cases in the cold war between East and West, it will be a crowning element in the long-term legacy of the crisis.

APPENDIX

Memoranda from
October–November 1962

TEN memoranda written during the Cuban missile crisis and referred to in the text are reproduced in this Appendix to provide additional data. Most were declassified with no deletions, except for documents G and I, and one reference to a diplomatic source in document E.

Document A

G/PM

TOP SECRET [Declassified November 20, 1981]

MEMORANDUM   October 23, 1962

TO: S/P—Mr. [Walt W.] Rostow
FROM: G/PM—Raymond L. Garthoff
SUBJECT: Reflections on the Confrontation over Cuba

The Soviets have doubtless had a number of motives in establishing missile bases in Cuba. They have probably been tempted by the first opportunity to establish a counterpart to American bases encircling the Soviet Union. There can be little doubt that they have recognized that such an action is provocative to Washington, though they may have underestimated the compulsion to react vigorously.

The Soviet leaders probably calculate that the new period of tension (which, incidentally, they had sought in advance to moderate by their relatively quiescent stand of late on Berlin, Laos, and the like) can be exploited to their advantage. While there are several ways in which the United States could have reacted, and may still react, each would offer certain opportunities for Soviet maneuver.

From a period of exuberant confidence following the first Soviet *sputnik* and first ICBM test in late 1957, the Soviets have thrice marched up the hill on Berlin and down again. From a period of publicly anticipated and acknowledged Soviet superiority in over-all military power in 1960, the military balance has by late 1961 and since swung more and more against them, and above all this is publicly accepted. It may appear in Moscow that missile bases in Cuba represent both the first, and probably the last, opportunity to place a lever under the US positions of strength on the Eurasian periphery.

At the extreme, the United States might militarily neutralize Cuba, at a cost to the American posture of peace, but also at the price of impairing the image of the USSR as a global power. Since the United States has chosen to act in the first instance resolutely, but not drastically, both sides will have the opportunity of assessing world reactions to the limited measures undertaken.

The chief Soviet "strategic" assets are: an intercontinental capability which works to restrain the United States from sharp escalation; a powerful nuclear missile force poised against Western Europe; a quantitative advantage in conventional strength in Europe, and especially on the access

195

routes to Berlin; a highly vulnerable situation in Laos; and now, the missile bases in Cuba. "Tactically" the Soviets have the advantages of: ability to match a selective blockade of Cuba by a comparable selective "filter" on Allied weapons allowed to go to Berlin; doubtless some sympathy for the view that "defensive" long-range missiles in Cuba are not essentially different from defensive long-range missiles in Turkey; the ability to trade off their Cuban bases for some inroads into the US overseas base system; and the "opportunity" to make the United States fire the first shot if they wish to precipitate an incident in the blockade.

The chief weaknesses in the Soviet position are: a basic military inferiority in the event of general war, compounded by Western alert and possible Western preemption in some cases; ineffective sea power either to challenge the American naval blockade, or to institute strictly reciprocal measures; and the inability to interpose their own power between that of the United States and Cuba at any acceptable risk.

These remarks are an incomplete draft of thoughts stemming from your request of this morning; being now fully engaged on more immediate aspects of the problem I am passing this on now without waiting for the chance to complete it, though I may return to it later.

cc: G　　　— Mr. Johnson
　　S/AL — Mr. Thompson
　　G/PM — Mr. Kitchen
　　INR　 — Mr. Hilsman

G/PM: R L Garthoff: pep

Document B

TOP SECRET [Declassified November 20, 1981]

MEMORANDUM   October 25, 1962

TO: S/P—Mr. Walt W. Rostow
FROM: G/PM—Raymond L. Garthoff
SUBJECT: Concern over the Course and Outcome of the Cuban Crisis

I am increasingly disturbed over indications that in all of our planning for the development of the Cuban crisis we have to our peril neglected one particular contingency: that the Soviets would react mildly and with great caution. A week ago we were concerned about strangulation of West Berlin, missile firings and exchanges of cities within the US and USSR, and other drastic and dangerous possibilities. Now the danger that looms large is not exchange of cities, but exchange of bases—at the extreme, the unhinging of our whole overseas base and alliance structure. It would be a remarkable thing if the Soviets were able to make substantial gains in achieving their main objective of weakening the alliances militarily and politically simply by exhibiting caution and indecision in the face of our initial stand. I can think of nothing that would more encourage the Soviets to create new Cubas and new distant military bases and local conflicts than would a net gain from their Cuban venture.

I am, as you know, in fullest accord with the objectives so resolutely outlined in the President's address. Yet I can not escape the conclusion that unintentionally we may be moving in a direction which in the eyes of Moscow, the American people, and history could make mockery of the statement that "further steps" may be necessary; it was presumed, of course, these would be further steps forward if they were necessary to achieve the objective of the "withdrawal or elimination" of the missile bases in Cuba. But a rush to find concessions that we can offer to achieve this objective could, to change the arithmetic in Lenin's phrase, mean "one step forward, two steps backward."

Negotiation is vastly to be preferred to direct military action, so long as it can achieve our objectives. That it is sometimes necessary to brace our diplomatic stand by resort to carefully considered military measures is, of course, manifest in the quarantine action itself. There are also still available means of increasing the pressure which we can bring to bear on the other side short of direct military action, in particular, broadening the blockade or commando raids on the missile bases. But any irresolution in enforcing the present quarantine, or in accepting a "freeze" on the present situation (thus closing off all options for intensifying pressure), or premature indications that we would "trade" other bases, would weaken greatly such strength as we now have to bring to bear in negotiation.

At the time of the President's address, and perhaps still today, the Soviet leaders have probably been quite uncertain as to whether the "initial step" was in fact only the first of a "one-two punch." Their caution to date has been a result of this uncertainty. But this is a wasting asset, if indeed not already a wasted one. When they realize the other shoe is not going to drop, they are likely to be emboldened in their actions and certain to raise their price in negotiations. If we seem to display a certain fear in our own actions, Soviet fear of these actions cannot fail to be lessened.

The terms for eventual negotiation might well include some give by the United States as well as by the USSR. But unless we are very careful, the business of letting the Soviets "save face" may come to involve losing our arm. The Soviets simply will not expect the United States to be offering concessions at a time when they have brought no counterpressure to bear on us in response to the quarantine. Any such indication (and the press is already rife with such rumors of trading off bases in Turkey, etc.) will mean to Moscow only that the United States is *not* prepared to *compel* the retraction of Soviet offensive power from the Western Hemisphere. One doesn't buy what is already his. If we concede that we must purchase the Soviet withdrawal, we undermine our right to compel it. The longer we haggle over terms, the more this is so. Moreover, the Soviets may be able to "sell" their missile bases in Cuba several times over. They can play us along on a deal exchanging Turkey for Cuba and then insist on broadening it out to include more and more United States bases—having already achieved most of their purpose simply by stimulating lack of confidence in the US alliance commitments. The missile bases in Turkey and Italy are not militarily important; this is, however, almost irrelevant. Berlin, too, is not *militarily* significant. The Turks and Italians have already shown alarm at unofficial indications of possible trade-off, and this alarm will both deepen and spread out to other areas, no matter how we seek to present the case in terms of suddenly acknowledged obsolescence and of renewed efforts to provide more modern long-range missile support from other locations and by multilateral agreements. There is a real danger that some of our Allies may believe that the United States is not only excessively concerned about the military threat to itself, but also that it is prepared to sacrifice some elements of its power and of its commitment to them in order to allay a selfish concern about a base near our shores.

I believe that the United States should make very clear that our objective remains the dismantling of present offensive bases in Cuba. We should emphasize our continuing readiness to discuss broader disarmament and other arrangements; and also our willingness to permit a United Nations presence to monitor the dismantling of existing offensive bases—but without raising the quarantine before the patient is cured. Discussions in a Summit meeting or other appropriate diplomatic interchange would almost certainly have to involve broad questions such as nuclear non-diffusion. However, it seems to me that we should approach such negotiations from a position of strength rather than a feeling of weakness. If we maintain the original resolve to use whatever means are necessary, though not more than are necessary, to effect the withdrawal of Soviet striking power from Cuba, I believe that the Soviets will in fact recognize that the United States does have the high cards.

cc: G   — Mr. Johnson
    G/PM — Mr. Kitchen
G/PM: RL Garthoff: pep

Document C

[For U. Alexis Johnson]
DEPARTMENT OF STATE
Deputy Undersecretary
G/PM

SECRET [Declassified November 20, 1981]

MEMORANDUM   October 27, 1962

SUBJECT: The Khrushchev Proposal for a Turkey-Cuba Tradeoff

Khrushchev now recognizes that his position is weak. The whole Soviet ploy with Cuban missile sites was probably based on a three-level course of action.

First, the Soviets hoped for, and probably expected, US acquiescence in the buildup of a Soviet missile complex in Cuba which would substantially augment Soviet strength in negotiations over Berlin, and in general. The appreciable military gain, while not seriously affecting the strategic military balance, could have been converted into a high card at the negotiation table.

Second, as a first-line fallback position, the Soviets could react to a US blockade or similar pressure short of direct military invasion or attack on the bases by proposing a trade of Turkish, Italian, and UK IRBMs for those in Cuba. It is the lower end of this range of action to which the Soviets have now fallen back.

Third, at worst, the Soviets would react to US military action against the bases by whatever forms of political protest were warranted by world reactions—even up to breaking diplomatic relations. The Khrushchev message of October 27 strengthens the conclusion that the USSR would not resort to direct military confrontation or reprisal—on the seas, in Cuba, or in Turkey. To date, the world reactions have not been what Moscow had hoped for; in particular, the unanimous OAS action must have been a severe disappointment.

The third course is still the remaining Soviet recourse if we reject their offer at the second level. The Soviet statement clearly evades any commitment to military action if the US should decline its offer and eliminate the missile site by unilateral military action. It states that the missiles in Cuba are in Soviet hands and would be used only if there were (a) an invasion of Cuba, or (b) an attack on the Soviet Union or any of her allies. It can scarcely be an oversight that the contingency of a strike to neutralize the missiles is not included in this commitment. The Soviets can probably still be compelled to withdraw the missile bases if they see the only alternative will be our destruction of them. However, even that outcome would almost certainly not provoke even limited Soviet military escalation.

The Turks have already made abundantly clear that they do not want to be compared with the Cubans, used as a pawn, or shorn of the Jupiters which have always been to them a proud symbol of their ability to strike back if they are hit. Hasty surfacing of long-held US military evaluations of the obsolescence of the Jupiters would be ineffective in meeting these strongly held views. The Jupiters are not important as a military-strategic asset—but, then, neither is Berlin. Yet both have elemental significance as symbols of the integrity of the Alliance and especially of our commitment to stand by the interests of each of its members.

The United States can, while solving the Cuban base question with determination, forcefully reaffirm its readiness to reach agreements on arms control and disarmament. We could thus indicate our pursuit of peace at the same time that we disposed of the latest Soviet disruption of the peace.

The United States has a unique opportunity to deal a major setback to the Soviet leaders, and once and for all to disabuse them—and others—of any illusion that the alternative to any Soviet gamble for high stakes will be not fallback advantages, but a defeat. Precisely such an outcome is the way to discourage such ventures in the future.

G/PM: RLGarthoff

Document D

[For the Executive Committee of the National Security Council]
DEPARTMENT OF STATE
Deputy Under Secretary
G/PM

TOP SECRET [Declassified November 20, 1981]

MEMORANDUM   October 27, 1962

SUBJECT: The Military Significance of the Soviet Missile Bases in
           Cuba

1. The presence of 24 1,020 n.m. MRBM launchers and 12 or 16 2,200 n.m. IRBM launchers in Cuba provides a significant accretion to Soviet strategic capabilities for striking the continental United States. In view of the relatively limited numbers of Soviet operational ICBM launchers—at present an estimated 75—the missiles in the Caribbean will increase the first-strike missile salvo which the USSR could place on targets in the continental United States by over 40 percent.

2. At present, 20 of the 24 MRBM launchers are believed to be fully operational, and the remaining four will be within a few days. The first 4 IRBM launchers will probably reach emergency capability by November 15, and full operational status on December 1. The 8 other confirmed IRBM launchers will probably reach emergency capability by December 1, and be fully operational by December 15. An additional four IRBM launchers will probably be completed, but it is possible that the quarantine has stopped them. The current threat is thus 24 MRBMs; by December it will—unless construction is effectively stopped within a month—be augmented by at least 12 and up to 16 IRBMs. Each launcher is assumed to have the standard two missiles, allowing one reload (for refire in 4–6 hours). In at least one of the nine bases more missiles than launchers have been positively confirmed, and in general the number of identified MRBM missiles at least is sufficient to man all the launchers for an initial strike. Earth-covered bunkers suitable for storage or checkout of nuclear weapons are under rapid construction, and at least two of them now appear to be complete. There is one such bunker for each pair of launch sites.

3. The strategic significance of the Cuban missile complex is due not only to the substantial quantitative increase in megatons deliverable in a surprise first strike, but also by their effect on the US deterrent striking force. Approximately 40 percent of the SAC bomber force is now located

202

on air bases within range of Soviet MRBMs in Cuba, and almost all of it is in range of the IRBMs. If the present base complex in Cuba is completed late in 1962, and taking into account the estimated Soviet ICBM force for the end of 1962, a Soviet attack without warning could destroy an appreciably larger proportion of over-all United States strategic capability than it could if the Cuban complex were not included. The number of US *weapons* surviving and ready to retaliate on targets in the USSR would be decreased by about 30 percent, and would thus leave only about 15 percent of the number in our pre-attack force. This force could still cause considerable destruction in a US retaliatory strike, the Soviets could not rely on the degree of surprise assumed in the above calculation, and it is very unlikely that the Soviets would be tempted toward resort to war by the change in the military balance. Nonetheless, this represents a serious dilution of US strategic deterrent capability.

4. The reasons for the strategic significance of the Cuban bases are: (a) the size of the Soviet ICBM force does *not* allow coverage of SAC bomber bases and soft ICBM sites; the addition of the MRBM/IRBM force already on the island of Cuba *does* permit coverage of *all* such points, thus bringing under fire an *additional* 26 US ICBMs and over 100 B-47s; (b) the Cuban based missile systems have high reliability (80 percent), accuracy (1 to 1.5 n.m. CEP), and warhead yield (up to 3 megatons each for the MRBMs, and up to 5 megatons for the IRBMs); (c) the United States does not have BMEWS or other early warning radar on the southern approaches; and (d) as taken into account earlier, many SAC bomber bases are concentrated in the South and Midwest.

5. All of the discussion above is concerned with the missile complex now being completed in Cuba. There is no reason why the Soviets could not, if unimpeded by an effective quarantine, literally multiply the number of launchers to a force large enough to threaten the entire strategic balance of power. The Soviets have deployed over 500 MRBMs and IRBMs on their own territory, and the lesser cost compared to ICBMs would make a major expansion in Cuba very attractive.

Raymond L. Garthoff

Special Assistant for Soviet Bloc,
Office of Politico-Military Affairs

Commentary on Document D
A Retrospective Evaluation
of the Soviet Missiles in Cuba in 1962

It is clear in retrospect that the Soviet motivation for deploying medium-range missiles in Cuba did not arise from a belief that growing Soviet strength could be exploited, but from a perceived need to offset growing *American* strength and the prospect that it would outpace Soviet strategic growth over at least the following five years. In 1962 the American intelligence and policy community did not fully appreciate this fact because it tended to hedge uncertainty about future Soviet military programs by overestimating them; the Soviet leaders knew better. And the Soviet leaders, while probably also overestimating American programs, did not need to do so in order to see their own strategic position worsening. In one sense, the United States failed to anticipate the Soviet action in Cuba because it failed to recognize how desperate the Soviet plight seemed in Moscow.

One of the considerations in American decisions during the Cuban missile crisis in October 1962 was an evaluation of the military significance of the Soviet deployment in Cuba of medium- and intermediate-range ballistic missiles (MRBMs and IRBMs). It is well known that Secretary of Defense Robert McNamara said at the outset of the crisis that the military significance of the Soviet deployment was not unmanageable and could be offset without having to remove the missiles—whether by compelling Soviet withdrawal or, if that could not be done, by American military action. Not all agreed with that judgment, but the matter was quickly set aside because of President John F. Kennedy's assessment of the *political* consequences, both international and domestic, if the United States were to acquiesce in the Soviet deployment in Cuba. McNamara did not question that judgment, and he did not deny that there was military significance to the deployment. How the deployment would actually affect the military balance, therefore, did not become an issue of contention. Indeed, it was not even fully analyzed in the hectic week of initial decisions. But it remained a factor in subsequent decisions throughout the thirteen days of the confrontation until Khrushchev agreed to dismantle and remove the missile systems.

To this day in the voluminous published commentary on the Cuban missile crisis there has been little assessment of the *military* significance of the Soviet missiles. Many—although not all— analysts have discounted that factor far too much, not going beyond reference to McNamara's judgment or comments on the overall force levels of the two sides. It is, therefore, of interest to see a now declassified Top Secret analysis made at the climax of the crisis.

On October 26, 1962, I was asked to prepare for the Executive Committee of the National Security Council (Ex Comm) an analysis of the military significance of the Soviet missiles in Cuba. On the following day I submitted the requested memorandum, reproduced here as document D.[1] Two recent accounts refer to this memorandum, suggesting that its effect, and perhaps that of most analyses in such cases, was to reinforce views already held. McGeorge Bundy, in his excellent memoir-history, notes that the military analysis failed to alter the judgment of the president, McNamara, himself, or others who were not originally influenced by the possible impact of the Soviet-missile deployment on the strategic balance, in contrast to Nitze, Dillon, McCone, and the Joint Chiefs.[2] In a

1. I had been in constant touch with colleagues working on the crisis in the Pentagon and the Central Intelligence Agency and quickly prepared the brief analysis. My recollection is that I did not formally "clear" the memorandum with anyone (in those remarkable and heady days, it was possible to prepare such a memorandum and submit it to the Ex Comm within hours with no lateral "clearances"!), but that I did informally clear it with Harry Rowen, deputy assistant secretary, International Security Affairs (ISA), in the Department of Defense, and Roger Hilsman, director of the Bureau of Research and Intelligence (INR) in the Department of State. I did not clear the paper with the CIA because of time pressures, but the current intelligence on the status of the Soviet missile deployment in Cuba was provided by the CIA, as were the agreed intelligence data concerning Soviet strategic forces and the SS-4 and SS-5 systems and capabilities. The information on American deployments was provided by the ISA, based on an analysis prepared by William Kaufmann, a consultant to the ISA, and Robert Trinkle of Systems Analysis.

2. McGeorge Bundy, *Danger and Survival: Choices About the Bomb in the First Fifty Years* (New York: Random House, 1988), pp. 451–52.

recent interview, Paul Nitze expressed this other point of view very clearly. After stating that he considered McNamara and Bundy to have been "dead wrong," in October 1962 and now, in their assessment of the effect on the strategic balance, he said, "I think it mattered a great deal to the Soviets, and I thought it properly mattered a greal deal to the Soviets. And it mattered a great deal to me. . . . The extraordinary thing was that the one person who agreed with me was Garthoff. At that time he wrote a memorandum which supported my conclusion. He went through the numbers and the strategic significance of these IRBMs and MRBMs and he came out with the same conclusion I'd come to. *Welch* [interviewer]: The one person apart from [General] Max [Maxwell] Taylor [chairman of the Joint Chiefs of Staff], you mean. *Nitze:* Well, Max Taylor is a great man, but I never thought Max was that good an analyst. Ray was then working for the CIA in an analytical function. It's a different kind of a way of looking at things."[3] Nitze had in mind that until September 1961 I had for four years been a senior intelligence analyst in the Office of National Estimates at the CIA.

The information in my memorandum is substantially self-explanatory. Although most of the information in it was correct, later additional information has modified the picture in a few respects.

First, the prevailing national intelligence estimate of seventy-five operational intercontinental ballistic missile (ICBM) launchers in the Soviet Union (revised in October to 60–65) was still high. U.S. intelligence later concluded that the Soviet ICBM force at that time numbered forty-four operational launchers (plus six test and training launchers that could have been used in an emergency). General Volkogonov, in January 1989, stated that the operational Soviet ICBM force in October 1962 was only "about twenty" ICBM launchers. The SS-7 ICBMs then being deployed were in groups of ten. It is possible that the United States evaluated two groups as "operational" on the basis of observed external comple-

---

3. James G. Blight and David A. Welch, *On the Brink: Americans and Soviets Reexamine the Cuban Missile Crisis* (New York: Hill and Wang, 1989), p. 150. Nitze found it "extraordinary" that my analysis corresponded to his because he knew that my policy position was more dovish.

tion, whereas they may not have been, explaining a discrepancy between twenty-four and forty-four (the four being the deployed SS-6 launchers, covered by Volkogonov's "about"). A correction to forty-four or to twenty-four reinforces the conclusion of the paper on the significance of the MRBMs and IRBMs in Cuba. Thus, completion of the deployment then under way, forty launchers, would in fact have nearly doubled or tripled the first-strike land-based missile salvo. In both cases, the ninety-seven Soviet short-range submarine-launched ballistic missiles (SLBMs) were not counted, because none was at that time deployed within range of the United States nor could they quickly have been brought here.

Critics might charge that even an increase that great in the Soviet first-strike missile salvo would not have altered the overall strategic balance. That, of course, was McNamara's point from the outset. As shown in table 1, the lineup (one cannot call it a "balance") of operational strategic forces at the end of October 1962 heavily favored the United States. Moreover, in quality the United States had a further lead (for example, all the Soviet SLBMs were short range and required surfacing of the submarine to fire, and two-thirds were on noisy, easily tracked diesel-powered submarines).

Nonetheless, the memorandum shows that the Soviet Union's move to increase its strategic capabilities by the Cuban deployment would in fact have posed "an appreciably heightened threat to the US strategic retaliatory forces" and hence to our deterrent capability. Thus a military concern existed in addition to the concern over Soviet intentions prompted by such a sudden and surreptitious gambit. Even if with hindsight these concerns can be considered excessive, they did not so appear at the time.

Second, the information in the memorandum represents the maximum extent of operational deployment before the resolution of the crisis on October 28.

Third, the United States did not know on October 27–28 the precise number of missiles in Cuba. We had identified thirty-three SS-4 missiles, but we knew that there might be more and that there might also be some SS-5 missiles. (Some supporting equipment unique to the SS-5 system had been identified, in addition to the distinctive SS-5 launchers.) In fact, the Soviet leaders then in-

Table 1. *U.S. and Soviet Strategic Forces, October 31, 1962*

Weapon system	United States		Soviet Union	
ICBM launchers[a]	172	(+7)	24–44	(+6)
SLBM launchers[b]	112	(+32)	0	(+97)
MRBM and IRBM launchers[c]	. . .	(105)	. . .	(24 in Cuba)
Strategic bombers[d]	1,450	. . .	155	(+)
Warheads (salvo)[e]	±3,000	. . .	±250	. . .

a. The figures in parentheses are additional test and training launchers also available for use. The 24–44 operational Soviet ICBMs were all liquid-filled missiles requiring several hours of preparation for firing.

In mid-October in response to the crisis the United States began to expedite completion of Atlas and Titan ICBM launchers then under reconstruction. While this effort could not of course affect the American force level more than marginally during the crisis, it did raise the number of operational American ICBM launchers from 112 in early October to 210 by January 30, 1963: 126 Atlas, 54 Titan I, and 30 Minuteman I (this concluded the Atlas deployment; 54 additional Titan II launchers under construction were completed within a few months; the Minuteman I deployment continued until early 1967). Incidentally, this expedited, or "crash," deployment resulted in lowered quality standards and reduced reliability, although in any event the Atlas and Titan I forces were phased out within a few years. By contrast, the Soviet Union by January 1963 had still not reached the 75 ICBM launchers earlier estimated for mid-1962 and only reached about 100 by mid-1963.

b. The U.S. figures conservatively assume seven of the nine operational U.S. Navy Polaris submarines with 112 of the 144 missiles would have been immediately available. The 97 relatively short-range ballistic missiles on thirty-five Soviet diesel and nuclear submarines were all in Soviet waters and unavailable for early commitment, in addition to being highly vulnerable.

c. The 60 Thor missiles in Great Britain were subject to British control, and the 45 Jupiters in Italy (30) and Turkey (15) were similarly subject to Italian and Turkish assent. These 105 missiles were, therefore, not counted in the Strategic Air Command (SAC) order of battle, although they were conditionally available for the Single Integrated Operational Plan (SIOP). The United States did not seek to alert these forces, and indeed on October 27 President Kennedy instructed that the Jupiters in Turkey be kept nonoperational.

On October 28, the last of the 24 SS-4 launchers in Cuba was counted as "operational" by the United States, with the assumption that nuclear warheads were available.

d. Strategic bombers are here defined as heavy bombers or as medium bombers with basing and refueling support for intercontinental strikes.

The SAC ready-strike bomber force rose from 652 on October 19, 1962, to 1,436 on October 24 with Defense Condition (DEFCON) 2, and 1,479 on November 4. It was supported by 1,003 aerial tankers. Between October 23 and November 26 SAC flew 2,511 operational sorties carrying 8,101 nuclear weapons on board.

The Soviet Long Range Aviation force had a total inventory of 155 Bison and Bear heavy bombers, and a large number of Badger and Bull medium bombers. The bomber force was not, however, supported by tankers for air refueling, and even the heavy bombers were dependent on limited Arctic advance bases for round-trip missions against North America. The force did not go on high-readiness under the nominal Soviet alert.

e. The SAC bomber and ICBM ready force grew from 1,433 warheads on October 19 to a peak of 2,952 on November 4. To this must be added the U.S. Navy Polaris force with 144 warheads on nine submarines.

These figures do not indicate the substantial nuclear delivery capability of other U.S. forces: strike aircraft on the navy's carrier force and in the European and Far Eastern theater commands.

It is difficult to estimate the number of Soviet warheads that were available for a strike, since the forces were not alerted and the time to generate the force would undoubtedly have had to be limited. It could have varied from less than 100 to several hundred.

In both cases, the figures represent potential "salvo" force delivery in a *first* strike, with no account for missile refire or bomber restrike capabilities. Warhead stockpiles were much larger, at least in the case of the United States, and not the limiting factor in the Soviet case. Second-strike capabilities would have been reduced in the case of the United States, and severely reduced in the case of the Soviet Union.

formed us that they had forty-two missiles in Cuba, and assisted us in observing the withdrawal of the forty-two missiles, all SS-4s.[4] No SS-4s, SS-5s, or other MRBMs or IRBMs have ever been seen in Cuba in the twenty-five years since, and there is no reason to doubt that these forty-two missiles were the total number there. The deployment under way would have brought the number to forty-eight SS-4 missiles and thirty-two SS-5 missiles—providing the standard single reload for each of the forty launchers, as was correctly estimated. Delivery of the last six SS-4 missiles and all thirty-two SS-5 missiles to Cuba was stopped by the "quarantine" blockade; five of the Soviet ships then en route, which immediately stopped and soon returned to Soviet ports, were identified by intelligence analysts as probably carrying some of the SS-5 missiles and the remaining SS-4 missiles.

No nuclear warheads were ever identified in Cuba, but there was evidence that some were en route from the Soviet Union when the quarantine began and interdicted them. As noted in the memorandum, standard Soviet nuclear weapons storage facilities were built at the missile sites (one for each eight launchers).

The reference to the nine "bases" for missiles should better have read nine "groups" (of four launchers each). The fourth group of SS-5 IRBM launchers, the tenth group in all, was clearly planned and in fact construction work had been started, but had not yet proceeded far enough to meet the intelligence analysts' criteria as "confirmed"—hence the reference to "12 or 16" SS-5 launchers. All forty MRBM and IRBM launchers were located at four complexes or bases, each with its own Soviet ground combat team to provide local security.

In short, the assessment erred in assuming that some of the SS-5 missiles might already be in Cuba and in assuming that the nuclear warheads might be there. These were, however, the only prudent assumptions to have made under the circumstances.

Fourth, it is worth noting that in 1962 an accuracy of 1.0 to 1.5

4. Some press reports at the time, mentioned in some later accounts, alleged that we had counted only thirty-seven outgoing missiles. These reports were incorrect and were based on the count on November 9, rather than the final count on November 10, when the last shipment departed.

nautical miles (for a very high yield missile payload) was considered good, and was indeed a threat to our early soft Atlas and Titan missile launchers and bomber bases, to say nothing of cities.

Finally, if the crisis had ended with the United States conceding a Soviet right to unlimited deployment of missiles in Cuba, we would have entered a period of increased strategic instability. The United States would undoubtedly have replied with an augmented airborne bomber alert force and probably an even more rapid program for submarine missile deployment. If a compromise resolution had allowed some twenty-four to forty Soviet missile launchers to remain, but no more, the period of American strategic force vulnerability would have been much briefer than under unlimited deployment, though it is difficult to estimate the psychological effects both of the missile capability and of the American retreat to its acceptance.

One other comment should be made. Some revisionist analysts have implied or charged that in 1962 the administration intentionally cultivated a false impression that the missile launchers were imminently to become operational and thus required urgent and extreme steps. This charge is not well founded. As indicated in the memorandum, by October 27 twenty MRBM launchers were "believed to be fully operational" (by October 28 all twenty-four) and the even more threatening IRBMs were expected to reach emergency operational status in two weeks. We now know that there were no IRBM missiles yet in Cuba, and the SS-4 MRBMs may have lacked nuclear warheads, owing to the timing and effectiveness of the quarantine, but those facts were not known and could not prudently have been assumed at the time. Official concerns were genuine and were justified, even if they were erroneous; expressions of these concerns were not knowingly made alarmist.

This discussion has not addressed the question of whether American strategic superiority, or American conventional superiority in the Caribbean, was predominant in influencing the Soviet leadership to withdraw the missiles. I would not disagree with the judgment, affirmed by several of the principal decisionmakers at the time, that "the decisive military element in the resolution of the crisis was our clearly available and applicable superiority in conventional weapons within the area of the crisis."[5] Nevertheless, the strategic balance undoubtedly did persuade the Soviet leaders not to counter in some other situation where they had decisive conventional superiority, such as Berlin. Both the strategic and conventional balances no doubt played a part. But even more decisive, in my judgment, was the balance of resolve, which also favored the United States. The Soviet leaders no doubt believed their action to have been justified, but they also knew they were taking the initiative in seeking to change the status quo. In that important sense they bore the responsibility for not permitting the situation to get out of hand as a result of any miscalculation of the American reaction.

For the American policymakers who dealt with the Cuban missile crisis in 1962, political considerations were dominant over military ones. Nevertheless, both political and military considerations reinforced their policy of resolve not to permit the deployment to remain.

5. Dean Rusk and others, "The Lessons of the Cuban Missile Crisis," *Time,* September 27, 1982, p. 85; from a joint statement by former Secretary of State Dean Rusk, Secretary of Defense Robert McNamara, Under Secretary of State George W. Ball, Deputy Secretary of Defense Roswell L. Gilpatric, Special Counsel to the President Theodore Sorensen, and Special Assistant to the President for National Security Affairs McGeorge Bundy.

Document E

DEPARTMENT OF STATE

OUTGOING TELEGRAM
SECRET [Declassified October 19, 1976]
ACTION: USUN New York 1133   Oct. 29, 1962

EYES ONLY UNDER SECRETARY BALL
FROM ALEXIS JOHNSON.

There follows the text of a memorandum by Garthoff, in my office, on the question of defining offensive weapons to be removed from Cuba which I feel might be helpful to your job up there. This memorandum has been discussed with Rowen in ISA but we have not sought formal DOD clearance:

The United States objective has been the removal of offensive weapons from Cuba. There is, of course, no generally accepted definition of "offensive weapons." We would like to see maximum military withdrawal from Cuba, but we must balance against this a reasonable interpretation of what is intolerable to us. On September 4, the President clearly indicated that weapons then in Cuba—including fighter aircraft, coastal defense, cruise-type missiles, missile armed patrol boats, and surface-to-air missiles—were not at that time regarded as "offensive weapons." On the other hand, the list of weapons, entry of which was prohibited under the quarantine proclamation, included all surface-to-surface missiles, bomber and fighter-bomber aircraft, bombs, and other support equipment for the above systems.

It is clear that the weapons systems which must be removed are the 1,000 n.m. and 2,200 n.m. surface-to-surface missiles, IL-28 jet light bombers, and the warheads and support equipment for these systems.

We cannot reasonably insist that the MIG fighters, surface-to-air missiles, or non-missile ground force weapons should be removed. Similarly, it would not be reasonable to demand that the planned fishing port not be built. The items on which there may be a legitimate difference of opinion are: short range (about 35 n.m.) coastal defense missiles, short range (about 15 n.m.) artillery rockets, and the short range (about 25 n.m.) missiles carried on patrol craft. Of these, the missile carrying patrol boats are most susceptible of offensive employment. None of these three systems, incidentally, has a nuclear delivery capability.

212

We would recommend that the United States initially propose that "surface-to-surface missiles" be removed, and that on the actual implementation a low-key effort be made to secure the return to the USSR of the patrol craft and coastal defense missiles, but that if challenged we should fall back to exclude the three short range systems. In addition to the MRBMs and IRBMs, the IL-28s should definitely be included, but the MIG fighters should not be.

The question of excluding visits of Soviet submarines or bombers should best be handled by appropriate unilateral US declaration at some appropriate time that any new attempt to create Soviet offensive bases in Cuba, including submarines as well as missiles and bombers, would be an even more serious infringement of the security of the Western Hemisphere than had been the present Soviet attempt to build such bases, and would of course require use to take the necessary measures to secure their removal.

Khrushchev's message of October 28 flatly stated that, in view of US assurances against an invasion, "the motives which induced us to render assistance of such a kind to Cuba disappeared." In view of the fact that Khrushchev was referring to what he termed means of defense—and which would seem to cover all Soviet military assistance to Cuba—there is some foundation for a US demand that all Soviet military advisers return to the Soviet Union. While this would not be a *sine qua non* of our position, it would seem to be a useful line to pursue. The departure of Soviet military specialists would, in the judgment of the Intelligence Community, initially render inoperable the surface-to-air missile sites, coastal defense missile sites, and most of the MIG-21 force. The JCS proposed procedures for rendering offensive systems to Cuba inoperable, and creating suitable guidelines for the UN inspection, seem satisfactory.

Drafted and approved: G — U. Alexis Johnson
Cleared: S/S — Mr. Furnas
Signed: Rusk

Document F

[For Jeffrey C. Kitchen to U. Alexis Johnson]

G/PM

SECRET [Declassified June 10, 1977]

MEMORANDUM   October 29, 1962

SUBJECT: Significance of the Soviet Backdown for Future US Policy

1. *Short-Run Effects*

Political—The short-run effects should be very favorable to the US. Unquestionably the US will emerge from this confrontation with increased prestige world-wide. The Soviet action should demonstrate once again the offensive nature of Soviet motivations more clearly than anything we could say. It should also demonstrate that the Soviets are not prepared to risk a decisive military showdown with the US over issues involving the extension of Soviet power. (We should be clear however that this is not to be confused with Soviet lack of willingness to "go to the mat" over an interest vital to Soviet security.) More specifically, short-run political effects should include the following:

a. Soviet ability to penetrate Latin America should suffer a reversal, though a base for future penetration may remain in Cuba for some time. Soviet intentions have been unmasked, and Soviet inability to force its will clearly demonstrated. Our problems in assisting Latin America to achieve a higher state of political and economic development will still require all of our best efforts. However, our efforts should be focused on the fundamental nature of the problem, and it is important that we continue to pursue our Latin American country internal programs, along with our broader development programs.

b. NATO should be strengthened. The firmness of the US stand, and perhaps even more importantly the categorical refusal to barter NATO assets for immediate US security interests, should provide assurance of US commitment to the Alliance.

c. Our position on Berlin should be greatly strengthened. Our resolute willingness to act in Cuba should result in a complete reassessment by the Soviets as to how far they can safely push US will in general, including Berlin. Similarly it should provide our Allies with fortitude for meeting Soviet threats.

d. The effect upon the neutrals is more difficult to estimate, but in general is favorable. It must raise in the minds of many of the neutrals

214

who may have a pro-Communist leaning a question as to how far they may safely "get in bed" with the Soviets and still protect their own national interests.

   e. While there is probably very little immediate effect on Soviet-Satellite relations, it cannot help but plant the seed of doubt as to Soviet omnipotence. This could have important implications for the future.

   f. The effect on the USSR can be beneficial, but this will depend on how we further use our present strong position. It is conceivable that within the Soviet leadership the events of the past several days may be considered so serious a setback that changes may occur in the current Soviet leadership.

   Military—The military benefits secured as a result of the Soviet backdown are similarly immense. Agreement not to proceed with additional missiles, and to dismantle existing missiles and launch facilities, cancels out the temporary increase in capability vis-à-vis the continental United States, which the Soviets achieved in their short-lived attempt to offset the current US nuclear strategic advantage.

2. *Long-Run Effects*

   Political—An analysis of long-run effects is of course more uncertain. Unquestionably the Soviet defeat will have its impact on Soviet thinking and policymaking. Over the long run, one effect may be to make the Soviets far more responsive to our efforts at finding peaceful solutions to the whole range of world problems. However, and this is an important qualification, this effect is certain to take a considerable period of time. We should not delude ourselves into believing that great and rapid changes will result in Soviet policy. People and governments simply do not and cannot change that quickly, even assuming the stimulus for doing so. Thus while it is useful to explore all avenues of solutions to world problems, such as disarmament, we must not expect quick or easy solutions. We would expect that the US will meet with the usual Soviet criticism, resistance, and negotiatory pressure. In short, we must not slip into euphoria over the successful course of events, assuming it continues to develop favorably.

   Military—Viewed in its long-run perspective, the Soviet backdown does not affect the Soviet military position in any important essential other than, of course, the important removal of the missiles from Cuba and awareness in Moscow of US refusal to permit *any* such venture. It is possible that the effect of these events might be to set in motion a redoubled Soviet effort to close the gap to development by the Soviets of a secure second strike capability.

3. *General Conclusion*

Our over-all preliminary conclusion may be summarized as follows:

a. We have in the recent situation gained broad political and military assets, on which we should attempt to capitalize. We have probably gained important, but less definitive, long-range benefits.

b. In these circumstances, it is vitally important that the US take the initiative in offering to negotiate on major issues between East and West. Without being bellicose in the basis of our new-found strength, nor on the other hand making concessions which would adversely affect our position of strength, we should press for fair but safeguarded solutions to outstanding problems.

If we have learned anything from this experience, it is that weakness, even only apparent weakness, invites Soviet transgression. At the same time, firmness in the last analysis will force the Soviets to back away from rash initiatives. We cannot now, nor can we in the future, accept Soviet protestations of "peaceful" coexistence at face value. The words may sound the same, but the meaning is different. Their willingness to cooperate in common endeavors can only be judged by performance. The difficult task for US policy in the future is to strike the correct fine balance between seeking cooperation from a forthcoming posture, while retaining the necessary strength and skepticism to insure ourselves and our friends against future duplicity.

RL Garthoff: pep

Document G

DEPARTMENT OF STATE

Deputy Undersecretary

TOP SECRET

MEMORANDUM

October 30, 1962

SUBJECT: Comments on Items III and IV of the
Agreed Agenda for the State-Defense
Meeting of October 30

The key problems for immediate decision are the modalities for removal of the offensive weapons in Cuba and verification that no additional ones are imported. Longer run arrangements will depend importantly upon the nature and functioning of these short term expedients. Nonetheless, we must consider also the longer term requirements and arrangements which we desire.

Long term verification requirements must be [sic; meet] two criteria: they must provide reasonable assurance against clandestine introduction of nuclear delivery systems into Cuba or other countries covered by these arrangements, and they must limit our freedom of action as little as possible. We are seeking to modify the Brazilian Resolution in order to avoid limitations on our transporting nuclear weapons through the denuclearized zone, but our main effort may have to be made at the time that Latin American and possible African regional conferences convene to establish specific arrangements implementing this Resolution.

[Deletion]

The second major problem in connection with long term arrangements concerns the extent of US or Hemispheric guarantees not to invade Cuba, and obligations by Cuba in addition to denuclearization.

[Deletion]

The US should not, of course, assume any obligations [deletion] beyond reaffirmations of our UN and OAS Charter obligations.

[Deletion]

G/PM:RLGarthoff:pep

217

Document H

November 3 [1962]

DRAFT INSTRUCTION TO USUN
FOR CONSIDERATION BY THE EXECUTIVE COMMITTEE

CUBA: INSPECTION ARRANGEMENTS

We do not yet know whether Cuba will be willing voluntarily to have international inspection on his [sic; its] soil, either to verify dismantling and removal of offensive weapons or to assure such weapons do not later reappear. However, Mikoyan visit could conceivably soften Cuban policy on this point. Moreover, door is not necessarily closed to some agreed form of inspection provided it is not limited to Cuba but covers a broader area. We understand SYG [UN Secretary General] had impression Castro found interesting SYG's argument that UN presence in Cuba in itself constituted deterrent to invasion of Cuba.

On these assumptions, following are procedures that are being considered after general review of the matter here.

1. *PHASE I* (now).

Hopefully we can quickly implement ICRC [International Committee of the Red Cross] arrangement operating from vessels outside three-mile limit. This inspection of incoming vessels would make possible suspension of enforcement of quarantine, but U.S. ships would stay on station. ICRC, operating as agent of SYG, would continue until full verification of dismantling and removal made it possible for U.S. to lift quarantine altogether. At that point, ICRC arrangement presumably would lapse.

2. *PHASE II* (*beginning* when Soviets say the offensive weapons are out of Cuba and ending with Security Council confirmation.) There are two alternatives for inspection, depending on whether Cuba acquiesces in inspection procedures or not.

a. If Cuba does *not* acquiesce, we would:

(1) Call a meeting of the council of the Organization of American States, acting as its Organ of Consultation, to pass a resolution explicitly recommending to OAS members that "pending the establishment of adequate arrangements for surveillance and

218

inspection under the auspices of the United Nations . . . there be undertaken such aerial and other appropriate surveillance of Cuba as may be necessary to assure that all missiles and other weapons with any offensive capability are dismantled and withdrawn from Cuba and that such weapons are not reintroduced into Cuba." This would provide an OAS umbrella for the comprehensive air reconnaissance which will be required in absence ground inspection to give OAS members, including U.S., some reasonable assurance that Soviets have in fact removed weapons from Cuba and also give a sanction for continued air surveillance if no other measures are devised to give continued assurance against their reintroduction.

(2) Upon completion of removal of the weapons, the Secretary General would make a report to the Security Council, the U.S. and the U.S.S.R. make declarations on what has been done to carry out commitments contained in the Kennedy-Khrushchev exchange of letters, and the Security Council President would sum up what has been said in a consensus statement. This procedure and the statements would of course have to be negotiated in advance with the Soviet Union. This procedure would not involve any Security Council Resolution.

b. If Cuba *does* acquiesce:

(1) UNSYG would, with Security Council authorization, place in Cuba a UN presence to conduct ground inspection along lines of general negotiating instructions (paragraph 6 of Department's [telegram to US Mission UN no.] 1147). As indicated in those instructions, systematic aerial reconnaissance would be necessary part of process in this period, and we should encourage SYG to develop capability to do all or part of necessary aerial surveillance.

(2) Upon satisfactory completion of such UN inspection, there would be a meeting of the Security Council at which the Council would take note of the SYG's report that offensive weapons had been removed from Cuba, and the U.S. and the U.S.S.R. would make complementary declarations. It would probably be necessary that the U.S. declaration make reference to a prior OAS action with respect to "invasion."

3. *PHASE III.* (This phase would begin with the completion of Security Council action confirming the removal of the weapons from Cuba and would continue through whatever period Cuba may be dominated by a Communist Government.) There appear to be two alternatives for continued inspection during this period to assure that the weapons are not reintroduced into Cuba:

   a. If Cuba does *not* acquiesce it would be possible under the OAS resolution mentioned in paragraph 2 to continue the aerial surveillance program.

   b. If Cuba *does* acquiesce it should be possible to provide an arrangement under the Brazilian Latin American Denuclearized Zone proposal which is now in the General Assembly to establish a system of inspection covering all of Latin America, including Cuba.

Document I

DEPARTMENT OF STATE

Deputy Undersecretary

G/PM

SECRET [Declassified March 16, 1988]

October 31, 1962

MEMORANDUM

TO: IO   — Mr. Wallner
      ACDA   — Mr. Fisher
      ARA   — Mr. Martin
      ISA/DOD — Mr. Barber
      L   — Mr. Chayes

FROM: G/PM   — Raymond L. Garthoff

SUBJECT: Draft Instruction of Long Term Verification Arrangements
         Concerning Cuba

Attached is the draft initial section of instructions intended to provide guidance on Phase III assurances against reintroduction of offensive weapons into Cuba. IO [Bureau of International Organization Affairs] has prepared the more detailed section on consensual negotiations ratified by the UN, which is also attached. ARA [Bureau of Inter-American Affairs] and L [Legal Adviser] should be drafting the parallel discussion on the use of an OAS resolution to authorize necessary verification. ACDA [Arms Control and Disarmament Agency] has been asked to provide the discussion on use of a denuclearized zone in Latin America for such assurances and inspection arrangements. These draft sections (in several copies) should be in my hands as soon as possible in order to be incorporated in the over-all draft instruction which Mr. Johnson wishes to have for the 10:00 a.m. [Ex Comm] meeting on November 1.

ISA/DOD [International Security Affairs/Department of Defense] and INR [Bureau of Intelligence and Research] are preparing a related background paper on the technical requirements for surveillance and inspection, and it is hoped that this paper also can be available by that time.

cc: G/PM — Mr. Kitchen
    INR — Mr. Hilsman

G/PM: RLGarthoff:pep

SECRET

DRAFT INSTRUCTION ON LONG TERM VERIFICATION
ARRANGEMENTS CONCERNING CUBA

1. OBJECTIVE.

The purpose of this instruction is to provide guidance for negotiation of the arrangements governing long term assurances against the introduction of offensive nuclear weapons into Latin America, and especially against the reintroduction of such weapons into Cuba so long as that country is ruled by a Marxist-Leninist regime. Earlier instructions have been provided to cover arrangements for Phase I and Phase II (Department 1147 dtd October 31 to USUN). Phase III would begin when the Security Council has accepted the report of the SYG that offensive weapons have in fact been removed from Cuba.

2. METHODS OF GAINING ASSURANCE.

The chief means of insuring ourselves that the Soviets do not introduce nuclear weapons systems into Cuba or elsewhere in Latin America is unilateral intelligence. However, such intelligence should be considered and used as a supplement to internationally recognized procedures for verification of the non-introduction of offensive weapons. The three principal methods of overt verification would be: (a) aerial reconnaissance; (b) control over incoming shipping; and (c) ground inspection. Of the three, aerial reconnaissance is probably the most significant and the least obvious an intrusion. Control over shipping, by placement of inspectors at all ports and airfields, would also be generally effective. Ground inspection would not be practicable as a basic inspection mechanism, but it could be valuable for checking up in instances when aerial reconnaissance or unilateral intelligence had inconclusive evidence of a possible violation; in other words, it could be a valuable supplementary means for checking on suspicious events.

The selection or combination of these methods would depend heavily upon the political arrangements under which the inspection was undertaken. Moreover, the first purpose of such arrangements would be to deter potential violation, as well as to detect such violation if it were not deterred.

3. ALTERNATIVE COURSES OF ACTION.

[2½ pp. deletion]

G/PM: RLGarthoff:pep

CONFIDENTIAL
ANNEX A: SOLUTION 1

The exchange of letters between the President and Khrushchev constitute in review a firm undertaking for the establishment of safeguards against the re-introduction of offensive weapons into Cuba. (In his letter of October 27 the President said "you would . . . undertake, with suitable safeguards, to halt the further introduction of such weapons systems into Cuba.")

One way to obtain safeguards against re-introduction of offensive weapons into Cuba would be to attempt to reach agreement of the three parties concerned, i.e., US, USSR and Cuba, for the establishment of a continuing inspection of Cuba. An inspection system could then be set up under the UN to provide for aerial surveillance of Cuba and for ground inspection of suspicious events reported to the SYG by his inspectors or by a member of the Security Council. If tripartite agreement were possible on this basis, authorization for the establishment of such an inspection system could be incorporated into the same SC resolution which accepts the report of the SYG that offensive weapons have been removed from Cuba at the end of Phase II.

[1¼ pp. deletion]

IO:WWallner:pep

CONFIDENTIAL

ANNEX B: ADDENDUM TO SOLUTION 2

DRAFT RESOLUTION FOR POSSIBLE ADOPTION BY THE COUNCIL OF THE ORGANIZATION OF AMERICAN STATES ACTING PROVISIONALLY AS ORGAN OF CONSULTATION UNDER THE RIO TREATY

Whereas: The COAS/OC in its Resolution of October 23, 1962, recognizing that "incontrovertible evidence has appeared that the Government of Cuba, despite repeated warnings, has secretly endangered the peace of the Continent by permitting the Sino-Soviet powers to have intermediate and middle-range missiles on its territory capable of carrying nuclear warheads";

Called "for the immediate dismantling and withdrawal from Cuba of all missiles and other weapons with any offensive capability";

Whereas: The establishment of nuclear weapons or nuclear delivery systems on the territory of an American Republic which did not possess such capability at the date on which it adhered to the Inter-American Treaty of Reciprocal Assistance creates a situation which would endanger the peace and security of the continent and is thus inconsistent with the purposes and principles set forth in the Charter of the OAS;

The COAS/OC decides

1. That no American Republic referred to in the preceding paragraph shall establish or permit the establishment within its territory of nuclear weapons, missiles capable of carrying nuclear warheads or nuclear delivery systems;

2. That upon the allegation by any American Republic that a Member State is failing to comply with or is preparing to violate paragraph 1 of this Resolution, that State shall permit without delay duly qualified observers appointed by the appropriate body of the OAS to enter its territory [for the purpose of verifying the truth or falsity of the allegations].

ARA:EWMartin:WAllen:pep

Document J

[For U. Alexis Johnson]

DEPARTMENT OF STATE

Deputy Undersecretary
G/PM

TOP SECRET [Declassified November 20, 1981]

MEMORANDUM   November 5, 1962

SUBJECT: Reprisals to Interference with US Aerial Surveillance

Unless we make crystal clear to the Soviets and to the Cubans that we will brook no interference with our unilateral aerial inspection, we will undermine any credence in our insistence on longer-range inspection in addition to making exceptionally difficult our own interim unilateral effort. If we are not prepared to take forceful steps to counter the use of force against ourselves, we will rightly or wrongly (and either would be bad) undermine belief that we would ever resort to force to meet intransigence on all the unresolved issues concerning present and future verification arrangements.

The Soviets have flatly said that all antiaircraft weapons were in Cuban hands [source reference deleted]. If it became necessary to undertake military action against Cuban air defenses as a result of their interference in our reconnaissance, we could make public the fact that the Soviets had informed us that such weapons were all in Cuban hands. This would reduce the already very remote possibility that the Soviets would react in any serious way to such actions on our part in reprisal.

Soviet military advisors and technicians were present with the Egyptian forces at the time of the Suez invasion in October 1956. We do not know whether any were killed in the Anglo-French strafing and bombing, but in any case the Soviets made no protest whatsoever. They did quietly evacuate their technicians through the Sudan as soon as that was practicable.

While it would be undesirable to undertake unnecessary military action endangering Soviet personnel, it would be even more undesirable to give them the impression that our resolve was so weak that we would permit Americans to be killed in conducting operations which even the Soviets have possibly recognized must now occur. Finally, as noted above, the

Soviets have authoritatively (whether correctly or—more likely—not) washed their hands of Cuban air defense weapons.

The best course of action would probably be to eliminate the interfering missile or gun sites or aircraft if possible, or comparable weapons on a reprisal basis.

G/PM: RLGarthoff:pep

Index